public policy
analysis

public affairs and administration
(editor: James S. Bowman)
(vol. 9)

Garland reference library
of social science
(vol. 171)

the public affairs and administration
series: James S. Bowman, editor

1. career planning, development, and management
   an annotated bibliography
   Jonathan P. West
2. professional dissent
   an annotated bibliography and resource guide
   James S. Bowman
   Frederick A. Elliston
   Paula Lockhart
3. American public administration
   a bibliographical guide to the literature
   Gerald E. Caiden
   Richard A. Loverd
   Thomas J. Pavlek
   Lynn F. Sipe
   Molly M. Wong
4. public administration in rural areas and small jurisdictions
   a guide to the literature
   Beth Walter Honadle
5. comparative public administration
   an annotated bibliography
   Mark W. Huddleston
6. the bureaucratic state
   an annotated bibliography
   Robert D. Miewald
7. labor management relations in the public sector
   an annotated bibliography
   N. Joseph Cayer
   Sherry S. Dickerson
8. public choice theory in public administration
   an annotated bibliography
   Nicholas P. Lovrich
   Max Neiman
9. public policy analysis
   an annotated bibliography
   John S. Robey

public policy analysis
an annotated bibliography

John S. Robey
University of Texas-Austin

preface by Thomas R. Dye

Garland Publishing, Inc. • New York & London
1984

© 1984 John S. Robey
All rights reserved

Library of Congress Cataloging in Publication Data
Robey, John S.
  Public policy analysis.

  (Public affairs and administration ; vol. 9)
  (Garland reference library of social science ; vol. 171)
  Includes indexes.
  1. Policy sciences—Bibliography. I. Title.
II. Series: Public affairs and administration series ; 9.
III. Series: Garland reference library of social
science ; v. 171.
Z7161.R59 1984   [H97]   016.3616'1   82-49149
ISBN 0-8240-9150-7

Cover design by Laurence Walczak

Printed on acid-free, 250-year-life paper
Manufactured in the United States of America

contents

Series Foreword   vii
Preface by Thomas R. Dye   ix

PART I: INTRODUCTION
Chapter 1. A User's Guide to *Public Policy Analysis*   3

PART II: ANNOTATED BIBLIOGRAPHY
Chapter 2. Agricultural Commodities Policy   11
Chapter 3. Civil Rights, Minorities, and Women   18
Chapter 4. Economic and Monetary Policy   36
Chapter 5. Educational Policy   46
Chapter 6. Energy and the Environment   54
Chapter 7. Military and Foreign Policy   75
Chapter 8. Municipal, State, and Local Government   88
Chapter 9. Sex, Drugs, and the Regulation of Morality   109
Chapter 10. Social Welfare Policy   117
Chapter 11. Taxing and Collecting Public Revenues   133
Chapter 12. Policy Analysis   141
Chapter 13. Policy Making   155

PART III: INDICES
Author Index   171
Subject Index   180

series foreword

The twentieth century has seen public administration come of age as a field and practice. This decade, in fact, marks the one hundredth anniversary of the profession. As a result of the dramatic growth in government, and the accompanying information explosion, many individuals—managers, academicians and their students, researchers—in organizations feel that they do not have ready access to important information. In an increasingly complex world, more and more people need published material to help solve problems.

The scope of the field and the lack of a comprehensive information system has frustrated users, disseminators, and generators of knowledge in public administration. While there have been some initiatives in recent years, the documentation and control of the literature have been generally neglected. Indeed, major gaps in the development of the literature, the bibliographic structure of the discipline, have evolved.

Garland Publishing, Inc., has inaugurated the present series as an authoritative guide to information sources in public administration. It seeks to consolidate the gains made in the growth and maturation of the profession.

The Series consists of three tiers:
1. core volumes keyed to the major subfields in public administration such as personnel management, public budgeting, and intergovernmental relations;
2. bibliographies focusing on substantive areas of administration such as community health; and
3. titles on topical issues in the profession.

Each book will be compiled by one or more specialists in the area. The authors—practitioners and scholars—are selected in open competition from across the country. They design their work to include an introductory essay, a wide variety of bibliographic materials, and, where appropriate, an information resource section. Thus each contribution in the collection provides a systematic basis for managers and researchers to make informed judgments in the course of their work.

Since no single volume can adequately encompass such a broad, interdisciplinary subject, the Series is intended as a continuous project that will incorporate new bodies of literature as needed. The titles in preparation represent the initial building blocks in an operating information system for public affairs and administration. As an open-ended endeavor, it is hoped that not only will the Series serve to summarize knowledge in the field but also will contribute to its advancement.

This collection of book-length bibliographies is the product of considerable collaboration on the part of many people. Special appreciation is extended to the editors and staff of Garland Publishing, Inc., to the individual contributors in the Public Affairs and Administration Series, and to the anonymous reviewers of each of the volumes. Inquiries should be made to the Series Editor:

James S. Bowman
Tallahassee

foreword

The study of public policy is the study of "What governments do, why they do it, and what difference it makes." Public policy is simply whatever government chooses to do or not to do. Harold Lasswell and Abraham Kaplan, however, define public policy as "a projected program of goals, values, and practices," and Carl Friedrick writes: "It is essential for the policy concept that there be a goal objective or purpose." The problem with these definitions is deciding whether we could ever discern or agree upon what these goals, objectives or purposes really are.

It would be nice if government activities were characterized by consistency and repetitiveness, but too often government actions are inconsistent and non-repetitive. If we excluded such actions from our study of "public policy," we would be missing a very important component of political life itself. A more realistic definition of public policy, therefore, is all government activity, whether goals are understood or not.

We return to our simple definition: "public policy is whatever governments choose to do or not to do." Of course, this definition places a very great burden on a bibliographer. What should be included in a bibliography on so extensive a topic as "public policy"? John S. Robey's *Public Policy Literature: An Annotated Bibliography* is a praiseworthy effort to deal with this formidable question. It is difficult to envision a more useful bibliography of public policy studies from 1977 through 1982, a period of extensive scholarly activity in this field.

Governments do many things: they regulate conflict, organize society to carry on conflict with other societies, distribute both material and symbolic benefits to individuals and groups within society, regulate the behavior of individuals and organizations, and extract support, symbolic and financial, from society. Often, a single government policy does all of these things at once. So it is not really possible to classify particular government policies, programs, or acts, as regulative, distributive, or extractive.

Robey's bibliography classifies policy studies by substantive field, which is probably the most convenient approach for most of us. The categories are reasonably comprehensive and inclusive. The annotations are particularly useful—brief and pointed. Scholars, librarians, and students should find this bibliography a very helpful tool in policy studies.

Thomas R. Dye
Florida State University

part i:
introduction

Chapter 1

A USER'S GUIDE TO
PUBLIC POLICY ANALYSIS

This bibliography has been developed with the aim that it be used as a research tool in public policy analysis. Of course, it is not a comprehensive bibliography. Given the thousands of articles and books that have been published, true comprehensiveness would be cumbersome. Nevertheless, the more than 700 annotated references included in the bibliography offer coverage of the best known recent books, as well as articles that have been published in the most prestigious public administration, political science, and public policy journals. Thus, even if the reader does not find everything on one of the policy areas included in this volume, one could still make a good start. This user's guide will explain how to use this bibliography to full advantage.

The Field of Public Policy Analysis and
the Need for Interdisciplinary Inquiry

Policy analysis has always had an interdisciplinary flavor to it. Traditionally, policy analysts could easily have fit into history departments, philosophy departments, or into the study of law. Since the behavioral revolution in the social sciences, however, political science has expanded even more into disciplines such as sociology, anthropology, psychology, and economics. In his most recent book on public policy, Aaron Wildavsky of the University of California at Berkeley relates that ten years ago he was content to consider himself a political scientist; five years ago he was content to consider himself as a public policy analyst; but today he thinks of himself as a political economist.
Certainly the growth of survey research techniques and the use of census data within the discipline has increased the demand for some computer and statistical knowledge on the part of policy analysts. The influence of the University of Michigan's Survey Research Center as well as the growth in the number of methodologically oriented courses for graduate students is sound testimony to the fact that today's graduate students must acquire some mathematical or quantitative skills if they are to be successful in the discipline.
There are many who believe that policy analysis is the only field within political science which is continuing to grow. In what was once a small part of political science or public administration, now are found doctoral programs at some universities (e.g., The Florida State University, University of California at Berkeley). Further,

3

this interdisciplinary approach is turning out to be healthy, and much cross-fertilization of dynamic models and perspectives is occurring. Because of the interdisciplinary nature of policy analysis, defining the exact parameters of the discipline is a difficult chore. Generally speaking, however, policy analysis deals with "who gets what" in American politics. Empirically oriented scholars are more interested in explaining why certain policies are pursued rather than determining which policies are good or bad. Policy analysts are interested in what the consequences are when certain policies are pursued. Various models and concepts have been developed to explain and describe policy choices (e.g., the game theory model, systems model, incremental model, and the elite model). Probably most public policies are the result of several forces, and no one model is superior in all situations.

If policy analysis is to become a science, policy analysts must be prepared to search for the determinants of public policy from an interdisciplinary perspective; that is, from economic, social, cultural, historical, and technological factors, as well as political system characteristics. Thomas R. Dye maintains that policy analysis is finding out what governments do, why they do it, and what difference it makes. If these questions are to be adequately answered, it may not be wise to take too parochial a view as to what should and what should not be considered fair game for policy analysis. The consequences of public policies in areas as diverse as education, welfare, health, housing, the environment, national defense, the economy, and foreign affairs must be examined. Narrow definitions of what is "political" must be discarded, and the full range of forces shaping our fields of inquiry examined. Certainly the breadth of interests of those involved in policy analysis has increased in recent years. This volume is one testimony to that healthy trend.

For the reader who is just beginning the journey into this interesting field of inquiry, a number of excellent introductory texts are available. Among them are: Dye's *Understanding Public Policy*; Starling's *The Politics and Economics of Public Policy*; Anderson, Brady and Bullock's *Public Policy and Politics in America*; and Lineberry's *American Public Policy*.

Coverage of This Volume

Perhaps the first thing one should examine is just exactly what this bibliography is and what it is not. Since some efforts were made to be systematic and logical, it may be important to review the rules that were followed in compiling and annotating the volume. Simply put, why were some references included and others excluded?

First, only books and articles were included. There was a wealth of material from which to choose just annotating books and articles, so dissertations, monographs, and convention papers were not included. As with the other guidelines used, this should not necessarily be construed as a judgment on the merit of any particular piece of work. Rather, it was a consideration of space limitations and one of accessibility for the users of the bibliography.

Second, because of the great increase in the amount of work being conducted in public policy analysis, it was decided to limit the effort to annotating research that has been done in the last five years. In some respects, this was a trade off. Not included are

A User's Guide 5

dated articles and books (some of them, of course, of high quality), but the result is current and not unwieldy. The rationale for this approach is simply that the line must be drawn somewhere, and all other things being equal, current research is more useful than dated information. If a reader is interested in dated research, however, he or she may examine a recent publication and by backtracking through the footnotes compile a complete set of source materials.

Third, research was limited to that which has been published in the English language. Although there is valuable research being published in many foreign languages, it was assumed that the overwhelming majority of the users of this volume would be primarily interested in annotations in English. Further, the preponderance of research being published in the field is in English. A related rule was that, because of the limitations to the English language, the majority of the research annotated deals with the United States, Canada, or Great Britain.

Fourth, the amount of work being conducted in virtually dozens of specific policy areas was examined. This examination led to ten specific policy areas for inclusion in the volume because of the amount of scholarly interest that had been displayed in those fields. Utilizing this rationale, the following policy areas were selected for inclusion:
    Agricultural Commodities Policy
    Civil Rights, Minorities, and Women
    Economic and Monetary Policy
    Educational Policy
    Energy and the Environment
    Military and Foreign Policy
    Municipal, State, and Local Government
    Sex, Drugs, and the Regulation of Morality
    Social Welfare Policy
    Taxing and Collecting Public Revenues
In addition, two chapters on public policy analysis per se were included. These are:
    Policy Analysis
    Policy Making
Thus, the work being done in relatively minor areas of academic concern has been eliminated. Utilizing this rationale made it possible to confine the work to reasonable limitations, while at the same time to include current research in the policy areas receiving the most attention by scholars.

Fifth, even adhering to the aforementioned limitations, it soon became obvious that unless some books and journals were excluded, the volume would soon become unwieldy. Therefore, it was decided to include only those articles that were published in the most well-known and relevant journals and books that were for the most part considered worthy of review by the editors of particularly relevant journals. This resulted in the selection of the following journals: *The American Political Science Review*, *The Journal of Politics*, the *American Journal of Political Science*, *Western Political Quarterly*, *Polity*, *Policy Studies Journal*, *Public Administration Review*, *Policy Analysis*, and *Public Policy* (the latter two journals recently have been combined into one, the *Journal of Policy Analysis and Management*). Also included is one year of a new journal, *Policy Studies Review*.

In summary, then, this volume was produced by applying the aforementioned rules to an extremely large pool of potential items. This has resulted in a bibliography that contains English language references for the preceding five years that have been published in a book that was reviewed by, or an article that was published in, either a prestigious or particularly relevant journal.

How to Use This Bibliography

This book is divided into three parts. The first consists of this guide. The third section consists of a set of indices, author and subject, which are tools to make the bibliographic material more accessible. The real core of the bibliography is Part II. Here, the references are arranged by topic into twelve chapters. Each of the references is assigned a number. These numbers are ordered sequentially across the twelve chapters. Thus, the chapter on Agricultural Commodities Policy contains entries 1 through 35, the chapter on Civil Rights, Minorities, and Women contains entries 36 through 121, and so forth.

The reader should consider this topical organization to be the main reference system of the bibliography. Depending on the subject area in which the reader is interested, he or she has merely to turn to the appropriate chapter for an overview of the sources relating to that particular topic.

On some occasions, a citation could have fit into more than one of the topical areas. For example, a study on public school desegregation could just as appropriately have been included in the Educational Policy chapter as in the Civil Rights, Minorities, and Women chapter. When situations like this have occurred, a subject index which cross-references the citations has been provided. An equally important research tool is the index of authors. This is simply an alphabetical listing of all the authors whose work has been annotated, with the numbers of the entries associated with their names. This should be helpful to those seeking other work done by the same person in collaboration with others, or alone.

Resource Guide

There are a number of general reference pbulications that are invaluable for the reader who has developed an interest in policy analysis. The Policy Studies Organization has published several reference sources. Among them are: *Policy Research Centers Directory*, which lists 107 university and non-university centers, institutes, or organizations that conduct policy studies research; *Policy Publishers and Associations Directory*, which describes policy-relevant scholarly associations, journals, book publishers, and interest groups; and *Policy Grants Directory*, which describes eighty-three governmental and private funding sources for policy studies research. These volumes are available from:
    Policy Studies Organization
    361 Lincoln Hall
    University of Illinois at Urbana-Champaign
    Urbana, IL 61801

Also, two journals are essential for the serious student of policy analysis, the *Policy Studies Journal* and *Policy Studies Review*. Sub-

A User's Guide

scriptions to both journals are available by writing to the Policy Studies Organization at the address above.

Recent Policy Studies Developments

The reader may be interested in being apprised of several recent developments in the field of policy studies that are of related interest to this volume. First, the *Encyclopedia of Policy Studies* will be published shortly by Marcel Dekker. It will be comprised of thirty-four chapters that describe the state of the art of the authors' respective fields of interest.

Second, *Public Policy Studies: A Multi-Volume Treatise* will be published by JAI Press in the winter of 1983-84. The series will consist of seven volumes, each containing twenty chapters. Each volume will be edited separately and will cover new research in the major subdivisions of the policy sciences. Third, the Policy Studies Organization is developing a new policy studies series with ABC-Clio Press. Last, a bibliography entitled *The Policy Studies Field: Its Basic Literature* may be compiled by the Policy Studies Organization in the years ahead.

part ii:
annotated bibliography

Chapter 2

AGRICULTURAL COMMODITIES POLICY

1. Aviel, JoAnn F. "Effect of the World Food and Fuel Crisis on Israeli Policy-Making." *Western Political Quarterly*, 31 (September 1978), 317-33.

   The world food and fuel crisis in 1972-74 caused policymakers in many countries to reassess policies. This paper utilized interviews with policymakers in Israel to analyze the effects of the crisis on their decision making.

2. Berry, R. Albert and William R. Cline. *Agrarian Structure and Productivity in Developing Countries*. Baltimore: Johns Hopkins University Press, 1979.

   Throws light on the relationship between farm size and the productivity of agriculture. Its importance stems from the fact that with the recent concern to satisfy the basic needs of the population of poor countries, land redistribution has been suggested as a means to achieve this end.

3. Boles, Donald E. and Gary L. Rupnow. "Local Governmental Functions Affected by the Growth of Corporate Agricultural Land Ownership: A Bibliographic Review." *Western Political Quarterly*, 32 (December 1979), 467-78.

   Corporate farms vary substantially in size and in their goals. They run the gamut from the large industrial type to a small family farm corporation, which may have sought its charter for purposes of estate planning advantages. One problem in accurately assessing the impact upon rural communities of changes in corporate farm and land ownership patterns is traceable to the lack of an agreed upon definition of what a farm corporation is, or should be.

4. Browne, William P. and Charles W. Wiggins. "Resolutions and Priorities: Lobbying by the General Farm Organizations." *Policy Studies Journal*, 6 (Summer 1978), 493-99.

   This analysis of the lobbying activity of the general farm organizations refutes many of the claims made about the dominance of ideology over material farm interests.

5. Dahlberg, Kenneth A. *Beyond the Green Revolution: The Ecology and Politics of Global Agricultural Development.* New York: Plenum Press, 1979.

   Most intellectual maps dealing with agriculture fail to recognize it as the basic interface between human societies and their environment. When agriculture is analyzed from a global perspective that takes evolution seriously, one sees that the ecological risks as well as the energy and social costs of modern industrial agriculture make it largely inappropriate for developing countries.

6. Esseks, J.D. "The Politics of Farmland Preservation." *Policy Studies Journal*, 6 (Summer 1978), 514-19.

   Preserving farmland has become an agenda item for many state and local governments. The threat or actuality of urban sprawl has driven farming, environmentalist, no-growth, humanitarian, and other groups to champion "Farmland Preservation" or "Save Our Farms" as a means to protect their varying interests which sprawl endangers.

7. Gordon, Robert M. and Steve H. Hanke. "Federal Milk Marketing Orders: A Policy in Need of Analysis." *Policy Analysis*, 4 (Winter 1978), 23-31.

   Uses data from New Jersey to show that the costs to consumers of federal milk marketing orders can be estimated with modest effort and expense, suggesting that Congress should pursue a full-scale quantitative analysis of their benefits and costs.

8. Guither, Harold D. *The Food Lobbyists: Behind the Scenes of Food and Agri-Politics.* Lexington Books, D.C. Heath, 1980.

   Interest group politics is the phenomenon about which Guither writes. The book is a sequence of summaries about the new actors in farm-policy decision making. An almost unimaginable amount of work has gone into the collection of information about and positions of the various groups.

9. Gustafson, Thane. "Transforming Soviet Agriculture: Brezhnev's Gamble on Land Improvement." *Public Policy*, 25 (Summer 1977), 293-312.

   Agricultural modernization and land improvement were two of the highest priority programs of the Brezhnev leadership, the land reclamation program being a major test of the ability of the leadership to control the state bureaucracy and to execute successfully a complicated, many-faceted, and enormous task.

10. Guth, James L. "Consumer Organizations and Federal Dairy Policy." *Policy Studies Journal*, 6 (Summer 1978), 499-503.

    Since 1933 milk prices in the U.S. have been heavily influenced by two interrelated federal programs: price supports for manufactured products and federal marketing orders for fluid milk. Policy has usually been determined within a classic "subgovernment," consisting of the National Milk Producers Federation, other dairy industry and farmer organizations, the House and Senate agriculture committees, and the USDA marketing authorities.

11. Hadwiger, Don R. and William P. Browne, eds. *The New Politics of Food*. Lexington, Mass.: D.C. Heath, 1978.

    The politics of American agriculture demonstrates vividly the relationship between institutional change and policy change, as well as how one limits the other.

12. Hardin, Charles M. "Agricultural Price Policy: The Political Role of Bureaucracy." *Policy Studies Journal*, 6 (Summer 1978), 467-72.

    Like much other American policy, agricultural price policy has been strongly influenced by bureaucracy or "political subsystems."

13. Johnson, D. Gale, ed. *Food and Agricultural Policy for the 1980s*. Washington, D.C.: American Enterprise Institute for Public Policy Research, 1981.

    Consists of papers presented to the Conference on Food and Agricultural Policy in October of 1980, in an effort to make a contribution to the preparation of agricultural legislation that was required during the early part of 1981, the Food and Agriculture Act of 1977, expiring with the 1981 crop year.

14. Jones, Lamar B. and G. Randolph Rice. "Agricultural Labor in the Southwest: The Postbracero Years." *Social Science Quarterly*, 61 (June 1980), 86-94.

    Examines the wage and employment effects of exclusion of supplementary farm workers--braceros--from farm labor markets in Texas, California, New Mexico, and Arizona. The authors find through the use of econometric procedures that the effects of exclusion have not been positive. They suggest that the primary retardant to wage improvement has been the increased illegal entry of workers from Mexico.

15. Laird, Roy D. "Grain as a Foreign Policy Tool in Dealing with the Soviets: A Contingency Plan." *Policy Studies Journal*, 6 (Summer 1978), 533-37.

    The key to grain becoming a major tool of diplomacy will be quiet, behind-the-scenes, step-by-step movements, dependent upon a most careful monitoring of the actual situation that develops in the Soviet grain fields and meat counters and, most of all, changes in the weather.

16. Lurie, Jonathan. "The Commodities Exchanges and Federal Regulation, 1922-1974: The Decline of Self-Government?" *Policy Studies Journal*, 6 (Summer 1978), 488-93.

    The development of private commodities exchanges, and other kindred institutions, into quasi-public regulatory agencies is one of the more important but little studied aspects of American administrative law. The growth of federal regulation in commodity exchanges and trading raises troublesome questions.

17. McCalla, Alex F. "The Politics of the U.S. Agricultural Research Establishment: A Short Analysis." *Policy Studies Journal*, 6 (Summer 1978), 479-83.

    Discusses the set of organizations, public and private, which fund and/or do agricultural research in the United States. Its purpose is to attempt to unravel the "politics" of that establishment.

18. McGee, Leo and Robert Boone, eds. *The Black Rural Landowner-- Endangered Species: Social, Political, and Economic Implication*. Westport, Conn.: Greenwood Press, 1979.

    Exceedingly valuable as the first in-depth look at the problems surrounding black land ownership. Thirty percent of the black population still lives on the land but unless they are given some needed assistance, they will be driven to the urban ghettoes.

19. Meier, Kenneth J. "Client Representation in USDA Bureaus: Causes and Consequences." *Policy Studies Journal*, 6 (Summer 1978), 484-88.

    The power and durability of agricultural policy subsystems has been attributed to the size and strength of interest group coalitions that the bureaus in the Department of Agriculture have built. Since most analyses of interest group support have been in case study form, this research empirically examines interest group support for USDA bureaus.

20. Michie, Aruna Nayyar. "Agricultural Modernization and Economic Inequality: The Indian Experience." *Social Science Quarterly*, 59 (September 1978), 311-23.

    Discusses the reasons why economic inequality increases with growth, and the relationship between production organization and distribution. The survey data used illustrate how a class of economically marginal people is created by agricultural policies.

21. Ortiz, Isidro D. "The Politics of Collective Bargaining in Agriculture." *Policy Studies Journal*, 6 (Summer 1978), 510-13.

    On June 4, 1975 Governor Brown signed into law the California Agricultural Labor Relations Act of 1975. As passed by the legislature and signed by Governor Brown, this legislation granted farmworkers the right to choose by secret elections which union, if any, would represent them and created a five-member board to be appointed by the governor to administer the law--the Agricultural Labor Relations Board. The purpose of the legislation, as declared in its preamble, was "to insure peace in the agricultural fields by guaranteeing justice for all agricultural workers and stability in labor relations.

22. Paarlberg, Don. "A New Agenda for Agriculture." *Policy Studies Journal*, 6 (Summer 1978), 504-6.

People think the central matter of public policy is the choice between alternative solutions to issues that are on the agenda. The real question is whether the issues on the agenda are the relevant ones.

23. ———. *Farm and Food Policy: Issues of the 1980's*. Lincoln: University of Nebraska Press, 1980.

Much of the book is devoted to the new agricultural agenda--making food available to all sectors of the population, reconciling environmental and production concerns, expanding international trade. The book's major contribution is the presentation of a broad perspective on this new agricultural policy agenda. Such broad views are rare in either public policy studies or in the specific field of agricultural policy.

24. ———, ed. *Food and Agricultural Policy*. Washington, D.C.: American Enterprise Institute for Public Policy Research, 1977.

Compiles papers presented at the Conference on Food and Agricultural Policy. The full range of farm and food policy was brought up for examination, but the sharpest focus was price and production policy for the major farm commodities.

25. Paarlberg, Robert L. "The Failure of Food Power." *Policy Studies Journal*, 6 (Summer 1978), 537-42.

Maintains that the value of food as an instrument of diplomacy is much less than meets the eye. For those foreign policy leaders who are yearning for some means to restore the U.S. to a position of unchallenged primacy on the world stage, this may be a disappointing lesson. But for those sensitive to the dangers of power abuse in the international system, this may be considered a happy discovery.

26. Payne, William C., Jr. "Implementing Federal Nondiscrimination Policies in the Department of Agriculture, 1964-1976." *Policy Studies Journal*, 6 (Summer 1978), 507-9.

There is a long history of minority group concerns in the agricultural policies of the United States from colonial times to the present. It is apparent that minorities do not participage in nor do they benefit from agricultural programs and policies to the degree that might be expected in an environment free of discrimination based on race, color or national origin.

27. Porter, Laurellen. "Congress and Agricultural Policy." *Policy Studies Journal*, 6 (Summer 1978), 472-79.

Reviews the demographic forces that have altered the constituency base of the House of Representatives, the congressional reforms of the 1970's, the new congressional budget process, and the impact of these changes as they were manifest in the making of agriculture policy.

28. Porter, Roger B. "The U.S.-U.S.S.R. Grain Agreement: Some Lessons for Policymakers." *Public Policy*, 29 (Fall 1981), 527-51.

The 1975 U.S.-U.S.S.R. Grain Agreement negotiations illuminate the parameters and constraints faced by policymakers in a democratic, pluralistic political system. The negotiations reveal the interaction between formulating a policy and implementing it, suggesting that who is seen as responsible for a policy is often as important as the content of that policy.

29. Richard, John B. "The Scramble for Water: Agriculture versus Other Interests in Wyoming." *Policy Studies Journal*, 6 (Summer 1978), 519-23.

The international food crisis, energy requirements and shortages, "hit" lists on water projects, and the western states' drought demonstrate the importance of adequate water resources throughout the nation and the world especially in relation to agriculture and food supplies.

30. Rushefsky, Mark E. "Policy Implications of Alternative Agriculture." *Policy Studies Journal*, 8 (Spring 1980), 772-84.

Suggests that there has been a small shift in American agricultural practices, and more importantly in policy making in this area, toward what can be called organic or alternative agriculture. These policy changes are partially due to triggering devices, exogenous forces that have led to changes in the policy agenda. Two major exogenous factors are reviewed--the energy crisis and environmental factors.

31. Sampson, R. Neil. *Farmland or Wasteland: A Time to Choose: Overcoming the Threat to America's Farm and Food Future.* Emmaus, Pa.: Rodale Press, 1981.

Demands for agricultural products are accelerating at an ever-increasing pace, while, simultaneously, the ability of the U.S. land to produce is being wasted faster than at any point in our history. It is clear that these two trends cannot continue indefinitely.

Agricultural Commodities Policy 17

32. Wallerstein, Mitchel B. *Food for War--Food for Peace: United States Food Aid in a Global Context.* Cambridge, Mass.: MIT Press, 1980.

    Defines the problem of American food aid, which is examined in four ways: the history of American food aid, the framework of international food aid, the foreign policy objectives of American food aid, and the resulting implications for international programs.

33. Weinbaum, Marvin G. "Political Risks in Agricultural Development and Food Policy in the Middle East." *Policy Studies Journal*, 8 (Spring 1980), 734-48.

    Analyzes agricultural and food policies in the Middle East, and finds that they are inescapably political.

34. Wilson, Graham K. *Special Interests and Policymaking: Agricultural Policies and Politics in Britain and the United States of America, 1956-1970.* London: John Wiley & Sons, 1977.

    Outlines how inertias of agricultural policies flow from more complex dynamics than simple interest-group political power. Can be recommended as a sobering, informative study of the politics of government/economy interaction.

35. Youngberg, Garth. "The Alternative Agricultural Movement." *Policy Studies Journal*, 6 (Summer 1978), 524-30.

    Alternative agriculturalists believe that conventional agriculture is destructive of both human and natural resources and is therefore destined to destroy itself as well as the larger population and are deeply committed to the reorientation of agricultural practices and techniques. This analysis attempts to assess the politics and policy prospects of this diffuse, dedicated and growing movement.

Chapter 3

CIVIL RIGHTS, MINORITIES, AND WOMEN

36. Adams, William and Suzanne Albin. "Public Information on Social Change: TV Coverage of Women in the Workforce." *Policy Studies Journal*, 8 (Spring 1980), 717-34.

   Analyzes the thematic and visual content of ten years of nightly television news coverage of women in the workforce and employment discrimination.

37. Baer, Judith A. "Sexual Equality and the Burger Court." *Western Political Quarterly*, 31 (December 1978), 470-91.

   The Burger Court has dealt severe blows to women's rights, notably in rulings on pregnancy benefits and public assistance for abortions. Analysis of several major decisions shows that the Court's record in this area is mixed because it has no real commitment to sexual equality. The favorable decisions result from factors other than feminist sympathies, and cases where the women lose reveal a striking insensitivity to feminist claims.

38. Becker, Susan D. *The Origins of the Equal Rights Amendment: American Feminism between the Wars.* Westport, Conn.: Greenwood Press, 1981.

   Provides the first comprehensive study of the National Woman's Party (NWP), although the major theme is the Equal Rights Amendment (ERA) which that party spent many years supporting. Places major emphasis on the 1920s and the 1930s since those were the decades of major promotion of the ERA by the NWP.

39. Black, Merle. "Racial Composition of Congressional Districts and Support for Federal Voting Rights Legislation in the American South." *Social Science Quarterly*, 59 (December 1978), 435-50.

   Support for federal voting rights legislation is related to racial composition in three time periods: (1) prior to the emergence of massive participation by blacks (1957 and 1960), (2) during the rapid expansion of the black electorate (1965 and 1969-1970) and (3) a decade after passage of the original act (1975).

40. Boneparth, Ellen, ed. *Women, Power and Policy*. New York: Pergamon Press, 1982.

   A feminist perspective is presented on a number of policy problems facing the country. The editor maintains that, "The feminist perspective that runs through the chapters in this volume argues that changes in the status of women are necessary and can be effected through public policy."

41. Bridges, William P. and Richard A. Berk. "Sex, Earnings, and the Nature of Work: A Job-Level Analysis of Male-Female Income Differences." *Social Science Quarterly*, 58 (March 1978), 553-65.

   The authors find that differential qualifications account for approximately 15 percent of the income gap between male-labeled and female-labeled jobs; underemployment of workers in female jobs accounts for another 15 percent; and residual effects for 70 percent. In addition, using job content measures, differential rewards are found for variability in job complexity for those working male- and female-typed jobs.

42. Brown, Lawrence D. "The Scope and Limits of Equality as a Normative Guide to Federal Health Care Policy." *Public Policy*, 26 (Fall 1978), 481-532.

   In recent years policy analysts have begun to insist that the equal access issue be viewed in the context of the national cost of medical services relative to that of other social goods, the cost effectiveness of medical services, and the degree to which health and illness result from behavior in an individual's power to pursue or avoid. Attracted by the new revisionist thinking, but unwilling to follow its arguments to their logical policy implications, federal policymakers have institutionalized their ambivalence.

43. Brown, Michael K. and Stephen P. Erie. "Blacks and the Legacy of the Great Society: The Economic and Political Impact of Federal Social Policy." *Public Policy*, 29 (Summer 1981), 299-330.

   Argues that the principal effect of the social policy initiatives of the 1960s for black Americans was the development of a social welfare economy of publicly funded middle-income service providers and low-income service recipients. By 1976 federal social policy had shifted from the human capital strategy of the Johnson years to an income maintenance strategy based on cash and in-kind transfers.

44. Buell, Emmett H., Jr. and Richard A. Brisbane, Jr. "The Politics of School Desegregation: An Emerging Literature." *Polity*, 11 (Spring 1979), 418-29.

   If not wholly representative, the five books reviewed at least suggest some of the avenues explored in a rapidly growing literature within American political science. As is so often the case with new areas of interest, some questions have been explored much more thoroughly than others.

45. Bullock, Charles S., III. "Congressional Voting and the Mobilization of a Black Electorate in the South." *The Journal of Politics*, 43 (August 1981), 662-82.

   Using data for the 86th through 95th Congresses, Bullock finds substantial variation over time in the relationship between percent black and southern representatives' roll call behavior. However, legislators who have a high black proportion in their districts or who are junior Democrats have, in recent years, shown greater responsiveness to black policy interests. Differences in patterns reported by other scholars are largely products of the time of their research.

46. ──── and Joseph Stewart, Jr. "The Justice Department and School Desegregation: The Importance of Developing Trust." *The Journal of Politics*, 39 (November 1977), 1036-43.

   Elimination of Southern segregated dual schools resulted from efforts of two federal departments, Justice and Health, Education and Welfare (HEW). The lasting consequences of the division of labor between Justice and HEW prompt this attempt to explain why Justice became involved in the districts which it first prosecuted.

47. Butler, John S. and Kenneth L. Wilson. "The American Soldier Revisited: Race Relations and the Military." *Social Science Quarterly*, 59 (December 1978), 451-67.

   Examines the classic finding that there is a positive relationship between racial contact and racial attitudes. This relationship is examined in the context of the recent development of racial separatism in the military.

48. Button, James. "The Quest for Economic Equality: Factors Related to Black Employment in the South." *Social Science Quarterly*, 62 (September 1981), 461-74.

   In terms of black employment in six Florida communities, the results of interviews conducted with the owners of 163 private establishments indicate that blacks are still rarely found in professional positions, that black employment progress has been greatest in Old South communities and that affirmative action programs have been moderately effective.

49. ──── and Richard Scher. "Impact of the Civil Rights Movement: Perceptions of Black Municipal Service Changes." *Social Science Quarterly*, 60 (December 1979), 497-510.

   Relying primarily on perceptual data on black municipal services changes from knowledgeable citizens in six carefully selected Florida communities, an impact of the civil rights movement is examined. Suggests that conventional political strategies have contributed only moderately to absolute and relative changes in such services since 1960.

50. Camp, Roderic A. "Women and Political Leadership in Mexico: A Comparative Study of Female and Male Political Elites." *The Journal of Politics*, 41 (May 1979), 417-41.

   Examines briefly the literature available on Mexican women in general, and their political roles in particular. Suggests several hypotheses concerning the political role of women on the basis of this literature and studies of women political leaders in other countries.

51. Campbell, Bruce A. "The Interaction of Race and Socioeconomic Status in the Development of Political Attitudes." *Social Science Quarterly*, 60 (March 1980), 651-58.

   Using a sample including 116 upper-status blacks to test indirect and isolation theories, finds indirect effects theory is supported, while isolation theory is not.

52. Carver, Joan S. "Women in Florida." *The Journal of Politics*, 41 (August 1979), 941-55.

   Carver discusses an array of data which reveals the status of women in the politics of Florida. She finds it paradoxical in view of Florida's progress in equalizing the treatment of women at law, that neither the national Equal Rights Amendment nor a state constitutional prohibition against discrimination based on sex has been able to win approval in the state.

53. Cayer, N. Joseph and Lee Sigelman. "Minorities and Women in State and Local Government: 1973-1975." *Public Administration Review*, 40 (September/October 1980), 443-50.

   Examination of state and local government workforce figures for 1973 and 1975 reveals that the number of white male employees fell both absolutely and proportionally over that period. Marked gains were made by white women and by black men and women. Nonetheless, by 1975, state and local governments were still a long way from reflecting the demographic makeup of the American population.

54. Claggett, William. "The Life Cycle and Generational Models of the Development of Partisanship: A Test Based on the Delayed Enfranchisement of Women." *Social Science Quarterly*, 60 (March 1980), 643-50.

   Notes that Converse has proposed that reinforcement through voting causes partisan intensity to increase and that his hypothesis implies that the mean partisan strength of women born before 1899 should be weaker than that of men the same age, and presents an analysis of current survey data showing no differences of this nature. The finding supports a generational explanation of partisan strength.

55. Costain, Anne N. "Eliminating Sex Discrimination in Education: Lobbying for Implementation of Title IX." *Policy Studies Journal*, 7 (Winter 1978), 189-95.

The relatively new and untested lobby supporting women's rights won a significant victory by getting Title IX implemented. Yet, this case illustrates the heavy burden placed on new lobbies to demonstrate their worth as potential clientele groups for federal agencies. In some respects this is more difficult than the public and often relatively short-term effort necessary to gain initial congressional passage of bills.

56. ———. "The Struggle for a National Women's Lobby: Organizing a Diffuse Interest." *Western Political Quarterly*, 33 (December 1980), 476-91.

Examines how diffuse interests are organized and what political strengths they display in gaining legislative victories. Two factors, drawn from the formation and early development of a national lobby for women, seem particularly significant in accounting for this legislative success: first, the ability to organize through ad hoc issue coalitions, and second, the exceptional diversity of some of the coalitions entered into.

57. ———. "Representing Women: The Transition from Social Movement to Interest Group." *Western Political Quarterly*, 34 (March 1981), 100-13.

Argues that policy change has been assisted by the shift of the women's movement from social movement to interest group. In analyzing this, the author points to the association of women's movement groups with older established women's organizations as critical for gaining access to the policy-making process.

58. Dye, Thomas R. and James Renick. "Political Power and City Jobs: Determinants of Minority Employment." *Social Science Quarterly*, 62 (September 1981), 475-86.

Minorities and women are underrepresented in "administrative," "professional" and "protective" jobs in cities. Minority employment in these jobs is independently affected by minority representation on city council, as well as by the size and percentage of the minority population of the city.

59. Erie, Steven P. "Public Policy and Black Economic Polarization." *Policy Analysis*, 6 (Summer 1980), 305-17.

Black economic development since the mid-1960's has been polarized, with an urban underclass developing alongside a fledgling middle class. Appraises how government policies--specifically, public employment, public assistance, and worker training—may cause or perpetuate this polarization, and considers the possible political consequences of simultaneous economic progress and growing dependence on government assistance.

60. Farley, Reynolds and Diane Colasanto. "Racial Residential Segregation: Is It Caused by Misinformation about Housing Costs?" *Social Science Quarterly*, 61 (December 1980), 623-37.

    Tests the hypothesis that blacks overestimate housing costs in white neighborhoods and thereby fail to seek housing they can afford. Finds that blacks are knowledgeable about such costs.

61. Frye, Hardy T. *Black Parties and Political Power: A Case Study.* Boston: G.K. Hall, 1980.

    A study of the origins, development, and effectiveness of the largely black National Democratic Party of Alabama, written by a sociologist who was a participant in its early activities and returned for a scholarly study of its later history conducted by extensive interviews, observations, and use of sometimes fugitive printed sources.

62. Garcia, John A. "Self-Identity among the Mexican-Origin Population." *Social Science Quarterly*, 62 (March 1981), 88-98.

    Self-labeling choices of the Mexican-origin population in the Southwest and the extent of sociodemographic differentiation among the variuos ethnic label choices are examined. The "Mexican-American" label was selected with greatest frequency, but also appeared to include the most differentiated group. Nonetheless, this label was even more strongly preferred by those in the 35-50 age group, those with a high school education and those with higher incomes.

63. Garcia, Jose A., Cal Clark, and Janet Clark. "Policy Impacts on Chicanos and Women: A State Case Study." *Policy Studies Journal*, 7 (Winter 1978), 251-57.

    Examines changes in the representation of Hispanics and women in the New Mexico state government workforce from 1971 to 1978. Finds that in spite of the passage of a state ERA in New Mexico, in spite of the state's affirmative action program, and in spite of a seemingly more favorable public atmosphere signalled by the election of a Hispanic governor, the inequalities in state employment which existed in 1971 persist.

64. Gatlin, Douglas S., Micheal W. Giles, and Everett S. Cataldo. "Policy Support within a Target Group: The Case of School Desegregation." *The American Political Science Review*, 72 (September 1978), 985-95.

    Empirically tests three theoretical approaches to explaining specific support for a policy output.

65. Gelb, Joyce and Marian Lief Palley. "Women and Interest Group Politics: A Comparative Analysis of Federal Decision-Making." *The Journal of Politics*, 41 (May 1979), 362-92.

    Considers the extent to which emergent feminist groups have been successful in influencing the American policy-making system. The techniques most useful in achieving political goals are surveyed. The Equal Credit Opportunity Act of 1974, the anti-sex discrimination provisions of the Title IX of the Education Amendments of 1972, the anti-abortion Hyde Amendments of both 1976 and 1977, and the Amendment to Title VII of the Civil Rights Act of 1964, which would end discrimination in employment on the basis of pregnancy or pregnancy-related disabilities are examined.

66. Gillespie, J. David and Michael L. Mitchell. "Bakke, Weber, and Race in Employment: Analysis of Informed Opinion." *Policy Studies Journal*, 8 (Winter 1979), 383-91.

    Reports research on informed opinion as to linkage between Bakke and the discretionary use of race in private employment practice.

67. Githens, Marianne and Jewel Prestage. "Women State Legislators: Styles and Priorities." *Policy Studies Journal*, 7 (Winter 1978), 264-70.

    From the literature the marginal man emerges as one who experiences stress as a result of the unique position he occupies. Overall, the data seem to support the hypothesis that women state legislators are objectively marginal. Most notable among the data that suggest experiential marginality are the women's high level of self-motivation on the one hand and the importance they attach to family attitudes about their involvement in elective politics on the other.

68. Goldman, Alan H. *Justice and Reverse Discrimination*. Princeton, N.J.: Princeton University Press, 1979.

    One of the most important social issues of the past decade is whether there should be preference, or "reverse discrimination," in employment and education for racial minorities and for women. The argument of the book is that preference should be provided as warranted for individuals, but should not be granted on a group basis.

69. Goldstein, Leslie F. "The Politics of the Burger Court toward Women." *Policy Studies Journal*, 7 (Winter 1978), 213-18.

    Maintains that despite the setbacks encountered by women's group litigants during the 1976-77 Supreme Court term, the fact remains that the Burger Court has contributed more to the development of American women's legal equality and constitutional freedom than any previous judicial body.

70. Greenberg, Stanley B. *Race and State in Capitalist Development: Comparative Perspectives.* New Haven, Conn.: Yale University Press, 1980.

    Attempts to investigate the reasons for the persistence of ethnic and racial divisions in advanced capitalist societies and argues that at the initial stages of capitalist development racial and ethnic divisions are rigidly institutionalized.

71. Gruhl, John, Cassia Spohn, and Susan Welch. "Women as Policymakers: The Case of Trial Judges." *American Journal of Political Science,* 25 (May 1981), 308-22.

    Examines the convicting and sentencing behavior of men and women judges in over 30,000 felony cases and compares the behavior of men and women judges in convicting and sentencing male and female defendants. The findings indicate that women judges generally did not convict and sentence defendants differently than men judges did.

72. Hall, Grace and Alan Saltzstein. "Equal Employment Opportunity for Minorities in Municipal Government." *Social Science Quarterly,* 57 (March 1977), 864-72.

    Finds Spanish-surnamed employment more strongly related to characteristics of that minority population than was the case for blacks in Texas. Indicates that substantial differences existed between the political activity and attitudes of black and white federal employees and that these were somewhat congruent with differences found within the general population.

73. Hanks, Michael. "Race, Sexual Status and Athletics in the Process of Educational Achievement." *Social Science Quarterly,* 60 (December 1979), 482-96.

    A model to investigate high school athletic participation effects on access to college is estimated separately for males and females, blacks and whites and by disposition to matriculate, using longitudinal data from a national sample of adolescents. Results indicate that participation in athletics facilitates the formation of educational goals and enhances one's prospects for attending an institution of higher education.

74. Hardy, Richard J. and Donald J. McCrone. "The Impact of the Civil Rights Act of 1964 on Women." *Policy Studies Journal,* 7 (Winter 1978), 240-43.

    The purpose is to determine whether the relative income of black women has improved systematically and significantly since the implementation of civil rights policies in 1965. The authors find that while civil rights policies have a salutary effect on the economic condition of black women, the median income of black women nationally in 1976 was only 34 percent that of white male income.

75. Henderson, Lenneal J. "The Impact of the Equal Employment Opportunity Act of 1972 on Employment Opportunities for Women and Minorities in Municipal Government." *Policy Studies Journal*, 7 (Winter 1978), 234-39.

    Argues that, in spite of policy minotoring and evaluation procedures incorporated into the Act, premise assessment of the impact of the 1972 EEO Act on women and minorities in municipal government remains problematical. Recommendations for moving analyses of the impact of the EEO Act from its present symbolic base to a more substantive foundation are made.

76. Hershey, Marjorie R. "Racial Differences in Sex-Role Identities and Sex Stereotyping: Evidence against a Common Assumption." *Social Science Quarterly*, 58 (March 1978), 583-96.

    Suggests that sex roles are not more egalitarian among blacks than among whites. Family income levels, father's absence or unemployment, and mother's employment have only slight effects on sex differences in attitudes toward sex-role identities and stereotyping of activities.

77. Hoole, Francis W., David H. Handley, and Charles W. Ostrom, Jr. "Policy-Making Models, Budgets, and International Organizations." *The Journal of Politics*, 41 (August 1979), 923-32.

    Reports an evaluation of the ability of four alternative budgeting models (incremental, share-of-the-pie, action-reaction, and environmental forces) to explain expenditures for five different international governmental organizations.

78. Huckle, Patricia. "The Womb Factor: Pregnancy Policies and Employment of Women." *Western Political Quarterly*, 34 (March 1981), 114-26.

    As Huckle reveals in her case study, barring discrimination in employment benefits based on the capacity to reproduce, while responsive to the problem of equity for women workers, does little to restructure employment opportunities for women who must fill dual roles of worker and mother.

79. Hunt, Larry L. and Janet G. Hunt. "Religious Affiliation and Militancy among Urban Blacks: Some Catholic/Protestant Comparisons." *Social Science Quarterly*, 57 (March 1977), 821-33.

    Shows Catholics to be of higher secular status and to hold distinctive orientations toward the issues of civil rights and social change. The finding that Catholics have an aversion to corporate forms of identity and militancy is interpreted as reflecting the historic linkage between Catholicism and individuated upward mobility among blacks.

Civil Rights, Minorities, and Women 27

80. Jackman, Mary R. "General and Applied Tolerance: Does Education Increase Commitment to Racial Integration?" *American Journal of Political Science*, 22 (May 1978), 302-24.

   Challenges the long-standing proposition that higher education produces stronger commitment to the democratic norm of tolerance. Replicated, national survey data that measure both abstract and applied commitment to racial integration are used to examine three important contributions to that perspective made by Prothro and Grigg (1960), Converse (1964), and Greeley and Sheatsley (1974).

81. Jacobs, David. "Dimensions of Inequality and Public Policy in the States." *The Journal of Politics*, 42 (February 1980), 291-306.

   If economic elites really do control the political process and use their influence to insure that low income groups receive less (as advocates of elite theory suggest), then differences between the poor- and middle-income groups should be of diminished importance. This study reveals a trend which is opposite to this expectation: the most politically significant income difference is the gap between low- and middle-income recipients.

82. Jones, August J. *Law, Bureaucracy and Politics: The Implementation of Title VI of the Civil Rights Act of 1964.* Washington, D.C.: University Press of America, 1982.

   This well-researched analysis of Title VI--the non-compliance provision--of the Civil Rights Act of 1964 focuses on implementation of the Act rather than the underlying politics of its development.

83. Joseph, Lawrence B. "Some Ways of Thinking about Equality of Opportunity." *Western Political Quarterly*, 33 (September 1980), 393-400.

   Argues against the common view that "equality of opportunity" and "equality of results" are polar concepts. The relationship between equality of opportunity and equality of results must be understood in terms of their application to two different social processes--the recruitment of individuals to social roles and the attachment of rewards to those roles. While the two normative principles are conceptually distinct, they are not mutually exclusive.

84. Kassiola, Joel. "Compensatory Justice and the Moral Obligation for Preferential Treatment of Discriminated Groups." *Polity*, 11 (Fall 1978), 46-66.

   Public policy aimed at remedying past injustices has created a further moral dilemma through reverse discrimination. But advocates of preferential treatment have rejected the charge of reverse discrimination on various grounds. The author examines the problem with reference to the principle of compensatory justice, applying the methodological controversy between individualists and holists to the issue.

85. Livingston, John C. *Fair Game? Inequality and Affirmative Action.* San Francisco: W.H. Freeman and Col, 1979.

    Of the spate of publications on affirmative action since the Supreme Court's Bakke decision, John Livingston's book is among the most intellectually stimulating. The book is a comprehensive, scholarly defense of affirmative action.

86. Long, James E. "Productivity, Employment Discrimination, and the Relative Economic Status of Spanish Origin Males." *Social Science Quarterly*, 58 (December 1977), 357-73.

    Concludes that both employment discrimination and low productivity have contributed to the inferior economic status of Spanish origin males compared with white males. The data also suggest that recent efforts to upgrade their economic status have not been very successful.

87. Lopez, Manual Mariano. "Patterns of Interethnic Residential Segregation in the Urban Southwest." *Social Science Quarterly*, 62 (March 1981), 50-63.

    The striking similarity of the overall pattern of residential segregation among Mexican Americans, blacks and Anglos for 1960 and 1970 masks some important changes. City characteristics found to be good predictors of segregation for 1960 fail to adequately account for the same types of segregation in 1970.

88. Lyon, Larry and Holley Rector-Owen. "Labor Market Mobility among Young Black and White Women." *Social Science Quarterly*, 62 (March 1981), 64-78.

    The National Longitudinal Surveys of young females provide the data for the construction of causal models of occupational mobility for both black and white workers.

89. McCarrick, Earlean M. "Equality v. Liberty: An Unresolved Constitutional Conflict." *Polity*, 10 (Winter 1977), 241-60.

    Controversies involving the Fourteenth Amendment in recent times have been viewed by the courts as conflicts between individual persons and state government. Argues that this treatment frequently bypasses the real issue, which is conflict between competing and equally valid individual rights. Finds, in examining cases involving access to privately owned property and school desegregation, that the courts have failed to provide unambiguous standards.

90. McCrone, Donald J. and Richard J. Hardy. "Civil Rights Policies and the Achievement of Racial Economic Equality, 1945-1975." *American Journal of Political Science*, 22 (February 1978), 1-17.

   Attempts to determine whether civil rights policies since 1964 have succeeded in systematically decreasing the gap between black and white male incomes, both nationally and regionally.

91. Martin, John Frederick. *Civil Rights and the Crisis of Liberalism: The Democratic Party 1945-1976*. Boulder, Colo.: Westview Press, 1979.

   An important contribution to the literature on liberalism and civil rights in the United States. It focuses on the growing tension within the Democratic party from 1945 to 1976 as the civil rights movement gathered momentum and then the consequent reaction set in.

92. Meier, Kenneth J. "Constraints on Affirmative Action." *Policy Studies Journal*, 7 (Winter 1978), 208-13.

   Achieving equal employment opportunity for minorities has been a federally imposed goal of state and local government since the mid-1960s. Examines how three different environmental constraints--economic, political, and administrative/labor pool-- restrict equal employment programs in state and local government bureaucracies.

93. Milward, H. Brinton and Cheryl Swanson. "The Impact of Affirmative Action on Organizational Behavior." *Policy Studies Journal*, 7 (Winter 1978), 201-7.

   Minority and women's groups have been highly critical of efforts to implement affirmative action programs, yet very little systematic research has been done to evaluate their impact. This research proposes to remedy this situation by using a theoretical model derived from the literature on organizational-environmental interaction to assess the implementation of federally mandated affirmative action programs.

94. Murray, Richard and Arnold Vedlitz. "Race, Socioeconomic Status, and Voting Participation in Large Southern Cities." *The Journal of Politics*, 39 (November 1977), 1064-72.

   By integrating census data with precinct level electoral data, seeks to examine more closely how socioeconomic variables within racial populations relate to differences in voting behavior. Black and white populations in five Southern cities are analyzed. The cities are Atlanta, New Orleans, Memphis, Dallas, and Houston.

95. O'Neill, Timothy J. "The Language of Equality in a Constitutional Order." *The American Political Science Review*, 75 (September 1981), 626-35.

   Illuminates the metaphorical structure of law and language and concludes that the restricted range of metaphorical thinking in law weakens the law's capacity to mediate struggles over social goals.

96. Pharr, Susan J. *Political Women in Japan: The Search for a Place in Political Life.* Berkeley, Calif.: University of California Press, 1981.

   Rests on intensive fieldwork in Japan (1971-1975), including some four hundred hours of in-depth interviews with one hundred young politically active women. From the study of these individuals, and of the sample at large, traces the process of role redefinition by which prevailing ideas about woman's status undergo change.

97. Preston, Michael B. "Black Elected Officials and Public Policy: Symbolic or Substantive Representation?" *Policy Studies Journal*, 7 (Winter 1978), 196-201.

   The increase in black elected officials nationwide has led to a renewed interest in electoral politics by the black community. There is, however, some question about the utility of this approach for solving the problems of black Americans. Indeed, it may be argued that there is "no one best way." Electoral politics is a vital and necessary weapon among others. To the degree that blacks use the ballot wisely, they will not only be able to achieve symbolic results, but substantive ones as well.

98. Price, Robert M. and Carl G. Rosberg, eds. *The Apartheid Regime: Political Power and Racial Domination.* Institute of International Studies, 1980.

   Subjects include analyses of Afrikaner politics, black politics, urban Africans, labor issues, current reforms, and opportunities for further change.

99. Quester, Aline O. and Janice Olson. "Sex, Schooling, and Hours of Work." *Social Science Quarterly*, 58 (March 1978), 566-82.

   For professional-technical occupations, earnings variance is greater for males and hours of work variance is greater for females; and, by occupation, male schooling exceeds that of females. The findings suggest that men prefer to maximize their earnings while women prefer to vary their hours, and in a lower direction than do men.

100. Regens, James and Charles S. Bullock, III. "Congruity of Racial Attitudes among Black and White Students." *Social Science Quarterly*, 60 (December 1979), 511-22.

    Examines the similarity in the pattern of organization and constraint of racial attitudes among a biracial sample of high school students and finds that the organization of racial attitudes is most similar for blacks and whites who are middle class, academically average or above, young, and attend racially balanced schools.

101. Rent, George S. and J. Dennis Lord. "Neighborhood Racial Transition and Property Value Trends in a Southern Community." *Social Science Quarterly*, 59 (June 1978), 51-59.

    Compares price trends in a racially changing and an all-white neighborhood. Finds a lower rate of property value appreciation in the racially changing neighborhood, apparently as a result of panic selling by white residents.

102. Robinson, Ted and Robert E. England. "Black Representation on Central City School Boards Revisited." *Social Science Quarterly*, 62 (September 1981), 495-502.

    An extension of Welch and Karnig's (1978) school board study analyzing black representation. The sample size has been increased from their forty-three to seventy-five central cities. Finds at-large electoral systems significantly reduce proportionally based equitable black representation.

103. Rose, Winfield H. and Tiang Ping Chia. "The Impact of the Equal Employment Opportunity Act of 1972 on Black Employment in the Federal Service: A Preliminary Analysis." *Public Administration Review*, 38 (May/June 1978), 245-51.

    After sketching the background of equal employment opportunity in the federal service, includes not only the General Schedule but other pay schedules as well. Also includes data from the post-EEOA period, compares pre- and post-EEOA progress, and concludes that the Act had little effect in increasing the proportion of blacks in the upper levels of the federal service as of May 31, 1974.

104. Schoen, Robert. "Toward a Theory of the Demographic Implications of Ethnic Stratification." *Social Science Quarterly*, 59 (December 1978), 468-81.

    Presents an outline relating ethnic stratification, the economic status of the country and the typical nature of demographic change. Notes that in ethnically stratified societies some lower socioeconomic groups have a "demographic opportunity" to move into a middle niche, while others do not. Illustrates this opportunity differential's explanatory utility by examining the Asian and colored groups in South Africa, and the demographic differences between Japanese Americans and Mexican Americans.

105. Sears, David O., Carl P. Hensler, and Leslie K. Speer. "Whites' Opposition to 'Busing': Self-Interest or Symbolic Politics?" *The American Political Science Review*, 73 (June 1979), 369-84.

Contrasts the "self-interest" and "symbolic politics" explanations for the formation of mass policy preferences and voting behavior.

106. Segers, Mary C. "Equality, Public Policy and Relevant Sex Differences." *Polity*, 11 (Spring 1979), 319-39.

In light of discussions concerning theories of equality and social justice, argues against an employment policy prescribing identity of treatment to secure equality of opportunity for the sexes. Examines the theoretical and practical deficiencies of such an approach and finds that contemporary employment policies, which profess to be neutral, penalize one sex by applying a pattern designed for the other.

107. Semyonov, Moshe. "Changing Roles of Women: Participation in Olympic Games." *Social Science Quarterly*, 62 (December 1981), 735-43.

Women's participation in sports is a recent phenomenon characterizing changes in female roles in society. Investigates whether indicators of female participation in the Olympic Games parallel models and theories of female participation in the labor force.

108. Slawson, John. *Unequal Americans: Practices and Politics of Intergroup Relations*. Westport, Conn.: Greenwood Press, 1979.

Addresses a very broad range of issues that have affected intergroup or minority group relations between the years 1930 and 1975. The work should be of interest to a general audience and a particularly valuable supplemental reading in introductory policy and minority relations courses.

109. Stewart, Debra W. "Organizational Variables and Policy Impact: Equal Employment Opportunity." *Policy Studies Journal*, 8 (Summer 1980), 870-78.

Explores how administrative organization practices mediate the impact of equal employment opportunity policy. Extra organizational variables are discussed as factors influencing the significance of organizational action.

110. Stoper, Emily and Roberta Ann Johnson. "The Weaker Sex and the Better Half: The Idea of Women's Moral Superiority in the American Feminist Movement." *Polity*, 10 (Winter 1977), 192-217.

   The question as to why so few women hold positions of power in American government leads the authors of this article to examine the sources and implications of one of the major arguments of American feminists: that woman's nature is morally superior to and mysteriously different from the nature of man. Although this claim has produced certain political benefits, it is argued that the overall effect has been to limit women's role in politics as well as to perpetuate their psychological weaknesses.

111. Thompson, Frank J. "Civil Servants and the Deprived: Socio-Political and Occupational Explanations of Attitudes toward Minority Hiring." *American Journal of Political Science*, 22 (May 1978), 325-47.

   Focuses on the attitudes of public administrators toward one politically important issue, minority hiring. The central hypothesis is that the receptivity of civil servants to hiring minorities will be more a function of their occupational concerns and of certain of their socio-political characteristics than of their perceptions of public sentiment and external group pressure. The data provide some support for this hypothesis.

112. Uhlman, Thomas M. "Black Elite Decision Making: The Case of Trial Judges." *American Journal of Political Science*, 22 (November 1978), 884-95.

   Presents the first extensive study of black elite decision making. The behavior of sixteen black trial court judges is the principal focus of analysis.

113. Waldman, Loren K. "Types and Measures of Inequality." *Social Science Quarterly*, 58 (September 1977), 229-41.

   Defines five types of inequality, classifies indices according to type(s) measured, and discusses the consequences of the use of inappropriate types in previous studies. Criteria for the selection of one of several alternative measures of a type are presented.

114. Welch, Susan and Dianne Levitt Gottheil. "Women and Public Policy: A Comparative Analysis." *Policy Studies Journal*, 7 (Winter 1978), 258-64.

   A brief overview of a project examining the impact of social, political and economic environmental factors on the presence of a number of state policies relating to women. Examines several types of policies to see if there are significant and consistent differences among the states: that is, do some states consistently treat women more equally, while others usually discriminate?

115. Wilcox, Jerry and Wade Clark Roof. "Percent Black and Black-White Status Inequality: Southern versus Non-Southern Patterns." *Social Science Quarterly*, 59 (December 1978), 421-34.

    Using 1970 data for 146 metropolitan areas, finds that racial inequality in education, occupation and income covaries positively with percent black in the South, but that elsewhere patterns are erratic and much less conclusive.

116. Wilson, William Julius. *The Declining Significance of Race: Blacks and Changing American Institutions*. Chicago: University of Chicago Press, 1978.

    An incisive analysis of the role of race and class in American society and their impact on race relations. Argues that the basis of racial strife has been eroded by economic changes calculated "to mediate or resolve class and racial conflicts grounded in the social relations of production."

117. Wohlenberg, Ernest H. "Correlates of Equal Rights Amendment Ratification." *Social Science Quarterly*, 60 (March 1980), 676-84.

    Finds that states with more innovative legislatures, those ratifying earlier suffrage amendments and those with more liberal religious and political views to be significantly more likely to have ratified ERA than those with opposite characteristics.

118. Worcester, Dean A., Jr. "Discrimination in Labor Markets: Cause, Consequences, and Culpability." *Policy Studies Journal*, 5 (Spring 1977), 320-25.

    Sets forth a deductive framework to explain why it is that a variety of equal opportunity legislation does more harm than good. Such legislation can cause unemployment among the minority groups the legislation purportedly is designed to assist. Yet this unemployment can easily be mistaken as evidence of discrimination, thereby bringing about calls for even stronger legislation.

119. Wright, Gerald C. "Racism and Welfare Policy in America." *Social Science Quarterly*, 57 (March 1977), 718-30.

    Finds that support for welfare is more closely tied to measures of racism than to general economic liberalism at the mass opinion level. At the state level, race variables are found to have a very substantial influence on four measures of AFDC policy liberalism.

120. Zashin, Elliot M. "Affirmative Action and Federal Personnel Systems." *Public Policy*, 28 (Summer 1980), 351-80.

When President Carter's Federal Personnel Management Project studied the civil service to determine what reforms were desirable, equal employment opportunity and affirmative action were among the major areas of concern. This paper traces its way through the personnel systems obstacle course and concludes that the prospects for achieving a more representative federal workforce are not greatly improved by the reforms.

121. Zetterbaum, Marvin. "Equality and Human Need." *The American Political Science Review*, 71 (September 1977), 983-98.

Is in part an exploration of how and whether it may be said that value arises from human need, how the concept of human need itself can be understood, and, specifically, how and whether the value of equality may be said to arise from some particular human need.

Chapter 4

ECONOMIC AND MONETARY POLICY

122. Allen, Michael P. "Economic Interest Groups and the Corporate Elite Structure." *Social Science Quarterly*, 58 (March 1978), 597-615.

Examines the ten principal interlock groups among the 250 major corporations of 1935 and 1970 in terms of their characteristics as economic interest groups. The results indicate that family and financial interest groups with centers of common control have declined relative to geographical interest groups without centers of common control, although family and financial interest groups have not been entirely eliminated.

123. Blair, John P. and David Nachmias, eds. *Fiscal Retrenchment and Urban Policy.* Beverly Hills, Calif.: Sage Publications, 1979.

Confronted with a future of slowly growing public revenues and unremitting demands for existing and expanded governmental services, the nation's central cities are entering an era of fiscal retrenchment during which tight budgets will force urban officials to make hard choices among competing governmental priorities and programs.

124. Bunce, Valeri. "Changing Leaders and Changing Policies: The Impact of Elite Succession on Budgetary Priorities in Democratic Countries." *American Journal of Political Science*, 24 (August 1980), 373-95.

Assesses the impact of electoral succession by examining how changes in the top leadership of seven advanced industrial democracies affected their budgetary allocations from approximately 1950 to 1976, with the guiding hypothesis that elections do not disturb the essentially linear and incremental nature of budgetary change in democratic states. This hypothesis, however, was not upheld by the analysis.

125. Burstein, Paul. "Party Balance, Replacement of Legislators, and Federal Government Expenditures, 1941-1976." *Western Political Quarterly*, 32 (June 1979), 203-8.

The work reported was designed to enhance the probability that political effects would be discovered. Two questions were asked: Do changes in the party balance in Congress, or changes in party control of Congress or the presidency, lead to changes in federal government expenditures in highly aggregated functional areas, such as health, agriculture, defense, etc.? Do changes in the rate at which legislators are replaced, regardless of party, lead to such changes in spending? Time series analysis of data for the period 1941-76 indicates that the answer to both questions is no.

126. Castells, Manuel. *The Economic Crisis and American Society*. Princeton, N.J.: Princeton University Press, 1980.

   Attempts to explain the economic crisis that has shaken advanced capitalism for roughly a decade by trying to explain the crisis for the core case of the United States. Characterizes the crisis as a structural one in which reproduction of the political economic system requires basic structural reform.

127. Clarke, Susan E. "Determinants of State Growth Management Policies." *Policy Studies Journal*, 7 (Summer 1979), 753-62.

   Two alternative explanations of why some states have a greater propensity than others to adopt state growth management programs--the spread of necessity and the emulation of virtue--are examined through linear multiple regression analysis.

128. Crandall, Robert W. *The U.S. Steel Industry in Recurrent Crisis: Policy Options in a Competitive World*. Washington, D.C.: Brookings Institution, 1981.

   Demonstrates that the profit motive simply cannot be relied upon to reindustrialize steel. A modernization would require either massive direct government subsidy, a bar to any steel imports, or a radical and permanent diminution of interest rates.

129. Edmunds, Stahrl W. "Who Pays the Costs of Inflation?" *Policy Studies Journal*, 7 (Spring 1979), 568-77.

   Inflation may be looked upon as a deferred consumption tax which reduces consumer purchasing power through high prices to compensate for earlier excess expansions of credit. A portion of this excess borrowing is by government to finance deficits. The inflation cost may then be compared by family-income class with the alternative income taxes needed to avoid inflation by eliminating the deficits.

130. Ehrlich, Paul R. "An Economist in Wonderland." *Social Science Quarterly*, 62 (March 1981), 44-49.

   Simon's criticism illustrates the types of errors some economists make when they deal with problems of population, resources, and environment. Issues associated with the data used are discussed.

131. Ervin, Osbin L. "Local Fiscal Effects of Coal Resource Development: A Framework for Analysis and Management." *Policy Studies Journal*, 7 (Autumn 1978), 9-17.

    Many small communities in coal-producing areas are likely to undergo energy-related growth over the next two decades. The conceptualizations and research discussed in this paper is the first step in the development of data-gathering and management approaches thought to be particularly appropriate to the coal communities of Illinois. The preliminary research focuses on impacts of a coal gasification facility. However, the conceptual framework and related data gathering and analysis should be applicable to other energy-related activities in small communities.

132. Flowers, George A., Jr., Jerome S. Legge, Jr., Paul E. Radford, and David H. Wiltsee. "Targeting Funds for Economic Development in Rural Georgia: The Experience of the Georgia Department of Community Affairs." *Public Administration Review*, 41 (July/August 1981), 485-88.

    During fiscal year 1980, the U.S. Farmers Home Administration (FmHA) desired that 10 percent of its Business and Industry Program loan guarantees be targeted to "highly distressed areas." Across the nation FmHA had neither a predetermined list of such areas nor did it have a set of criteria for identifying such communities. The purposes of this article are to present the experience of the Georgia Department of Community Affairs with targeting, and offer some guidance to practitioners in other states who are responsible for developing and applying measures of local economic distress.

133. Ginsburg, Helen. "Full Employment as a Policy Issue." *Policy Studies Journal*, 8 (Winter 1979), 359-68.

    Traces the origin of the legislative debate over full employment back to the 1940s.

134. Gist, John R. "Appropriations Politics and Expenditure Control." *The Journal of Politics*, 40 (February 1978), 163-78.

    Uncontrollability is politically intriguing because it seems to controvert the established dictum that control over the purse strings is fundamental to congressional power. Indeed, it seems highly likely that the pervasive nature of these uncontrollables in the budget will have certain non-trivial consequences for the congressional appropriations process. Two such consequences are the subject of this paper.

135. Green, Phyllis Strong. "Confounding Influences, Unintended Impacts, and Growth Management Policies." *Policy Studies Journal*, 8 (Summer 1980), 893-900.

    Demonstrates the relationship among inputs, indirect effects, and intended and unanticipated consequences in determining the content and scope of growth management policies in three California cities.

136. Hanke, Steve H. and James B. Anwyll. "On the Discount Rate Controversy." *Public Policy*, 28 (Spring 1980), 171-83.

    A history of cost-benefit procedures for water projects is presented, the discount rate controversy reviewed, and recommendations made.

137. Hansen, Susan B. and Patrick Cooper. "State Revenue Elasticity and Expenditure Growth." *Policy Studies Journal*, 9 (Autumn 1980), 26-33.

    Estimates the contribution of elasticity of tax revenues to the growth of expenditures in the fifty American states since 1960, based on elasticity measures for state revenue sources compiled by the Advisory Commission on Intergovernmental Relations, an index of state tax structural change, and controls for federal aid to states, population increase, and per capita growth in real income.

138. Huddleston, Mark W. "Assessing Congressional Budget Reform: The Impact on Appropriations." *Policy Studies Journal*, 9 (Autumn 1980), 81-86.

    Assesses changes in patterns of spending decisions since 1974, and concludes that the legislation has, to date, had little discernible impact in these areas.

139. Hula, Richard C. "Public Needs and Private Investment: The Case of Home Credit." *Social Science Quarterly*, 62 (December 1981), 685-703.

    Seeks to shed some light on the process of private sector credit allocation in a large, urban county. An initial attempt to explain geographic variation in home credit is based on five simple models of market expectation. The analysis continues with an examination of residuals from these models and the potential explanatory power of selected discrimination variables. Evidence is presented that suggests that previous efforts to explain the allocation of home credit may understate the importance of such discrimination variables.

140. Humphrey, Craig R. and Frederick H. Buttel. "The Sociology of the Growth/No-Growth Debate." *Policy Studies Journal*, 9 (Winter 1980), 336-45.

    This theoretical analysis focuses on the properties of conservative, liberal, and radical paradigms in social science and their application to the growth/no-growth debate in environmental policy literature.

141. Keehn, Norman H. "Liberal Democracy: Impediment to Anti-Inflation Policy." *Polity*, 13 (Winter 1980), 207-29.

Traces the ineffectiveness of governmental efforts to deal with inflation to American liberal-democratic institutions and social values. Contends that the political economy of liberal democracy is so structured as to give public authority limited room to maneuver and little power to institute an effective anti-inflationary program. Consequently, measures designed to curb inflation have yielded disappointing results.

142. Kemp, Kathleen. "Symbolic and Strict Regulation in the American States." *Social Science Quarterly*, 62 (September 1981), 516-26.

In controlling industrial externalities, the American states fall into three groups: nonadopters, symbolic adopters, and strict adopters. These state groupings are best distinguished by the strength of their middle classes, poor innovativeness in regulating the industry, energy self-sufficiency and state decentralization.

143. Kenski, Henry C. "Partisanship and Ideology in the Revenue Act of 1978." *Policy Studies Journal*, 9 (Autumn 1980), 74-81.

The Revenue Act of 1978 was basically a tax policy written in Congress and supported by a broad coalition of moderate and conservative Democrats uniting with Republicans. Ideological divisions in Congress are such that building a majority coalition of liberally oriented tax-cut and tax-reform legislation is difficult. Party and ideology were both salient in the Kemp-Roth vote in each chamber and also in the Corman amendment vote in the House. In the Senate, the relationship between party and tax-cut benefits was unimpressive, although a modest relationship emerged between ideology and the latter.

144. Keyserling, Leon H. "The Problem of High Unemployment: Result of Muddled National Economic Policies." *Policy Studies Journal*, 8 (Winter 1979), 349-59.

Addresses the need for reconstruction of national economic policies, including abandonment of (1) the unemployment-inflation "trade-off," (2) attempts to balance the federal budget at the expense of the economy and the people, (3) the prevalent monetary policy with soaring interest rates, and (4) excessive reliance on tax reductions in lieu of increased public outlays or investment.

145. Kiewiet, D. Roderick. "Policy-Oriented Voting in Response to Economic Issues." *The American Political Science Review*, 75 (June 1981), 448-59.

Explores the hypothesis that voting in response to economic problems is policy-oriented; voters concerned about unemployment are predicted to give greater support to Democratic candidates,

Economic and Monetary Policy 41

while those concerned about inflation are predicted to vote more Republican. In light of evidence from previous research, investigates the electoral effects of inflation and unemployment as (1) problems directly experienced by the individual, and (2) problems deemed serious for the nation as a whole.

146. Lewis-Beck, Michael S. "Maintaining Economic Competition: The Causes and Consequences of Antitrust." *The Journal of Politics*, 41 (February 1979), 169-91.

After considering the purposes and measurement of antitrust efforts, evaluates leading hypotheses on the political and economic determinants of antitrust enforcement, then analyzes the impact of antitrust policy to see whether it actually helps or hinders economic competition.

147. McTighe, John J. "Management Strategies to Deal with Shrinking Resources." *Public Administration Review*, 39 (January/February 1979), 86-90.

While the effects of shrinking revenues are being felt throughout the intergovernmental system, from the White House to the neighborhood fire house, most public managers are finding themselves uncomfortably ill-prepared to deal with this phenomenon. Little, if any, formal training has been provided for managers in cutback management.

148. Parks, Roger B., Paula C. Baker, Larry Kiser, Ronald Oakerson, Elinor Ostrom, Vincent Ostrom, Stephen L. Percy, Martha B. Vandivort, Gordon P. Whitaker, and Rick Wilson. "Consumers as Coproducers of Public Services: Some Economic and Institutional Considerations." *Policy Studies Journal*, 9 (Summer 1981), 1001-11.

Explores the concept of coproduction in an effort to sharpen the definition of that concept and add rigor to the understanding of the effects of coproduction in local service delivery and the processes by which coproductive activity occurs.

149. Pastor, Robert A. *Congress and the Politics of U.S. Foreign Economic Policy, 1929-1976*. Berkeley, Calif.: University of California Press, 1980.

Covers several large items: an evaluation of paradigms for analyzing policy making, a brief history of U.S. trade policy since 1929, a survey of U.S. policies on foreign investments and foreign assistance. Arrives at some useful conclusions, particularly those that cause the reader to question some prevalent myths.

150. Porter, Roger B. *Presidential Decision Making: The Economic Policy Board*. New York: Cambridge University Press, 1980.

This book is a case study focusing on the structure and operation of an advisory body during the Ford administration.

Porter chronicles its history, notes its functions, and details its organization.

151. Prysby, Charles L. "Mass Policy Orientations on Economic Issues in Post-Industrial America." *The Journal of Politics*, 41 (May 1979), 543-65.

    Focuses on the relationship between objective economic situations and orientations on various economic issues. The vertical dimension of social stratification is examined to determine the degree to which differences in economic issue orientations can be explained by differences in such things as income, education, or occupational status.

152. Reid, J. Norman and William F. Fox. "Interregional Benefits from Federal Spending: A New Look at an Old Issue." *Policy Studies Journal*, 9 (Autumn 1980), 95-102.

    Though the distribution of federal expenditures among the regions of the country is an issue that has been much studied, comparison of overall spending totals obscures several important differences among the programs that make up those totals. This paper distinguishes among programs according to their expected community income multipliers and also according to the type of program.

153. Rhoads, Steven E. "Economists and Policy Analysis." *Public Administration Review*, 38 (April 1978), 112-20.

    Ever since the great depression economists have been entering government service in increasing numbers, and in recent years have been systematically analyzing and making recommendations about important questions of public policy. After a brief look at statistics on economists in government, the article focuses on the economists whose principal job is the analysis and evaluation of public policy.

154. Schlozman, Kay Lehman and Sidney Verba. *Injury to Insult: Unemployment, Class and Political Response*. Cambridge, Mass.: Harvard University Press, 1979.

    With this book we now have a guide to understanding the political consequences of being economically deprived, in general, and being unemployed, in particular.

155. Sederberg, Peter C. and Marcia Whicker Taylor. "The Political Economy of No-Growth." *Policy Studies Journal*, 9 (Spring 1981), 735-55.

    Recommends substituting more abundant political resources for scarce economic ones. Appropriate scenarios resulting from these substitution patterns are subjected to speculative analysis.

156. Shefrin, Bruce M. *The Future of U.S. Policies in an Age of Economic Limits.* Boulder, Colo.: Westview Press, 1980.

    Considers future U.S. political and economic systems based upon a slow-growth or no-growth American economy. Argues that consensus politics reduces political conflict mainly through the lower and middle classes' expectation of progress based on their belief in economic growth.

157. Shepsle, Kenneth A. "The Discount Rate for Public Investments: Should the Government Really Be Different?" *Policy Studies Journal*, 5 (Spring 1977), 332-40.

    Examines the choice among discount rates for public investment, a choice that can influence substantially the budgetary decisions of government. One prominent line of analysis argues that the public discount rate should be less than the private because of the greater capacity for risk spreading in government. Offers cogent argument why this line of analysis is erroneous, suggesting that, at least on these grounds, public and private investments should be treated identically.

158. Solomon, Arthur P., ed. *The Prospective City: Economic, Population, Energy, and Environmental Resources.* Cambridge, Mass.: MIT Press, 1980.

    Provides an up-to-date review of the socioeconomic trends shaping American cities, among other themes considering whether the rehabilitation of older central-core neighborhoods by young professionals will alter the economic and social prospects of cities.

159. Stein, Robert M. "The Allocation of Federal Aid Monies: The Synthesis of Demand-Side and Supply-Side Explanations." *The American Political Science Review*, 75 (June 1981), 334-43.

    Previous research on the distribution of federal aid monies has been dominated by the donor's perspective. Identifying a linkage between demand-side determinants of aid allocations, this article proposes and tests hypotheses derived from an integrated model of federal aid allocations.

160. Tassey, Gregory. "The Effectiveness of Venture Capital Markets in the U.S. Economy." *Public Policy*, 25 (Fall 1977), 479-97.

    Addresses two separate policy questions in evaluating the role of the U.S. venture capital market in economic growth. Attempts to identify each policy question as a separate issue in a framework for technology policy.

161. Teal, Roger and Alan Altshuler. "Economic Regulation: The Case of Aviation." *Policy Studies Journal*, 6 (Autumn 1977), 50-62.

    Analyzes the recent buildup of momentum for pro-competitive regulatory reform in the field of air transportation.

162. Teigen, Ronald L. "Trends and Cycles in the Composition of the Federal Budget, 1947-1978." *Policy Studies Journal*, 9 (Autumn 1980), 11-19.

    Systematic movements in the composition of the federal budget are studied, using a simple statistical structure which distinguishes trend, cyclical, and price-indexing phenomena.

163. Thurow, Lester C. *The Zero-Sum Society: Distribution and the Possibilities for Economic Change.* New York: Basic Books, 1980.

    Frozen pluralism is the essence of Thurow's diagnosis of the American malaise. His prescriptions for our condition offer a unique amalgam of competitive and egalitarian policies.

164. Wade, L.L. and A.J. Groth. "Politics, Policies, and Rapid Economic Growth in Developing Countries." *Policy Studies Journal*, 7 (Summer 1979), 781-87.

    Less-developed countries which have launched accelerated and sustained economic growth share certain political features (varieties of "authoritarianism") and have pursued broadly similar developmental policies. The implications for systems pursuing different strategies of development, for long-term stability, and equity require assessment.

165. Wallich, Henry C. "The Interface of Fiscal and Monetary Policy." *Policy Studies Journal*, 9 (Autumn 1980), 68-74.

    Examines the interface between fiscal and monetary policy, in the context of a symposium on taxation and spending policy.

166. Weatherford, M. Stephen. "Economic Conditions and Electoral Outcomes: Class Differences in the Political Response to Recession." *American Journal of Political Science*, 22 (November 1978), 917-38.

    Using data from the 1956-60 American panel study, data which span the worst recession [to that time] since the Great Depression, attempts to specify the sources of political responses to the recessions of 1958 and 1960.

167. Wilson, James Q., ed. *The Politics of Regulation.* New York: Basic Books, 1980.

    According to Wilson and the authors of the nine empirical studies of regulatory enterprises included in this volume, there is a politics of regulation. Although this book is not the first effort to grapple with disparities between conventional theories and regulatory behavior, it is an especially ambitious and successful one.

Chapter 5

EDUCATIONAL POLICY

168. Ambler, John S. "Politicization of Higher Education in Britain and France." *Policy Studies Journal*, 10 (Autumn 1981), 136-49.

The more highly politicized nature of French, as compared to British, universities can be explained only partially in terms of such cultural and political differences as the greater strength of the revolutionary tradition in France and the more conservative tenor of French governments in the 1960's and 1970's. Political tensions in French higher education are also in part the result of policy choices, notably the greater speed of expansion of enrollments in France as compared to Britain and the form of French university elections, which strengthened politicized unions.

169. Berne, Robert and Leanna Stiefel. "Measuring the Equity of School Finance Policies: A Conceptual and Empirical Analysis." *Policy Analysis*, 7 (Winter 1981), 47-69.

To measure the equity of school finance policies, numerous choices among alternative equity concepts and statistical techniques must be made. The authors develop a framework for equity analysis that highlights choices and interprets the choices as value judgments.

170. Boss, Michael O. and Harmon Zeigler. "Experts and Representatives: Comparative Basis of Influence in Educational Policy-Making." *Western Political Quarterly*, 30 (June 1977), 255-62.

Two bases of influence power in educational policy making are considered. Expertise, as employed by school superintendents, is countered by the claims of the school board to representational legitimacy. Assuming that boards who oppose the policies of the superintendent are attempting to exploit their unique resource, the highest proportion of boards fails to do so. The school board appears to have greatest influence over the educational program when it acts in a representative capacity on behalf of an aroused public.

171. Bresnick, David. "The Federal Educational Policy System: Enacting and Revising Title I." *Western Political Quarterly*, 32 (June 1979), 189-202.

   Examines the development and operation of the national educational policy system, including executive, legislative, and interest group sectors during the enactment of the Elementary and Secondary Education Act of 1965 and its revision in 1974. It finds that as the policy development process of 1965 changed to policy revision in 1974, a concomitant shift occurred from executive-centered to legislative committee-centered decision making.

172. Bullock, Charles S., III and Joseph Stewart, Jr. "Second Generation Discrimination in American Schools." *Policy Studies Journal*, 7 (Winter 1978), 219-24.

   Bullock and Stewart maintain that second generation discrimination lurks just below the surface in thousands of schools across the nation, doing untold damage to the students and faculty whom it touches. Our country has largely eliminated the poisonous influence of segregation which told blacks that they were not good enough to associate with whites. However, we allow policies to persist which convey the message to minorities that they are less intelligent, less diligent, less well-behaved, and less proficient as teachers, coaches, and administrators than are whites.

173. Chambers, M.M. "Long-Term Expectations for Financing Higher Education." *Policy Studies Journal*, 10 (Autumn 1981), 96-105.

   The view of higher education as a private purchase of a consumer's good, for private gratification and aggrandizement, is slowly changing to the salutary view that higher education is a public service whose benefits accrue chiefly to the whole society. An interlude of emphasis of federal tax cutting need not necessarily mean that the fifty states will abandon themselves to fiscal austerity for higher education.

174. Cleary, Robert E. "Federal Higher Education Policy: A View from the Campus." *Policy Studies Journal*, 10 (Autumn 1981), 85-95.

   During the last generation, the federal government became a major source of financial assistance to colleges and universities. There is a fear on many campuses that the increased scope and nature of federal activity is causing a fundamental change in the governance of American higher education.

175. Cohen, Ronald D. and Raymond A. Mohl. *The Paradox of Progressive Education: The Gary Plan and Urban Schooling.* Port Washington, N.Y.: Kennikat Press, 1979.

   Presents a well-researched, readable case study of the relationships between an extensive educational reform (the Gary plan), the established and the competing ideologies as played out through political struggles, and factionalism within the educational bureaucracies.

176. Comer, James P. *School Power: Implications of an Intervention Project.* New York: Free Press, 1980.

   Demonstrates a triad of concerns about public education: (1) returning power to principals and teachers, as well as to parents; (2) developing a working relationship between public schools and institutions of higher learning; (3) dispelling the concept that effective learning is associated only with a certain economic level, racial background or teaching strategy.

177. Comfort, Louise K. *Education Policy and Evaluation: A Context for Change.* New York: Pergamon Press, 1982.

   Explores the failure of public educational policies, the needs and policy prerequisites for education, the relationship of law and policy, and structure and policy. The author also discusses the means of implementing educational policies and how to evaluate them. Concludes with a model for educational change.

178. Dentler, Robert A. and Marvin B. Scott. *Schools on Trial: An Inside Account.* Cambridge, Mass.: Abt Books, 1981.

   The goal of the book is to help Boston and other northern city residents where school desegregation will have to take place within the coming years.

179. Engelbert, Ernest A. "University Education for Public Policy Analysis." *Public Administration Review*, 37 (May/June 1977), 228-36.

   Highlights the major features of policy analysis as an educational field. Focuses on (1) the origins of this field, (2) the major tracks of study, (3) the approach and content of the subject matter, (4) the developing relationships to the public service, and (5) some unresolved educational issues.

180. Ertur, Omer S. "School District Budgetary Elections: A Cost Redistributive Procedure?" *Policy Studies Journal*, 9 (Spring 1981), 699-706.

   Examines, theoretically and empirically, school district budgetary election voting behavior. Argues that the change from fiscally independent to state-funds dependent school district operations may have altered the traditional cost/quantity-based school budgetary voting behavior.

181. Gardner, David P. "Forces for Change in the Governance of British and American Universities." *Policy Studies Journal*, 10 (Autumn 1981), 123-36.

    Government control of colleges and universities has been increasing in recent years. The challenge for higher education is how to make institutions properly accountable but less controlled by government. The experience in this regard in the United Kingdom and the United States is compared.

182. Giles, Micheal W. and Douglas S. Gatlin. "Mass-Level Compliance with Public Policy: The Case of School Desegregation." *The Journal of Politics*, 42 (August 1980), 722-46.

    Studies factors influencing avoidance of public school desegregation policy. Finds that resort to private schools is explicable in cost-benefit terms and in terms of a sense of efficacy. Perception of elite positions does not appear to be an important influence on the decision.

183. Greer, Darryl G. "State-Level Coordination and Policy Implementation." *Policy Studies Journal*, 10 (Autumn 1981), 32-47.

    Presents general propositions about the policy resources of a state higher education coordinating board, some determinants of state-level coordination of institutions of higher education, the function of conflict in coordination, the role of a coordinating board in policy making, and conditions under which coordination of institutions and policy implementation may be successful.

184. Jackman, Mary R. "Education and Policy Commitment to Racial Integration." *American Journal of Political Science*, 25 (May 1981), 256-69.

    Evaluates at length the conceptual and empirical validity of the Support for Integration and Government Action scales.

185. Jud, G. Donald and James L. Walker. "Discrimination by Race and Class and the Impact of School Quality." *Social Science Quarterly*, 57 (March 1977), 731-49.

    Data from a sample of 1,215 males, all of whom were out of school for at least one year, fail to reveal evidence of significant class discrimination, but find continuing and substantial racial discrimination. Moreover, the findings suggest that the quality of early schooling influences achievement and earnings.

186. Kirst, Michael W. "The States' Role in Educational Policy Innovation." *Policy Studies Review*, 1 (1981), 298-308.

    Maintains, after examining control of educational policies, that since the 1960's the growth of state influence over local education has grown at an unprecendented rate. This trend was bound to continue into the decade of the 70's as well.

187. Levine, Erwin L. and Elizabeth M. Wexler. *PL 94-142: An Act of Congress*. New York: Macmillan Publishing, 1981.

    Subjects are the events and precedents leading to the passage of the Education for All Handicapped Children Act of 1975, and an evaluation of its implementation.

188. Lord, J. Dennis and John C. Catau. "School Desegregation Policy and Intra-School District Migration." *Social Science Quarterly*, 57 (March 1977), 784-96.

    Patterns of school transfers and residential shifts by whites within the Charlotte-Mecklenburg School District were found to be related to the black ratio of the school, whether or not the school was involved in busing for desegregation purposes, and the distance of the school from the center of the city.

189. Manus, Lawrence and Edward Hollander. "The Capitol and the Campus--Each in Its Proper Place." *Policy Studies Journal*, 10 (Autumn 1981), 19-32.

    While a reduction and redirection of regulation may serve the colleges well, a review of history indicates that the important developments in higher education have occurred during periods of government involvement.

190. Merelman, Richard M. "Democratic Politics and the Culture of American Education." *The American Political Science Review*, 74 (June 1980), 319-32.

    Argues that weaknesses in the school's socialization of democratic values can be traced to culturally patterned strains in American education.

191. Miller, Trudi C. "Political and Mathematical Perspectives on Educational Equity." *The American Political Science Review*, 75 (June 1981), 319-33.

    A selective review of the literature on equal educational opportunity supports an argument for explicit use of normative models in research.

192. Morgan, Patrick M. "Academia and the Federal Government." *Policy Studies Journal*, 10 (Autumn 1981), 70-84.

    In recent years a revolutionary shift has occurred in the federal government-higher education relationship. Why didn't higher education resist more vigorously federal encroachment in its autonomy?

193. Musgrove, Frank. *School and the Social Order.* Chichester: Wiley, 1979.

    Beginning with a review of various sociological theories of the social order, examines the meaning of social class and its relationship to schooling. Challenges the prevalent view that public (in American terms) schools are oriented toward the middle class.

194. Newacheck, Paul W. "Capitalization: The Price of School Finance Reform." *Policy Analysis*, 5 (Winter 1979), 21-36.

    Educational tax and expenditure capitalization is a market process whereby nominal gains and losses in educational spending and tax liabilities are translated into changes in property values within school districts. Presents an empirical analysis that simulates the effects of capitalization within the San Francisco Bay area under different hypothetical school finance reform plans.

195. Odell, Morgan and John Thelin. "Bringing the Independent Sector into Statewide Higher Education Planning." *Policy Studies Journal*, 10 (Autumn 1981), 59-70.

    The ideal of a comprehensive higher education planning agency was only partially fulfilled in the 1970's. It was especially limited in its ability to bring independent colleges and universities into statewide planning. The unfulfilled comprehensive statewide planning model makes an attractive case for decentralized decision making.

196. Orfield, Gary. *Must We Bus? Segregated Schools and National Policy.* Washington, D.C.: The Brookings Institution, 1978.

    Concerning one of the most divisive political issues of our time, this comprehensive book reflects an awareness of the historical, legal, sociological and political dimensions of the struggle over school desegregation.

197. Prestage, Jewel L. "Quelling the Mythical Revolution in Higher Education: Retreat from the Affirmative Action Concept." *The Journal of Politics*, 41 (August 1979), 763-83.

    Finds that so far affirmative action has not proven to be an efficacious response to the useful educational statuses of American blacks.

198. Rosenthal, Alan and Susan Fuhrman. "Higher Education Leadership in State Legislatures." *Policy Studies Journal*, 10 (Autumn 1981), 47-59.

   The distribution of higher education leadership in state legislatures is examined. It is based on questionnaire and interview information from 285 legislators who exercise influence on education policy in the fifty states, and one-third of whom give special attention to issues of higher education.

199. Schramm, Sarah Slavin. "Women's Educational Equity: Favorable Student Responses." *Policy Studies Journal*, 7 (Winter 1978), 243-50.

   The purpose is to determine if there are better and worse ways of handling the presentation of women's educational equity to college students, female and male. Specifically, will a more agreeable response to women's educational equity be forthcoming from a particular mode of presentation?

200. Schuman, David. *Policy Analysis, Education, and Everyday Life*. Lexington, Mass.: D.C. Heath, 1982.

   Schuman adopts a posture of "radical empiricism" in this analysis of the effects of post-secondary education. The book is organized first to present the details of the study, then to explore the emergent patterns of behavior Schuman discovers, and finally to discuss the implications for methodology and policy studies.

201. Sherman, Joel D. "Financing Local Schools: The Impact of Desegregation." *Policy Studies Journal*, 7 (Summer 1979), 701-7.

   Examines the impact of school desegregation--and concomitant white flight to private academies--on local financial support of the public schools in South Carolina.

202. Tropman, John E. "The Grade Tax." *Policy Analysis*, 5 (Summer 1979), 393-95.

   Suggests the possibility of applying a system of "tax" used in the financial realm to a different realm of value, school grades.

203. Weatherford, M. Stephen. "The Politics of School Busing: Contextual Effects and Community Polarization." *The Journal of Politics*, 42 (August 1980), 747-65.

   Previous studies of public opinion on the busing issue have sought the sources of opposition in the socialization and ideology of individuals. Hypothesizes that the process of political mobilization will heighten the salience of interpersonal contact regarding the issue.

204. Wise, Arthur E. *Legislated Learning: The Bureaucratization of the American Classroom.* Berkeley, Calif.: University of California Press, 1979.

    Criticism of the extraordinary growth of government regulation of education has been an insistent theme of academic professionals in recent years. Presents an analysis of this problem that makes an important contribution to the literature.

205. Wolf, Eleanor P. *Trial and Error: The Detroit School Segregation Case.* Detroit, Mich.: Wayne State University Press, 1981.

    Analyzes the Detroit case from the perspective of the logic and quality of the testimony (on residential and educational segregation and school violations) that utilized social science research, and not only deals with the issues related to school desegregation, but also raises key questions for social science, policymakers, and the judiciary.

206. Wright, Erik Olin. *Class Structure and Income Determination.* New York: Academic Press, 1979.

    Attempts to reconcile theoreticians' concepts of class in income determination with the growing body of empirical studies and quantitative data on status attainment and educational inequality.

Chapter 6

ENERGY AND THE ENVIRONMENT

207. Andrews, Richard N.L. "Values Analysis in Environmental Policy." *Policy Studies Journal*, 9 (Winter 1980), 369-78.

   The consideration of values in environmental policy decisions requires attention not only to substantive matters of environmental quality, but also to balancing such broader social values as science, democracy and authority. Current methods for values analysis can be grouped according to their relative emphasis among these values in order to better illuminate the implications of adopting such methods.

208. Aron, Joan B. "Intergovernmental Politics of Energy." *Policy Analysis*, 5 (Fall 1979), 451-71.

   The effort by the Carter administration to draft a comprehensive energy policy accentuated the omnipresent problem of accommodating the states' preferences in the formulation of new national programs.

209. Axelrod, Regina S., ed. *Environment, Energy, Public Policy: Toward a Rational Future*. Lexington, Mass.: D.C. Heath, 1981.

   Is a collection of nine articles on the relationship between energy usage and environmental impact. Developed as a result of a conference on energy and the environment held at Adelphi University in June 1979, the book appears at a time when problems of energy supply, use, and cost threaten to defeat the environmental progress of the 1970's.

210. Beck, Paul A. "Correlates of Energy Conservation." *Public Policy*, 28 (Fall 1980), 451-71.

   Results from a study of the factors related to family energy conservation are employed to evaluate some assumptions of and prospects for energy policy. The study is based on a sample survey of 779 Pittsburgh families conducted in 1978.

211. Benedict, Robert, Hugh Bone, Willard Leavel, and Ross Rice. "The Voters and Attitudes toward Nuclear Power: A Comparative Study of 'Nuclear Moratorium' Initiatives." *Western Political Quarterly*, 33 (March 1980), 7-23.

   Focuses upon recent ballot propositions in four western states which proposed additional state regulations for nuclear power plants. A very high correlation is found between the variable of cost-benefit analysis and the vote.

212. Berry, Linda and Lois Martin Bronfman. "Research Strategies for Evaluating the Adoption Potential of Energy Technologies." *Policy Studies Journal*, 9 (Spring 1981), 721-34.

   Three noneconomic models evaluating adoption potential are examined for technological innovations whose diffusion potential is not yet known. Applications of the general models are suggested with specific references to development of solar total energy systems.

213. Berry, Marvin P. "Water Management in Crisis." *Public Administration Review*, 37 (September/October 1977), 472-77.

   Evidence indicates that a very pronounced shortage of water is imminent in some areas and that the number of such areas will increase with time. Changes in the present patterns of allocation and use must be made in the face of political opposition by numerous and well-organized constituencies which are supported by proven and repeated arguments on their behalf. The distributive mode of water development, with its dependence on the public treasure, is deeply entrenched.

214. Bonnicksen, Thomas M. and Thomas S. Robinson. "Constraints on the Development of National Seashores and Lakeshores: A Political Perspective." *Public Administration Review*, 41 (September/October 1981), 550-57.

   A political perspective is used to clarify some of the constraints involved in a pending decision by the Park Service to consider expanding recreational developments on the Apostle Islands National Lakeshore in Wisconsin. These political constraints and the issues in question are similar to those faced by the Park Service for other national seashores and lakeshores.

215. Boschken, Herman L. "Public Control of Land Use: Are Existing Administrative Structures Appropriate?" *Public Administration Review*, 37 (September/October 1977), 495-504.

   In the post-World War II period, a transformation of urban processes has occurred which raises questions about the appropriateness of "territorial" government.

216. Bowman, Ann and Michael A. Maggiotto. "The Effect of Environmental Policy Orientations: Lobbying Florida's Legislators." *Social Science Quarterly*, 62 (September 1981), 547-54.

Upon discovering two competing orientations to air pollution among state legislators (health/environmental versus business/economics), the role of these perceptions in the information/influence process is examined. Finds that policy orientation affects a legislator's (1) exposure to information, (2) evaluations of its utility and (3) assessments of cue-givers' influence.

217. Brunner, Ronald D. "Decentralized Energy Policies." *Public Policy*, 28 (Winter 1980), 71-91.

Suggests that the federal government can encourage more local communities to take an active, effective role in developing and implementing local energy policies, without prescribing what those policies should be. Also proposes a federal program for this purpose.

218. Bucknell, Howard. *Energy and the National Defense*. Lexington, Kent.: University Press of Kentucky, 1981.

Presents a general overview of the energy future for the U.S. in the 1980's and includes all aspects of energy use, energy ideologies, conservation, international dimensions, energy wars, the politics of energy, and others.

219. Buttel, Frederick H. "Economic Growth and the Welfare State: Implications for the Future of Environmentalism." *Social Science Quarterly*, 58 (March 1978), 692-99.

Analyzes the connection between support for economic growth and welfare-state attitudes among the American public. The results show that persons who favor the expansion of the American welfare state tend to favor accelerated economic growth, although the relationship is much more pronounced among the working class than the middle class. The data suggest the possibility of fractionalization of the American left over the issue of controlling economic expansion and environmental degradation.

220. Calvert, Jerry W. "The Social and Ideological Bases of Support for Environmental Legislation: An Examination of Public Attitudes and Legislative Action." *Western Political Quarterly*, 32 (September 1979), 327-37.

The immense pressures to develop the natural resources of the West require assessments of public preferences concerning energy and environmental policy in the states affected. The degree to which public sentiments are reflected in legislative choice is examined.

Energy and the Environment

221. Charney, Jonathan I., ed. *The New Nationalism and the Use of Common Spaces: Issues in Marine Pollution and the Exploitation of Antarctica.* Allanheid, Osmun, 1982.

    Covers economic and international political issues of marine pollution and Antarctica, including pollution by ships, pollution of oceans by land-based sources, and the legal, economic, and political aspects of these pollution sources.

222. Cigler, Beverly A. "Organizing for Local Energy Management: Early Lessons." *Public Administration Review*, 41 (July/August 1981), 470-79.

    Local governments could play a large role in U.S. energy conservation policy, while maintaining their own fiscal stability. Data from a survey of 72 percent of all municipalities in North Carolina with populations over ten thousand were used to explore the current and planned levels of program commitment in energy, the organization for energy management, and perceived needs for enhancing the local efforts.

223. Conrad, Jon M. "Oil Spills: Policies for Prevention, Recovery, and Compensation." *Public Policy*, 28 (Spring 1980), 143-70.

    A simple model of petroleum production and transport is developed that contains a stochastic spill process. Pending U.S. legislation is examined in light of theoretical policy prescriptions, and conclusions and recommendations are offered for better coordinating spill policy and research.

224. Convisser, Martin. "Transportation and the Environment." *Policy Studies Journal*, 6 (Autumn 1977), 40-49.

    Reviews some of the most significant ways in which environmental statutes and concerns have influenced the activities of the Department of Transportation during the past decade. Emphasizes that environmental protection is a latecomer in the hierarchy of mandates and concerns that Congress has imposed on the transportation agencies.

225. Conway, Nicholas T. and Gregory L. Simay. "The Energy Research and Development: A Partnership between Federal and Local Government." *Public Administration Review*, 37 (November/December 1977), 711-13.

    Today, energy research and development are more critical than ever before. The federal government is developing systems, equipment, and economic incentives to conserve energy and develop new energy sources. To enjoy public support, approaches must be carried out in harmony with the total social and economic environment of the nation's cities.

226. Cook, Constance E. *Nuclear Power and Legal Advocacy: The Environmentalists and the Courts.* Lexington Books, D.C. Heath, 1980.

    A successful, readable effort to refine interest group theory to accord with present-day realities. Surveys and analyzes the battles environmentalists have fought before the Nuclear Regulatory Commission and in the courts against nuclear power, focusing on the effort to stop construction of a nuclear plant at Midland, Michigan.

227. Cook, Earl. "The Tragedy of Turfdom." *Social Science Quarterly*, 62 (March 1981), 23-29.

    Suggests that the American university, a federation of turfdoms rather than a community of scholars, may be ecologically unfit for the rapidly changing social environment that will result from depletion of energy and material resources.

228. Cortner, Hanna J. "Formulating and Implementing Energy Policy: The Inadequacy of the State Response." *Policy Studies Journal*, 7 (Autumn 1978), 24-29.

    A 1977 study for the Four Corners Regional Commission of the member states of Arizona, Colorado, Nevada, New Mexico, and Utah reveals that present state organizational arrangements for energy policy planning, administration and coordination are grossly inadequate. Briefly describes the principal findings of that report, examining the administrative and legislative mechanisms, decision-making resources, functional and coordinative planning capabilities, and environmental assessment practices in the five states.

229. Cuzan, Alfred G. "A Critique of Collectivist Water Resources Planning." *Western Political Quarterly*, 32 (September 1979), 320-26.

    In most regions of the United States, but especially in the West, demand for water is fast outstripping its supply. This problem has led many analysts and decision makers to conclude that what is needed is state and federal allocation of water to competing uses according to comprehensive plans designed to maximize social welfare. This paper criticizes such approaches.

230. Daneke, Gregory A. "The Political Economy of Nuclear Development." *Policy Studies Journal*, 7 (Autumn 1978), 84-90.

    Critics contend that, all safety issues aside, the nuclear industry is not cost-competitive in comparison to coal and solar. Within the context of this larger debate the nuclear enterprise has been put forth as a model of government involvement.

231. Deese, David A. and Joseph S. Nye, eds. *Energy and Security.* Cambridge, Mass.: Ballinger Publishing Co., 1981.

The final project of a multidisciplinary project on problems of interruptions in energy flows, focusing for the most part on oil. The chapters cover some general propositions on energy security, the problems facing six key regions or countries, the particular issues in American energy security, and include some conclusions.

232. Del Sesto, Steven L. "Conflicting Ideologies of Nuclear Power: Congressional Testimony on Nuclear Reactor Safety." *Public Policy*, 28 (Winter 1980), 39-70.

Examines the ideologies of pro- and anti-nuclear witnesses appearing at the Congressional hearings on *The Status of Nuclear Reactor Safety*, held by the Joint Committee on Atomic Energy in 1973-1974.

233. _____. "Nuclear Reactor Safety and the Role of the Congressman: A Content Analysis of Congressional Hearings." *The Journal of Politics*, 42 (February 1980), 227-41.

By means of a content analysis this study shows that the now defunct Joint Committee on Atomic Energy conducted its business with a pro-nuclear stance and appeared antagonistic and unresponsive to environmentalists and other outside groups who brought their views before the Committee hoping for support.

234. Doerksen, Harvey. "Water, Politics, and Ideology: An Overview of Water Resources Management." *Public Administration Review*, 37 (September/October 1977), 444-48.

The physical attributes of water create substantial uncertainties for the decision maker that are only partially reduced by technological advances. The highly diverse political and legal system for managing water resources creates uncertainties which defy comprehensive management. The managers themselves bring to the decision-making arena preconceived notions of public interest based on professional training, agency traditions, and ideological value frameworks. All these factors work against attempts at meaningful coordination and cooperative decision making.

235. Doran, Charles F. "OPEC Structure and Cohesion: Exploring the Determinants of Cartel Policy." *The Journal of Politics*, 42 (February 1980), 82-101.

OPEC sets a single price for a single grade of petroleum. Decisions are by consensus. If price increases occur too rapidly, security relations with specific consumer nations may be threatened. Conversely, if price increases too slowly, consensus may break down; the cartel leadership may face unacceptable levels of regional turbulence. Excessive price increase in the medium term is likely to induce massive energy substitution. For all of these reasons price decisions within OPEC are perilous and highly politicized.

236. Dye, Thomas R. and Dorothy K. Davidson. "State Energy Policies: Federal Funds for Paper Programs." *Policy Studies Review*, 1 (1981), 255-62.

Finds that neither economic nor political structures explain the great variation that exists among state energy program expenditures. However, the urbanized, energy-rich, economically growing states were found to have higher expenditures on energy problems.

237. Edgmon, Terry D. "Energy as a Disorganizing Concept in Policy and Administration." *Policy Studies Journal*, 7 (Autumn 1978), 58-67.

Broadly reviews our past energy organizing concepts, patterns of energy politics, and emerging energy "ideologies," so as to assess the potential impact of the latest federal energy reorganization upon energy decision making. It is the author's contention that energy, because of its seeming abundance in our recent past, has led us to ignore its significant ramifications for social organization.

238. Edmunds, Stahrl W. "Environmental Policy: Bounded Rationality Applied to Unbounded Ecological Problems." *Policy Studies Journal*, 9 (Winter 1980), 359-69.

The interaction among myriad species and chemicals in the food chain often yields potential outcomes which are difficult to foresee. In policy terms, these interactions comprise an information load beyond human cognition, resulting in unexpected side effects.

239. Ehrlich, Paul R. "Environmental Disruption: Implications for the Social Sciences." *Social Science Quarterly*, 62 (March 1981), 7-22.

The common problems of social scientists and ecologists should help to unite them in dealing with the population-research-environment crisis. The reasons demographers and economists are often in conflict with environmental scientists could help with the world "problematique."

240. Erickson, Kenneth P. "Public Policy and Energy Consumption in Industrialized Societies." *Policy Studies Journal*, 7 (Autumn 1978), 112-21.

Is energy consumption necessarily a function of economic output, so that reducing the United States' consumption of

Energy and the Environment 61

energy will inevitably draw down our economic output and, with it, our standard of living? The Chase Manhattan Bank answers "Yes!" The Ford Foundation argues to the contrary. This article examines these conflicting hypotheses in the light of data from a number of capitalist industrial societies.

241. Fowler, Kenneth S. "On Cutting Down Trees: Socioeconomic Trade-Offs of Selected Harvest Policies." *Policy Analysis*, 3 (Summer 1977), 341-56.

   Develops estimates of the changes in employment, gross regional product, property-tax assessed valuation, and productive capacity of the forest that result from four timber-cutting schedules applied to a specific region over a twenty-year period.

242. Game, Kingsley W. "Controlling Air Pollution: Why Some States Try Harder." *Policy Studies Journal*, 7 (Summer 1979), 728-38.

   The uneven and slow compliance of the states with their duties under the 1970 Clean Air Amendments was measured in terms of state air quality spending levels, Environmental Protection Agency subsidies, and the relation between the two, across fifty states. Independent variables ranging from actual aggregate pollution to form of bureaucratic organization were hypothesized as influences on these policy outputs and tested by multiple regression.

243. Goodwin, Craufurd D., ed. *Energy Policy in Perspective: Today's Problems, Yesterday's Solutions*. Washington, D.C.: The Brookings Institution, 1981.

   Students continually ask how we got into the current mess; here is the answer. A review of the energy policy process since the Truman years, this is a collection of essays by five authors on each presidency.

244. Graves, Philip E. and Ronald J. Krumm. *Health and Air Quality: Evaluating the Effects of Policy*. Washington and London: American Enterprise Institute for Public Policy Research, 1981.

   It is agreed that the efforts to control air quality have not sufficiently taken into account the economic costs and benefits of clean air. The book starts from this premise and contends present policy requires substantial revision in order to take into account the economic impact of regulation.

245. Gremillion, Lee L., James L. McKenney, and Philip J. Pyburn. "Program Planning in the National Forest System." *Public Administration Review*, 40 (May/June 1980), 226-30.

   The National Forest System's program planning system is the mechanism by which the organization formulates medium-range plans and generates budget requests for congressional consideration. This system allows NFS managers to examine and negotiate different strategies for deploying their resources within broad politically determined guidelines.

246. Griffin, Kenyon N. and Robert B. Shelton. "Coal Severance Tax in the Rocky Mountain States." *Policy Studies Journal*, 7 (Autumn 1978), 29-40.

   Examines the coal severance tax policies of six coal exporting states in the Rocky Mountain West--Arizona, Colorado, Montana, New Mexico, Utah and Wyoming--and concludes with observations about the consequences of the coal severance tax for the states and the nation.

247. Gustafson, Thane. "The New Soviet Environmental Program: Do the Soviets Really Mean Business?" *Public Policy*, 26 (Summer 1978), 455-76.

   The Soviet government has begun, for the first time, a large environmental program, aimed chiefly at preserving clean water. The question is, will the new program have any effect?

248. Hamilton, Mary A. "Energy Policy and Changing Public-Private Sector Relationships." *Policy Studies Journal*, 7 (Autumn 1978), 90-96.

   Attempts to determine the changes in public-private relations that are required to achieve energy policy objectives and to examine those changes that have already occurred. To do this, the discussion focuses on one broad facet of joint public-private activity in energy policy--the development and commercialization of new energy technologies, such as solar technologies, which are intended to reduce reliance on nonrenewable resources.

249. Harrison, David. "Controlling Automotive Emissions: How to Save More Than $1 Billion per Year and Help the Poor Too." *Public Policy*, 25 (Fall 1977), 527-53.

   Analyzes federal policy on automotive tailpipe emissions, suggesting that the current strategy be modified to permit new car emissions to vary for cars sold in different areas.

250. Ingram, Helen and John R. McCain. "Federal Water Resources Management: The Administrative Setting." *Public Administration Review*, 37 (September/October 1977), 448-55.

   The administrative setting of federal water resources management reflects the pattern of politics in the larger arena of water policy. Describes the long-standing administrative structure and policy arena of water resources, examines the forces for change in administrative arrangements, particularly the mandate of the Environmental Protection Agency, and assesses the administrative setting and long-range opportunities for further modification of the policy arena in the future.

251. _____. "Distributive Politics Reconsidered--The Wisdom of the Western Water Ethic in the Contemporary Energy Context." *Policy Studies Journal*, 7 (Autumn 1978), 49-58.

    Examines what energy development demand for water could mean for the prevailing patterns of water use in the principal river basin in the arid West--the Colorado River Basin. The existing public and state legislative attitudes about water allocation and traditional relationships among water users are examined.

252. Ingram, Helen, Nancy Laney, and John R. McCain. "Water Scarcity and the Politics of Plenty in the Four Corners States." *Western Political Quarterly*, 32 (September 1979), 298-306.

    Examines how states, particularly state legislatures, are likely to use their recently reasserted preeminence in determining water allocation. Using the arid Four Corners states of Arizona, New Mexico, Colorado, and Utah as case examples, the article establishes the compelling reality of growing water demand pressing close upon limited water supply.

253. Jones, Bryan D., Saadia R. Greenberg, Clifford Kaufman, and Joseph Drew. "Bureaucratic Response to Citizen-Initiated Contacts: Environmental Enforcement in Detroit." *The American Political Science Review*, 71 (March 1977), 148-65.

    When citizens contact local government agencies, they generally attempt to influence service delivery decisions made by these bureaucracies. Examines the nature of citizen contacts, and the results of such contacts, with respect to the enforcement of environmental ordinances in Detroit, Michigan.

254. Jorgensen, Joseph G. "Social Impact Assessments and Energy Developments." *Policy Studies Review*, 1 (1981), 66-86.

    Between 1964, when the Wilderness Act was passed, and 1978, with the passage of the Endangered American Wilderness Act, the federal government enacted more than twenty pieces of major legislation pertaining to protection of the environment of the United States. In his capacity as a social scientist, Jorgensen addresses the social impacts of such legislation.

255. Kenski, Henry C. and Margaret C. Kenski. "Partisanship, Ideology, and Constituency Differences on Environmental Issues in the U.S. House of Representatives." *Policy Studies Journal*, 9 (Winter 1980), 325-35.

    Three cross-sectional data sets for the U.S. House of Representatives are analyzed for 1973 to 1978.

256. Kerrigan, Mark L. "Decision Making in the Management of Energy Regulation." *Public Administration Review*, 39 (November/December 1979), 553-55.

   The management information systems approach divorces management from the knowledge of prior decision-making approaches. Implementing new systems is like charting new waters, and the direction for the Federal Energy Regulatory Commission is more comprehensive than what has existed in prior administrations. The extent of deviation from the remainder of the concepts in Lindblom's "successive limited comparisons" approach is strictly a matter of degree.

257. Lambright, W. Henry and Albert H. Teich. "Policy Innovation in Federal R & D: The Case of Energy." *Public Administration Review*, 39 (March/April 1979), 140-47.

   In just a handful of years, energy research and development expenditures have moved from a few hundred million dollars in predominantly one technology (atomic energy) to several billion dollars distributed among a wide range of energy technologies. Here is a process of policy formation that is still at a relatively early state.

258. Lave, Charles A. "Transportation and Energy: Some Current Myths." *Policy Analysis*, 4 (Summer 1978), 297-315.

   Much of the debate on transportation problems in general, and on President Carter's energy plan in particular, has been based on implicit assumptions that hardened into "wisdom" ten to twenty years ago. Draws upon a substantial body of research to examine these received ideas and to demonstrate that many of our most cherished beliefs about transportation and energy simply are not true.

259. Light, Alfred R. "The Carter Administration's National Energy Plan: Pressure Groups, and Organizational Politics in the Congress." *Policy Studies Journal*, 7 (Autumn 1978), 68-76.

   Highlights several important lessons that we might draw from the 1977 energy history. These are: (1) maximize "real" policy-making participation in the early stages; (2) get your act together; (3) let others do the compromising after you are committed; and (4) adopt flexible timetables so as to exploit opportunities.

260. MacEwen, Ann and Malcolm MacEwen. *National Parks: Conservation or Cosmetics*. Winchester, Mass.: Allen & Unwin, Inc., 1982.

   Traces the establishment of, and describes the national parks of England and Wales, including their physical and vegetational characteristics. Emphasis is given to the contribution that parks make to the national social structure and to the economic viability of local communities.

Energy and the Environment 65

261. McKean, Margaret A. *Environmental Protest and Citizen Politics in Japan.* Berkeley, Calif.: University of California Press, 1981.

   Thanks to citizens' protests, Japan now has the strictest antipollution standards in the world. After a general treatment of popular participation, this study analyzes pollution litigation, case histories of citizens' movements, political attitudes, and behavior of environmental activists.

262. McKean, Roland N. "Enforcement Costs in Environmental and Safety Regulation." *Policy Analysis*, 6 (Summer 1980), 269-89.

   Discusses practicable aids to decisions involving enforcement issues: reminders of the right questions to ask, econometric evaluations of existing regulations that allow for enfocement, and descriptions of factors on which enforcement difficulties depend.

263. McNeil, Mary, ed. *Environment and Health.* Washington, D.C.: Congressional Quarterly, 1981.

   A factual, straightforward discussion of a wide variety of topics ranging from protecting our air, land, and water to nuclear power, food, the dangers of our workplaces, and the costs of regulation.

264. Martin, Dolores T. "Energy Policy, Information Costs, and Secondary Demand Effects." *Policy Studies Journal*, 5 (Spring 1977), 301-7.

   Examines the impact of the federal imposition of the 55 MPH speed limit on the development of means to avoid the limit. Since people generally like to drive faster than 55 MPH, this limit increased the desire for means to exceed the limit without being caught. The proliferation of CB radios was one such means.

265. Medler, Jerry and Alvin Mushkatel. "Urban-Rural Class Conflict in Oregon Land-Use Planning." *Western Political Quarterly*, 32 (September 1979), 338-49.

   Looks at citizen support for and opposition to state land-use regulation in Oregon as reflected in the outcome on a 1976 referendum to repeal that state's land-use statutes. Four hypotheses concerning electoral support for land-use planning are examined using county, city, precinct and individual data.

266. Menzel, Donald C. "Implementation of the Federal Surface Mining Control and Reclamation Act of 1977." *Public Administration Review*, 41 (March/April 1981), 212-19.

   Analyzes the rule-making events and decision processes associated with the implementation of the recently enacted

Surface Mining Control and Reclamation Act of 1977, with particular attention centered on the implementation experience in West Virginia. And, more broadly speaking, the paper is concerned with the design of national policies that rely heavily on the states for their effective implementation and administration.

267. Milbrath, Lester W. "Incorporating the Views of the Uninterested but Impacted Public in Environmental Planning." *Policy Studies Journal*, 8 (Summer 1980), 913-20.

    Due to a variety of factors, the great proportion of the public is excluded from participation in environmental planning. A well-designed sample survey is one viable method for incorporating the views of the uninterested but impacted public in environmental decision making. Such a study was carried out on the Niagara Frontier. Experience with that study is instructive for delineating the conditions needed for maximum utilization of the information such a study can generate.

268. Mitnick, Barry M. "Incentive Systems in Environmental Regulation." *Policy Studies Journal*, 9 (Winter 1980), 379-94.

    An incentive systems framework, featuring the concept of incentive relation, is offered as a means of integrating and systematizing discussion of alternative means of regulation. The distinction of incentive and directive means of environmental regulation, together with the levels of their targets and the penalties for enforcement, are employed to develop a typology of regulatory means and to categorize environmental regulatory alternatives.

269. Morris, David. *Self-Reliant Cities: Energy and the Transformation of Urban America*. San Francisco, Calif.: Sierra Club, 1982.

    First reviews the past history of American cities' reliance on first wood, then coal, and then petroleum as principal sources of energy. Presents an optimistic prognostication of the future when American cities will humanly scale energy systems and gain energy autonomy.

270. Mushkatel, Alvin H. and Dennis R. Judd. "The State's Role in Land Use Policy." *Policy Studies Review*, 1 (1981) 263-74.

    Focuses upon the political opposition from rural dwellers and land developers toward the enactment of effective land use legislation.

271. Navarro, Peter. "The 1977 Clean Air Act Amendments: Energy, Environmental, Economic, and Distributional Impacts." *Public Policy*, 29 (Spring 1981), 121-46.

    The 1970 Clean Air Act was a laudable response to a serious air pollution problem. In contrast, its 1977 Amendments were primarily aimed at attaining an assortment of distributional goals for a powerful coalition of special interests. The energy, environmental, economic, and distributional impacts of Title I of the 1977 Amendments, which primarily regulates coal-burning power plants, are analyzed relative to the base case 1970 Act.

272. Nelkin, Dorothy. "Some Social and Political Dimensions of Nuclear Power: Examples from Three Mile Island." *The American Political Science Review*, 75 (March 1981), 132-42.

Draws examples from the Three Mile Island accident to review several characteristics of nuclear technology, its scale and costs, its complexity, its uncertain and unpredictable physical effects, and its indirect risks. It then explores the implications for social, political and administrative institutions as they grope for ways to manage the risks of nuclear power in the context of critical public scrutiny. Finally, it identifies a range of issues calling for policy research.

273. Nikolai, Loren A., Rick Elam, and Barry Bozeman. "Financial Statement Modeling: Analyzing the Pollution-Control Tax Incentive." *Policy Analysis*, 5 (Spring 1979), 243-54.

Financial statement modeling is an approach to policy analysis which employs data similar to that used by economists in such analytic approaches as cost-benefit analysis, but which is rooted in concepts used by accountants. The authors apply this approach to an evaluation of the congressionally mandated pollution-control tax incentive in order to assess the effectiveness of this policy.

274. Nivola, Pietro S. "Energy Policy and the Congress: The Politics of the Natural Gas Policy Act of 1978." *Public Policy*, 28 (Fall 1980), 491-543.

Much of the great congressional debate over energy policy during 1977-78 centered on the problem of natural gas pricing. Reform of the regulatory structure for natural gas came to be considered the centerpiece of President Carter's National Energy Plan. This paper analyzes the gas pricing controversy and the new legislation finally adopted.

275. Okrent, David. *Nuclear Reactor Safety: On the History of the Regulatory Process*. Madison: University of Wisconsin Press, 1981.

A chronological description of technical requirements and practices involved in licensing nuclear reactors, the primary focus is upon safety issues involved in siting nuclear generating stations.

276. Olson, Laura K. "Approaches to the Study of Public Policy and the Environment." *Polity*, 11 (Winter 1978), 270-79.

The various approaches to policy analysis are almost as numerous as the political scientists in the field. The books considered here all address themselves to questions of public policy, particularly environmental problems, and reflect divergent approaches to policy studies. Attempts to assess the relative strengths and weaknesses of their modes of analysis.

277. Orbell, John M. and L.A. Wilson, II. "The Governance of Rivers." *Western Political Quarterly*, 32 (September 1979), 256-64.

When external effects (such as pollution) flow in a "sequential" or "cumulative" manner (as in pollution of rivers) collective decision making under majority rule will never produce an equilibrium outcome--at the socially optimal level of pollution or at any other level. Implications are drawn for understanding U.S. water pollution policies.

278. Orr, David W. "In the Tracks of the Dinosaur: Modernization and the Ecological Perspective." *Polity*, 11 (Summer 1979), 562-87.

Analyzes the man-nature relationship in the perspective of a number of interrelated propositions. Finds a notable consensus concerning the steady-state, the self-actualization of man, and the need for a cooperative approach to nature, smaller and more independent communities, and concentration on intermediate techniques. In the author's view, the crisis is one of perception, which calls for solution through a holistic science.

279. ―――. "U.S. Energy Policy and the Political Economy of Participation." *The Journal of Politics*, 41 (November 1979), 1027-56.

Notes that energy policy is commonly regarded as a highly technical subject. In contrast, the thesis of the essay is that "energy policy most directly involves politics and ethics." Debate about a national energy policy "concerns which risks we as a society accept, which we avoid, who decides, and by what process." Argues for greater public involvement in the energy sector as a means for broadening the concept of the public interest, promoting equity in the distribution of payoffs, increasing public accountability, and improving social resiliency, but at the cost of a more technologically modest future.

280. ――― and Stuart Hill. "Leviathan, the Open Society, and the Crisis of Ecology." *Western Political Quarterly*, 31 (December 1978), 457-69.

To the extent that political implications of the "crisis" have been addressed, it is widely assumed that solutions will require the creation of highly centralized, authoritarian governments. Argues that such a course would not only fail to solve ecological problems, but might well intensify them. Presents a case for a middle approach of "selective decentralization" which is designed to foster societal resiliency.

281. Orr, Lloyd D. "Social Costs, Incentives Structures, and Environmental Policies." *Western Political Quarterly*, 32 (September 1979), 286-97.

Some basic technological and economic factors in environmental quality control are discussed as background for a description and critique of environmental policy. A version of effluent charges that emphasizes incentives for innovation, rather than short-term adjustments to environmental standards, is recommended as an appropriate direction for public policy.

282. Perry, Charles S. "Energy Conservation Policy in the American States: An Attempt at Explanation." *Social Science Quarterly*, 62 (September 1981), 540-46.

States' adoption of energy conservation policies depends on their tendency to adopt consumer laws, legislative professionalism, coal energy base and recent increases in electrical generating capacity. It does not notably depend upon factors influencing adoption of other energy policies less oriented to conservation.

283. Pierce, John C. "Conflict and Consensus in Water Politics." *Western Political Quarterly*, 32 (September 1979), 307-19.

Compares the general public, members of citizen advisory committees, group leaders, and water managers in the distribution of their perceptions of the importance of water resource issues, their satisfaction with water resource policy, their identification of important water resource problems, and their ranking of alternative water resource uses. The Gini Index of Inequality is employed to assess the level of concurrence.

284. Regens, James L. "State Policy Responses to the Energy Issue: An Analysis of Innovation." *Social Science Quarterly*, 61 (June 1980), 44-57.

Research by Regens reveals that the states have formulated and implemented innovative policy responses beyond those mandated by the federal government in the energy area and suggests the latter appears to be related primarily to the structural composition of states, particularly their existing energy supply-demand system, rather than to public perceptions of the importance of energy as a problem.

285. _____ and Robert W. Rycroft. "Administrative Discretion in Energy Policy-Making: The Exceptions and Appeals Program of the Federal Energy Administration." *The Journal of Politics*, 43 (August 1981), 875-88.

At a time when granting broad discretionary authority to federal regulatory agencies has generated heated debate, this research reveals that commonly held explanations are inadequate and even dysfunctional in the energy policy arena. Suggestions of oil company conspiracies or agency capture by corporate elites appear overly simplistic. The alternative picture of a hopelessly fragmented system in which the Federal Energy Administration is dominated by veto politics and interest brokerage is also not supported.

286. Rider, Robert. "Decentralizing Land Use Decisions." *Public Administration Review*, 40 (November/December 1980), 594-602.

Reviews the process of policy formation, the role of discretion in land use planning, and the purpose of the land use plan to arrive at an operational alternative to the comprehensive plan. A framework is suggested as a starting point in designing the land use plan to serve as a management tool in the process of interaction on land use issues.

287. Rosenbaum, Walter A. *Energy, Politics and Public Policy*. Washington, D.C.: Congressional Quarterly, 1981.

Stresses the *political* choices and problems involved in responding to the energy issues confronting the U.S. since 1973. Only a small portion of the books published since 1973 have specifically addressed the political obstacles to forming adequate energy policies in America, and none of these has focused on the topic as explicitly or exclusively as this one.

288. Russell, Clifford S. "What Can We Get from Effluent Charges?" *Policy Analysis*, 5 (Spring 1979), 155-80.

Clarifies the debate over effluent charges as instruments of environmental quality policy.

289. Rycroft, Robert W. "Bureaucratic Performance in Energy Policy-Making: An Evaluation of Output Efficiency and Equity in the Federal Energy Administration." *Public Policy*, 26 (Fall 1978), 599-627.

Defining efficiency in terms of the ratio between resource expenditures and bureaucratic effort, and equity as the distribution of such effort, this study focuses on the compliance and enforcement aspects of the Federal Energy Administration's (FEA) fuel allocation and pricing programs, and assesses the performance of the FEA by subjecting agency policy outputs to the evaluative criteria of efficiency and equity.

290. ——. "Energy Policy Feedback: Bureaucratic Responsiveness in the Federal Energy Administration." *Policy Analysis*, 5 (Winter 1979), 1-19.

Assesses the performance of the Federal Energy Administration by subjecting the agency's policy feedback mechanisms to the evaluative criterion of "bureaucratic responsiveness."

291. Sabatier, Paul and Geoffrey Wandesforde-Smith. "Major Sources on Environmental Politics, 1974-77: The Maturing of a Literature." *Policy Studies Journal*, 7 (Spring 1979), 592-604.

Provides a brief review of the major works published since 1974 on the formulation and implementation of policy dealing with air and water pollution, land use (from an environmental perspective), and the protection of natural resources.

292. Schaller, David A. "An Energy Policy for Indian Lands: Problems of Issue and Perception." *Policy Studies Journal*, 7 (Autumn 1978), 40-48.

Indian energy development questions are being heightened in public debate. The dominant perceptions of decision groups, together with their preferred arenas for political transactions, will greatly influence a number of important energy policy outcomes. The opportunity for the policy studies and intergovernmental coordination raised here should not be neglected.

293. Schooler, Dean and Helen Ingram. "Water Resource Management." *Policy Studies Review*, 1 (1981), 243-53.

Examines the influences of both the state and federal governments on water resource policy and the cooperation and conflict that exist between these two levels of government.

294. Sears, David O., Tom R. Tyler, Jack Citrin, and Donald R. Kinder. "Political System Support and Public Response to the Energy Crisis." *American Journal of Political Science*, 22 (February 1978), 56-82.

Considers the impact of diffuse support for the political system on public compliance with official policy by studying citizens' reactions to the energy crisis of 1974. Using data from a survey of Los Angeles residents, the paper examines three specific hypotheses. The main results were that diffuse support for the political system had only a weak relationship to attitudinal agreement with the official "line" on the energy crisis, overshadowed by the role of political partisanship.

295. Simon, Julian L. "Environmental Disruption or Environmental Repair?" *Social Science Quarterly*, 62 (March 1981), 30-43.

Ehrlich says that the environment now faces unprecedented disruption. But data presented here suggest the opposite--that

U.S. pollution is declining, world resources are getting less scarce, food availability is increasing, and population growth is not a threat to us.

296. Stoff, Michael B. *Oil, War, and American Security: The Search for a National Policy on Foreign Oil, 1941-1947.* New Haven, Conn.: Yale University Press, 1980.

    Offers a well-footnoted, terse history of this country's wartime essay into the petroleum business and the early postwar skirmish between the governmental advocates of the continued public voice in oil policy (to vouchsafe adequate and secure oil supplies) and the private sector advocates of leaving the oil business to the private sector, whose viewpoint had come to prevail by 1947. Above all, the book details the interacting forces influencing the direction of postwar oil policy in the U.S.

297. Stucker, James P. "The Distributional Implications of a Tax on Gasoline." *Policy Analysis*, 3 (Spring 1977), 171-86.

    On an analysis of household survey data, concludes that the gas tax is quite regressive and that public policies designed to reduce energy consumption or oil imports must be designed carefully so as not to involve undesirable redistributions of income.

298. Swanson, Gerald C. "Politics, Policy and Public Administration: Breakfast of Champions?" *Polity*, 9 (Spring 1977), 364-72.

    At a time when problems facing governments and the institutions which publicly administer their programs appear so overwhelming--particularly in the areas of natural resources and energy, environment, employment, and research and development, to name but a few--attempts at refining the instrumental tools and theoretical concepts of public administration seem wanting.

299. Vietor, Richard H.K. *Environmental Politics and the Coal Coalition.* College Station: Texas A&M University Press, 1980.

    Examines the evolution of federal environmental policies relevant to coal energy and the political processes that guided that evolution. The thesis is that this evolution represents a new "modernized" stage in the relationship between business and government, one which is inimical to democratic decision making.

300. Wardwell, John M. and C. Jack Gilchrist. "The Distribution of Population and Energy in Nonmetropolitan Areas: Confluence and Divergence." *Social Science Quarterly*, 61 (December 1980), 567-80.

    Notes that dependable supplies of relatively low-cost energy underlie most of the reasons offered for the growth of population and economic activities in non-metropolitan areas in the past decade. Accordingly, increasing energy costs and supply uncertainties constitute a reconcentrating influence. This influence may be ameliorated by small-scale, community-based efforts to reduce petroleum dependence through conversion to alternative energy sources and technologies.

301. Watts, Nicholas and Geoffrey Wandesforde-Smith. "Postmaterial Values and Environmental Policy Change." *Policy Studies Journal*, 9 (Winter 1980), 346-58.

    Advances the proposition that environmental policy may be particularly suited as a vehicle for the articulation of postmaterial values in advanced industrial societies, and that recognition of this is likely to prove enormously helpful in future comparative and cross-national research into the origins of environmentalism and the causes of environmental policy change.

302. Weingast, Barry R. "Congress, Regulation, and the Decline of Nuclear Power." *Public Policy*, 28 (Spring 1980), 231-55.

    The determinants of regulatory decision making in the area of nuclear power are studied in this paper. The major contention is twofold. First, the promotional measures of Congress and the Atomic Energy Commission during the 1950's and early 1960's did not carry over into the 1970's. Second, the change occurred largely in response to the active opposition of the environmental groups.

303. Wengert, Norman I. "The Energy Boom Town: An Analysis of the Politics of Getting." *Policy Studies Journal*, 7 (Autumn 1978), 17-23.

    Deals specifically with the politics of getting funds and other benefits to mitigate adverse consequences of energy boom town growth. The merits or needs for actions to mitigate negative impacts are often very important, although identification of negative impacts, particularly those of a secondary character may prove difficult.

304. Wenner, Lettie M. "Pollution Control: Implementation Alternatives." *Policy Analysis*, 4 (Winter 1978), 47-65.

    Economists argue that the present method of implementing environmental goals, administrative permits based on effluent/emission standards, is both ineffective and inefficient. The author investigates two alternative methods of pollution control, effluent charges and sale of pollution rights, by projecting their likely theoretical impacts and by analyzing the limited empirical information concerning their use in the U.S.

305. Weyant, John P. "Quantitative Models in Energy Policy."
     Policy Analysis, 6 (Spring 1980), 211-34.

   To what extent have quantitative models been used in the
   formulation of American energy policy? Addresses this question
   by examining two issues confronted by the Ninety-Fourth Congress, oil price decontrol and synthetic fuels commercialization.

306. White, Irvin L., Steven C. Ballard, and Timothy A. Hall.
     "Technology Assessment as an Energy Policy Tool." *Policy
     Studies Journal*, 7 (Autumn 1978), 76-83.

   Technology assessment was first introduced as a kind of
   applied policy analysis in 1966. In this brief paper, technology assessment as a kind of applied policy analysis is described and its contribution to better informed energy policy
   making is discussed.

307. Wilcox, Fred, ed. *Grass Roots: An Anti-Nuke Source Book*.
     Trumansburg, N.Y.: Crossing Press, 1980.

   A how-to book for those interested in opposing nuclear
   energy. It comprises a collection of articles by leading nuclear opponents and ranges from the theory of civil obedience
   to self-representation in court cases.

308. Wilson, Robert B. "Management and Financing of Exploration
     for Offshore Oil and Gas." *Public Policy*, 26 (Fall 1978),
     629-57.

   The present method of leasing the rights to offshore exploration for oil and gas is reviewed and found to provide effective incentives for efficient management of the resource in
   most respects. The major exception is an inefficient transfer
   of risk from the government to private firms.

309. Yandle, Bruce. "Fuel Efficiency by Government Mandate: A Cost-
     Benefit Analysis." *Policy Analysis*, 6 (Summer 1980), 291-
     304.

   The 1981-1984 fuel economy standard mandated in 1977 by
   the U.S. Department of Transportation imposed a set of strict
   performance rules on all domestic automobile producers. Cost-
   benefit analysis of the standard, based on the agency's underlying assumptions and on data contained in its background documents, indicates that the standard was barely cost-beneficial.

Chapter 7

MILITARY AND FOREIGN POLICY

310. Anderson, Paul A. "Justifications and Precedents as Constraints in Foreign Policy Decision-Making." *American Journal of Political Science*, 25 (November 1981), 738-61.

   Foreign policy actions are accompanied, as a matter of course, by justifications in terms of precedent, consistency, and resolve. The proposition developed in this paper is that the necessity of justifying foreign policy decisions acts as a constraint on what counts as an acceptable alternative.

311. Bardes, Barbara and Robert Oldendick. "Beyond Internationalism: A Case for Multiple Dimensions in the Structure of Foreign Policy Attitudes." *Social Science Quarterly*, 59 (December 1978), 496-508.

   Finds public opinion on foreign policy to be organized along five dimensions and to be generally more structured than previous research has indicated.

312. Baugh, William H. "Deceptive Basing Modes for Strategic Missiles: An Exercise in the Politics of an Ambiguous Nuclear Balance." *Western Political Quarterly*, 33 (June 1980), 247-59.

   Unconstrained increases in strategic missile accuracies have led to a widespread perception that fixed land-based missiles are vulnerable to a disarming first strike. That perceived vulnerability has led to proposals for new deceptive basing modes which are said to restore a degree of safety. These claims about vulnerability and programs to counteract it are assessed using a nuclear exchange simulation model.

313. Bloomfield, Lincoln P. "American Approaches to Military Strategy, Arms Control, and Disarmament: A Critique of the Postwar Experience." *Policy Studies Journal*, 8 (Autumn 1979), 114-19.

   The U.S. has since World War II followed a defense policy and strategy that combined traditional national approaches with features especially typical of American attitudes toward war and peace as well as force and power. The deep dilemmas of nuclear deterrence confront the U.S. with an inescapable dilemma, which in turn motivates an increasingly serious arms control policy.

314. Bobrow, Davis B. "Arms Control through Communication and Information Regimes." *Policy Studies Journal*, 8 (Autumn 1979), 60-65.

More than a decade of emphasis on arms control through agreed numerical ceilings on weapons by type has failed to create a safer world or slowed the trend toward the increasing number, sophistication, and proliferation of destructive capacities. Priorities and possibilities in three areas merit pursuit: within U.S. and allied forces; between adversaries; and for potential third party sources of guarantees, sanctions, and mediation.

315. Brenner, Michael J. *Nuclear Power and Non-proliferation: The Remaking of U.S. Policy.* New York: Cambridge University Press, 1981.

An outstanding case study on the resurgence of official concern in the U.S. in 1974 pertaining to nuclear energy—more particularly, the worry that accelerating developments in peaceful nuclear energy were directly contributing to a parallel proliferation of nuclear weapons capabilities.

316. Butterworth, Robert Lyle. "The Arms Control Impact Statement: A Programmatic Assessment." *Policy Studies Journal*, 8 (Autumn 1979), 76-84.

In 1975 Congress required that budgetary requests for selected defense programs be accompanied by a statement assessing their arms control effects. Suggests that the requirement has been unsuccessful because of an inadequate appreciation both of the political dynamics of the bureaucratic process involved and of the objective problems of these arms control issues.

317. Canby, Steven L. "NATO Defense: The Problem Is Not More Money." *Policy Studies Journal*, 8 (Autumn 1979), 46-53.

Points out the shortcomings in NATO defense strategy and argues that there are at least three distinct solutions for obtaining a true conventional defense in NATO and that these can be obtained at no additional cost.

318. Chomsky, Noam. *Towards a New Cold War: Essays on the Current Crisis and How We Got There.* New York: Pantheon Books, 1982.

Linguistic scholar Noam Chomsky who became a leading critic of U.S. policy in Vietnam, continues his passionate and well-documented attack on U.S. foreign policy in general. In twelve essays written between 1973 and 1981 and in eighty pages of new commentary, Chomsky focuses on U.S. "complicity" and the media's suppression of news of the massacres in Timor, the new Cold War, the Middle East, Indochina, the Paris Accords of 1973, and the "generally ridiculous" memoirs of Henry Kissinger.

319. Coffey, Joseph I. "Arms, Arms Control and Alliance Relationships: The Case of the Cruise Missile." *Policy Studies Journal*, 8 (Autumn 1979), 37-45.

NATO may be confronting a crisis over the cruise missiles. Some allies may seek longer-range, nuclear-armed missiles which could enable them to strike at Soviet MR/IRBM's and at other targets inside the U.S.S.R.; others (along with many Americans) aim at restricting both the range and the missions of cruise missiles. The first option could jeopardize detente, inhibit further progress in SALT and conceivably weaken American control over the uses of nuclear weapons in time of war. The second could cause strains between the U.S. and its European allies.

320. Critchley, W. Harriet. "Defining Strategic Value: Problems of Conceptual Clarity and Valid Threat Assessment." *Policy Studies Journal*, 8 (Autumn 1979), 28-37.

The changing international environment for U.S. strategic policy formation is causing progressive uncertainty about the adequacy of threat assessment concepts and procedures. The concept of "strategic value," which plays a central role in decisions to use and control military force, is defined and elaborated in terms of three key elements--territory, worth and access.

321. de la Garza, Rudolfo O. "Chicanos and U.S. Foreign Policy: The Future of Chicano-Mexican Relations." *Western Political Quarterly*, 33 (December 1980), 571-82.

As Chicanos have begun to play a more significant role in domestic politics, Mexico, because of its recent oil discovery and the undocumented worker issue, has become increasingly important to U.S. policy makers. This has led to speculation regarding the development of a Chicano lobby which will support Mexican interests in the U.S. This paper addresses the feasibility of such a linkage developing from a number of perspectives.

322. Duval, Robert D. and William R. Thompson. "Reconsidering the Aggregate Relationship between Size, Economic Development, and Some Types of Foreign Policy Behavior." *American Journal of Political Science*, 24 (August 1980), 511-25.

In a reexamination of the relationship between the size of a nation-state and its foreign policy behavior, two sets of hypotheses which relate size to verbal/nonverbal and conflictual/cooperative dimensions of foreign policy activity are retested.

323. Etheredge, Lloyd S. "Personality Effects on American Foreign Policy, 1898-1968: A Test of Interpersonal Generalization Theory." *The American Political Science Review*, 72 (June 1978), 434-51.

   Whether personality characteristics of American leaders crucially determine major American foreign policy decisions has been a matter of considerable disagreement. A test of two hypotheses drawn from interpersonal generalization theory shows such influences have probably been crucial in a number of cases in American foreign policy between 1898 and 1968.

324. Harkavy, Robert. "Harmonizing Policies across Arms Control Domains: Dilemmas and Contradictions." *Policy Studies Journal*, 8 (Autumn 1979), 66-75.

   Examines some apparent dilemmas and possible contradictions in U.S. policies spanning several of the most important arms control domains. The analysis is centered on the triangular relationship connecting nuclear non-proliferation, SALT, and conventional arms transfers (CAT), with each analyzed as dependent and independent variables in relation to the others.

325. Hevener, Natalie, ed. *The Dynamics of Human Rights in U.S. Foreign Policy*. New Brunswick, N.J.: Transaction Books, 1981.

   Based on a colloquia series held at the University of South Carolina, the fourteen essays represent a critical appreciation of U.S. human rights policies in the last three decades.

326. Hollick, Ann L. *U.S. Foreign Policy and the Law of the Sea*. Princeton, N.J.: Princeton University Press, 1981.

   An excellent, detailed chronological study covering the forty-year period from World War II through the ninth session of the Third United Nations Conference on the Law of the Sea (UNCLOS III) in 1980, which focuses on the American decision-making process and portrays a constantly evolving American "policy" in response to domestic and bureaucratic politics, to new technological, strategic, and economic developments, and to a changing international political system.

327. Holsti, Ole R. and James N. Rosenau. "The Foreign Policy Beliefs of Women in Leadership Positions." *The Journal of Politics*, 43 (May 1981), 326-47.

   Surveys the beliefs of Americans in leadership positions. Women were found with almost equal frequency among the strongest and weakest supporters of Cold War positions, but women are inclined to favor a more limited international role for the United States.

328. Johnson, Loch and James M. McCormick. "The Making of International Agreements: A Reappraisal of Congressional Involvement." *The Journal of Politics*, 40 (May 1978), 468-78.

Examines by surveying systematically all non-classified U.S. foreign policy commitments from 1946 to 1972, seeking to determine the extent to which Congress and the Executive Branch have participated in the making of international agreements over the twenty-seven-year period.

329. Kaiser, Fred M. "Structural and Policy Change: The House Committee on International Relations." *Policy Studies Journal*, 5 (Summer 1977), 443-50.

Presents an interesting case because its jurisdiction is dramatic and controversial, epitomized by the war in Indochina. Foreign policy, moreover, has been an area in which Congress and the relevant committees have adopted innovative and independent policy positions vis-a-vis the Executive (Frye, 1975). Thus, the coincidental transformations, in structure and behavior, on international relations permit examination of the relationship between the two variables--both the impact of structure on behavior and their common dependency on other variables.

330. Korb, Lawrence J. "The Process and Problems of Linking Policy and Force Structure through the Defense Budget Process." *Policy Studies Journal*, 8 (Autumn 1979), 92-98.

The purpose of the defense budget process is to produce a force structure to support national security policy. To accomplish this task, the Department of Defense has designed a system built around planning, programming and budgeting and zero-based budgeting. However, while these two systems help to marry policy and force structure, for several interrelated reasons the fit is far from perfect.

331. Kushman, John E., Alexander Groth, and Robin Childs. "Political Systems and International Travel." *Social Science Quarterly*, 60 (March 1980), 604-16.

Applies a quantitative model from regional analysis to the most recent United Nations data on international travel to examine the relationships between different types of political systems and international travel. Finds that omitting political considerations from models based on "environmental" or "sociological" variables gives a seriously incomplete and potentially misleading picture of international travel.

332. Lunch, William M. and Peter W. Sperlich. "American Public Opinion and the War in Vietnam." *Western Political Quarterly*, 32 (March 1979), 21-44.

Describes American public opinion concerning the war in Vietnam from 1964 to 1973. Following an introduction and a discussion of methodological issues regarding wartime public opinion, reviews the flow of opinion about Vietnam, both in the aggregate and for various demographically defined sub-groups. Measures support and opposition to the war using both a broad "mistake" question and more specific policy questions, and examines differences revealed by the questions for age, sex, race, religious belief, social status and political party affiliation.

333. McCormick, James M. "International Crises: A Note on Definition." *Western Political Quarterly*, 31 (September 1978), 352-58.

   Discusses the first step in doing research on international crises: defining the nature of the phenomenon. First identifies the two definitional approaches used to define international crises--crises as decision-making situations and crises as interaction situations--then discusses the conceptual and empirical problems of employing only one approach to identify a crisis situation.

334. ——— and Young W. Kihl. "Intergovernmental Organizations and Foreign Policy Behavior: Some Empirical Findings." *The American Political Science Review*, 73 (June 1979), 494-504.

   Evaluates whether the increase in the number of intergovernmental organizations (IGO's) has resulted in their increased use for foreign policy behavior by the nations of the world.

335. Madar, Daniel. "Patronage, Position, and Policy Planning: S/P and Secretary Kissinger." *The Journal of Politics*, 42 (November 1980), 1065-84.

   While Henry Kissinger was Secretary of State, the department's policy planning staff was exceptionally effective in intervening in policy deliberations and decisions. Its effectiveness was directly related to the support of Kissinger, to his ability to dominate policy and decision making in the department and to the intermediary position the staff established during his tenure.

336. Mansbach, Richard W. and John A. Vasquez. "The Effect of Actor and Issue Classifications on the Analysis of Global Conflict-Cooperation." *The Journal of Politics*, 43 (August 1981), 861-74.

   International politics has long been dominated by a realist cognitive map that assumes that unitary states are the sole major actors and that they interact over the single issue of power. Compares that map with one that takes account of nongovernmental and subnational actors interacting over diverse issues in a European setting.

Military and Foreign Policy 81

337. Migdal, Joel S. "Policy and Power: A Framework for the Study of Comparative Policy Contexts in Third World Countries." *Public Policy*, 25 (Spring 1977), 241-60.

    Focuses on the effect of the level of political institutionalization on policy successes in the Third World.

338. Modelski, George. "Long Cycles and U.S. Strategic Policy." *Policy Studies Journal*, 8 (Autumn 1979), 10-17.

    The theory of long cycles is a set of propositions about the behavior of the global political system. It has its roots in a tradition of "oceanic" thought and it may be contrasted with two more conventional models of world politics, the states-system model and the imperial model. The theory offers a basis for strategic analysis and for the derivation of policy implications.

339. Molineu, Harold. "Carter and Human Rights: Administrative Impact of a Symbolic Policy." *Policy Studies Journal*, 8 (Summer 1980), 879-85.

    Begins with the assumption that since President Carter's human rights policy is largely an exercise in symbolic politics, the criteria for understanding its impact have more to do with the impression than with substantive improvement in human rights.

340. Morgan, Patrick M. "Arms Control: A Theoretical Perspective." *Policy Studies Journal*, 8 (Autumn 1979), 105-14.

    Offers a new definition of arms control and traces some of the implications of that definition. It also sets out a list of prerequisites for arms control. Within the framework, the current and future prospects for arms control are briefly assessed, as are the fundamental limitations of arms control as a strategy for peace and security.

341. Most, Benjamin A. and Harvey Starr. "Diffusion, Reinforcement, Geopolitics, and the Spread of War." *The American Political Science Review*, 74 (December 1980), 932-46.

    Reports the results of an examination of the possible diffusion of new war participations during the 1946-65 era. A theoretical argument is developed to yield more precise expectations about when, where, why, and how diffusion processes might operate.

342. Nau, Henry R. "Continuity and Change in U.S. Foreign Energy Policy." *Policy Studies Journal*, 7 (Autumn 1978), 121-31.

    The core of U.S. energy policy continues to be based on foreign policy considerations. Yet is foreign policy a sufficient basis to create and sustain a domestic consensus on energy policy? There are difficult trade-offs here between U.S. domestic and foreign interests. How these trade-offs are made will determine the future of U.S. energy policy.

343. Nelkin, Dorothy and Michael Pollak. "The Politics of Participation and the Nuclear Debate in Sweden, the Netherlands, and Austria." *Public Policy*, 25 (Summer 1977), 333-57.

    In Sweden, the Netherlands, and Austria, nuclear policies face wide opposition. Compares the efforts of these three countries to broaden public involvement in energy decisions.

344. Oldendick, Robert and Barbara Ann Bardes. "Multiple Dimensions in the Structure of Foreign Policy Attitudes." *Social Science Quarterly*, 62 (March 1981), 124-27.

    Despite differences in methods, item domains and purposes, Wittkopf's analysis is said to offer a great deal of support for the central theme of the original Bardes and Oldendick (1978) article: foreign policy beliefs are most accurately characterized as multidimensional and are not arrayed solely along an internationalism dimension.

345. _____. "Belief Structures and Foreign Policy: Comparing the Dimensions of Elite and Mass Opinions." *Social Science Quarterly*, 62 (September 1981), 432-42.

    Contrasts the structure of elite and mass foreign policy opinion. Factor analyses of the elite and mass data yielded a five-factor solution for the elites and a six-factor solution among the masses.

346. Ostrom, Charles W., Jr. "A Reactive Linkage Model of the U.S. Defense Expenditure Policy-Making Process." *The American Political Science Review*, 72 (September 1978), 941-57.

    Develops a working synthesis of three current approaches--Arms Race, Organizational Politics, Bureaucratic Politics--based on the insights and observations of Samuel Huntington (1961), Warner Schilling (1962), Colin Gray (1971), and James Rosenau (1971).

347. Pettman, Ralph. *Biopolitics and International Values: Investigating Liberal Norms*. Elmsford, N.Y.: Pergamon Press, 1981.

    Fashions an interesting turn in the ever growing debate about the place of politics in sociobiology.

348. Picard, Louis A. "The SALT I Negotiations: A Game Theory Paradigm." *Policy Studies Journal*, 8 (Autumn 1979), 120-27.

    Focuses on the negotiating process leading up to the SALT I agreements of 1972. Through the insights of game theory we can better understand the difficulties inherent in reaching accords in nuclear arms negotiations.

349. Pipes, Richard. *U.S.-Soviet Relations in the Era of Detente*. Boulder, Colo.: Westview Press, 1981.

    Consists of eight papers published by Pipes between 1970 and 1980 on Soviet foreign policy, ranging in focus from general background studies of the historical evolution of Russia's image of its role in the world and the operational principles of Soviet foreign policy to more specific analysis of issues.

350. Quandt, William B. *Saudi Arabia in the 1980s: Foreign Policy, Security, and Oil*. Washington, D.C.: The Brookings Institution, 1981.

    It is to "help Americans understand Saudi Arabia better" that Quandt, senior analyst with the Brookings Institution, has written this brief study.

351. Quester, George H. "Defining Strategic Issues: How to Avoid Isometric Exercises." *Policy Studies Journal*, 8 (Autumn 1979), 99-105.

    There is a risk that the threat of nuclear war will be exaggerated in ways injurious to arms control and will deliver to the Soviet leadership the political returns it may be seeking. This undesirable outcome is the result of logical tricks we play on ourselves in trying to be very precise about factors like the accuracy of missiles.

352. Ransom, Harry Howe. "Being Intelligent about Secret Intelligence Agencies." *The American Political Science Review*, 74 (March 1980), 141-48.

    Analyzes selected publications since 1974 on U.S. secret intelligence agencies.

353. Reppy, Judith. "Military R&D: Institutions, Output, and Arms Control." *Policy Studies Journal*, 8 (Autumn 1979), 84-92.

    There is a large well-funded program for military R&D in the U.S. Two kinds of questions are raised in connection with this program: the problem of optimizing the military effectiveness of the program through the allocation of resources among R&D projects and between R&D and other elements in the defense budget; and the problem of the long-range effects of new weapons technology on international stability.

354. Richardson, Neil R., Charles W. Kegley, Jr., and Ann C. Agnew. "Symmetry and Reciprocity in Dyadic Foreign Policy Behavior." *Social Science Quarterly*, 62 (March 1981), 128-38.

    Suggests how characteristic international interaction patterns may complement prior research that has attempted to explain foreign policy behavior on the basis of national actor attributes alone. Investigates two proposed interaction characteristics, quantitative symmetry and affective reciprocity. Quantitative symmetry is more characteristic of conflictive dyads than of cooperative ones. Meanwhile, cooperative dyads and, to a lesser extent, conflictive dyads feature nonreciprocal affective intensity.

355. Rochester, J. Martin. "The Paradigm Debate in International Relations and Its Implications for Foreign Policy Making: Toward a Redefinition of the 'National Interest.'" *Western Political Quarterly*, 31 (March 1978), 48-58.

Changing conditions in the international system have occasioned a large paradigm debate in the international relations field which has important implications for foreign policy making insofar as different definitions of the "national interest" tend to be arrived at depending upon which paradigm (or image of the world) one adopts. The analysis is applied to U.S. foreign policy making.

356. Rockman, Bert A. "America's Departments of State: Irregular and Regular Syndromes of Policy Making." *The American Political Science Review*, 75 (December 1981), 911-27.

The problems of defining foreign policy authority, assuring an integrated perspective, and effectively using specialized expertise are best seen in terms of the larger problem of governance in Washington against which all proposals for reform must be abraded.

357. Rothstein, Robert L. *The Third World and U.S. Foreign Policy: Cooperation and Conflict in the 1980s*. Boulder, Colo.: Westview Press, 1981.

An in-depth and thoughtful analysis of the policy courses available to the U.S. in its relations with Third World countries. Drawing on concepts and theories developed in earlier publications, critically reviews the North/South negotiating system and examines some of the issues raised by such international policy areas as food, energy, trade, and debt.

358. Rourke, John T. "Congress and Foreign Policy." *Polity*, 8 (Summer 1981), 688-96.

The works included in this review essay allow for two approaches to the study of Congress's role in the formation and conduct of American foreign policy. The first specifically focuses on the legislative role. The second approach examines congressional impact as part of a study which includes the overall foreign policy process.

359. Schoultz, Lars. *Human Rights and United States Policy toward Latin America*. Princeton, N.J.: Princeton University Press, 1981.

   Traces the development of human rights as a dimension of U.S. policy toward Latin America during the period 1960-80, and discusses a full range of policy considerations including domestic and foreign factors that influenced the evolution of U.S. positions, and the means of implementing a human rights standard.

360. Sigelman, Lee and Dixie M. McNeil. "White House Decision-Making under Stress: A Case Analysis." *American Journal of Political Science*, 24 (November 1980), 652-73.

   Three interrelated hypotheses about the impact of stress on organizational aspects of the decision-making process are synthesized from existing theory and research.

361. Siverson, Randolph M. and Joel King. "Attributes of National Alliance Membership and War Participation, 1815-1965." *American Journal of Political Science*, 24 (February 1980), 1-15.

   Aims at identifying those attributes of national alliance membership which tend to be associated with war participation.

362. Slater, Jerome. "Population Defense Reconsidered: Is the ABM Inconsistent with Stability?" *Policy Studies Journal*, 8 (Autumn 1979), 53-59.

   The argument of this essay is that current U.S. strategic postures and weapons systems, based essentially on mutual assured destruction (MAD), are defective, in that they over-deter and under-defend.

363. Snyder, William P. and James A. Davis. "Efficiency and Usefulness in Policy Research: The Case of the All-Volunteer Force." *Public Administration Review*, 41 (January/February 1981), 34-46.

   Finds that policy research sponsored by the Department of Defense on the all-volunteer armed force is, with some qualifications, relevant, timely, and nonduplicative. Unlike other researchers, the authors conclude such policy research is at least potentially useful to the Department of Defense and its branches.

364. Spanier, John and Joseph Nogee, eds. *Congress, the Presidency, and American Foreign Policy*. Elmsford, N.Y.: Pergamon Press, 1981.

   A collection of case studies bracketed by introductory and concluding chapters by each of the coeditors, this book is intended to be a critical examination of executive-legislative relations in a period of growing Congressional assertiveness--the 1970's.

365. Starr, John Bryan, ed. *The Future of US-China Relations*. New York: New York University Press, 1981.

A collection of seven essays by established students of China commissioned by the U.N. Association of the U.S. plus commentaries by four more authorities, all members of a panel who coordinated their studies during eight months in 1978 and 1979. In early '79 they traveled together to Japan, China, and Taiwan to observe and consult broadly at different levels of government and society.

366. Thompson, Kenneth W. "New Reflections on Ethics and Foreign Policy: The Problem of Human Rights." *The Journal of Politics*, 40 (November 1978), 984-1010.

Not since the days of Woodrow Wilson and Franklin D. Roosevelt with their "Fourteen Points" and "Four Freedoms" have ethical principles received greater prominence than in the political campaigning and presidential statements of Jimmy Carter. Washington observers have noted that the human rights issue fit Carter like a glove.

367. ———. *Morality and Foreign Policy*. Baton Rouge: Louisiana State University Press, 1980.

Thompson, who for three decades has consistently focused on the problems of morals in foreign policy, offers us a review of the issues and literature in this area from the days of ancient Rome to President Carter's emphasis on human rights in international relations. This study is a concise and clear presentation of the eternal dilemmas when morals and politics must cross paths.

368. Trice, Robert H. "Foreign Policy Interest Groups, Mass Public Opinion and the Arab-Israeli Dispute." *Western Political Quarterly*, 31 (June 1978), 238-52.

Considers the roles played by domestic interest groups and mass public opinion in the American foreign policy process.

369. von Beyme, Klaus. "Detente and East-West Economic Relations." *The Journal of Politics*, 43 (November 1981), 1192-1206.

Overall, socialist and western countries are willing to separate economic from political considerations in the conduct of East-West relations, and to assign greater priority to economic factors. Examines policies with both economic and political implications, including American embargo policies, the invasion of Afghanistan by the U.S.S.R., and the Jewish emigration policies of the U.S.S.R. in 1979 to qualify for American "most favored nation treatment."

370. Weintraub, Sidney, ed. *Economic Coercion and U.S. Foreign Policy: Implications of Case Studies from the Johnson Administration.* Boulder, Colo.: Westview Press, 1982.

   Focuses on American attempts in the 1960's to use economic pressure on Third World states for political purposes. The case studies cover U.S. relations with Indonesia, India, Egypt, Chile, and South Africa.

371. Wittkopf, Eugene R. "The Structure of Foreign Policy Attitudes: An Alternate View." *Social Science Quarterly*, 62 (March 1981), 108-23.

   Replication and extension of an earlier analysis of public attitudes toward foreign policy using a Likert approach rather than factor analysis to initially probe the data yields somewhat different interpretations of the attitudes of Americans and of the demographic correlates of those attitudes. A bifurcation of the pre-Vietnam war consensus underlying postwar American foreign policy is suggested.

Chapter 8

MUNICIPAL, STATE, AND
LOCAL GOVERNMENT

372. Adams, Bruce and Betsy Sherman. "Sunset Implementation: A Positive Partnership to Make Government Work." *Public Administration Review*, 38 (January/February 1978), 78-81.

Government at all levels is held in low esteem by the governed. The factors contributing to this public disenchantment are widely recognized. Certain essential services are not delivered, while others are provided in an inefficient and wasteful manner. Taxes continue to climb. Accountability is often undermined by secrecy and special interest domination. Public administrators are overwhelmed by the white plague of paperwork. And legislative bodies do not effectively perform their oversight function. In this atmosphere, Sunset legislation has emerged as one of the most significant public management issues.

373. Allen, Irving. "Suburban Preference of Urban Ethnic Groups." *Social Science Quarterly*, 62 (March 1981), 99-107.

European ethnic groups in three Connecticut SMSA's by the late 1960's had assimilated toward similar city and suburban settlement patterns. Among groups still in the cities, any early differences in preferences for community type were diminishing among contemporaneous ethnic generations.

374. Angel, William D., Jr. "Zenith Revisited: Urban Entrepreneurship and the Sunbelt Frontier." *Social Science Quarterly*, 61 (December 1980), 434-45.

Suggests that nonecological variables may also be instrumental in explaining regional economic shifts, and notes that urban entrepreneurs alter a city's infrastructure to accommodate leading-edge growth and thereby assume a major responsibility for such shifts. In this fashion, entrepreneurs in such cities as Dallas and Fort Worth transformed their cities into leading growth poles of the American south and helped spawn the rise of the Sunbelt.

375. Bahl, Roy, ed. *Urban Government Finance: Emerging Trends.* Beverly Hills, Calif.: Sage Publications, 1981.

   This collection of nine research papers is Volume 20 in the semiannual series of *Urban Affairs Annual Reviews* and constitutes the most recent empirical research on state and local government finances.

376. Beecher, Janice A., Robert L. Lineberry, and Michael J. Rich. "Political Power, the Urban Agenda, and Crime Policies." *Social Science Quarterly*, 62 (December 1981), 630-43.

   Urban crime rates increased significantly during the period 1948-1978. Local police policies varied from one city to another and over time as well. Examining ten cities during this time period and focusing on mayoral incumbencies as the unit of analysis, the associations among urban power configurations, urban issues agendas, and police policies are described.

377. Beer, Samuel H. "Political Overload and Federalism." *Polity*, 10 (Fall 1977), 5-17.

   The tendency of government expenditure to claim an increasing share of national product is the subject of much scholarly debate. Directs attention to forces within government itself that promote this tendency.

378. Bingham, Richard D. "Innovation, Bureaucracy, and Public Policy: A Study of Innovation Adoption by Local Government." *Western Political Quarterly*, 31 (June 1978), 178-205.

   The adoption of innovations by housing authorities, school districts, public libraries, and municipal governments is examined in an attempt to identify factors which lead to innovation adoption by local government and to study the process of adoption.

379. Boruch, Robert F., David Rindskopf, Patricia S. Anderson, Imat R. Amidjaya, and Douglas M. Jansson. "Randomized Experiments for Evaluating and Planning Local Programs: A Summary on Appropriateness and Feasibility." *Public Administration Review*, 39 (January, February 1979), 36-40.

   The main purpose of the randomized assignment here is to guarantee that the program participants are equivalent to nonparticipants in the long run, and consequently that comparison of the two groups will be as fair and as unequivocal as possible. Summarizes some of the authors' research findings on the feasibility of randomized tests for planning and evaluating local programs.

380. Boulay, Harvey. "Social Control Theories of Urban Politics." *Social Science Quarterly*, 59 (March 1979), 605-21.

Maintains that social control theories of urban politics hold that quiescence among potentially disruptive elements is a major goal of the political process in cities. This position is critically assessed with attention to its roots in Marxism, its logical structure and policy relevance.

381. Brecher, Charles and Raymond D. Horton, eds. *Setting Municipal Priorities, 1982*. New York: Russell Sage Foundation, 1981.

A collection of essays that examine public policy in New York City. More specifically, the essays consider population changes, taxing and spending, and service delivery.

382. Broadnax, Walter D. "The New Federalism: Hazards for State and Local Government?" *Policy Studies Review*, 1 (1981), 231-35.

Attempts to examine the effects of Reagan's "New Federalism" and examines whether the states have the talent and data collection apparatus to effectively regain control of many of the programs now administered by the federal government.

383. Brouthers, Lance Eliot. "Measuring Inequality in the Delivery of Urban Public Services: A Simplification." *Policy Studies Journal*, 9 (Summer 1981), 999-1000.

Attempts to revise a formula applicable to the delivery of urban public services.

384. Brown, Anthony. "Technical Assistance to Rural Communities: Stopgap or Capacity Building." *Public Administration Review*, 40 (January/February 1980), 18-23.

Examines the nature and effectiveness of the present technical assistance delivery as a response to the needs of small communities and the public administrators working in them, and suggests an alternative approach.

385. Bryan, Frank M. *Politics in the Rural States: People, Parties, and Processes*. Boulder, Colo.: Westview Press, 1981.

As description and analysis proceed from the social and economic status of the people through political participation, parties, primaries, and the legislature, many of today's ideas about rural areas begin to fall. Holds that ruralism and its politics are oriented to the new wave of technology that calls for bureaucratic, efficient, informed, and centralized decision making.

Municipal, State, and Local Government

386. Cayer, N. Joseph and Roger L. Schaefer. "Affirmative Action and Municipal Employees." *Social Science Quarterly*, 62 (September 1981), 487-94.

Examines how well rank-and-file employees of a Texas municipality understand and how deeply they support equality of opportunity and affirmative action. The authors used a survey instrument and found the attitudes of employees do not differ significantly from the views of managers, which have been the subject of much previous research.

387. Cingranelli, David L. "Race, Politics and Elites: Testing Alternative Models of Municipal Service Distribution." *American Journal of Political Science*, 25 (November 1981), 664-92.

Does the racial composition, political allegiance, or economic character of a neighborhood affect the share of municipal services it receives? This study of the distribution of police and fire protection resources in Boston in the early 1970's presents evidence that residential neighborhoods with high levels of previous support for the mayor and those containing high levels of business activity receive relatively high per capita service allocations.

388. Clark, Terry, ed. *Urban Policy Analysis: Directions for Future Research*. Beverly Hills, Calif.: Sage Publications, 1981.

A series of essays that are of a generally high caliber. The topics covered include urban fiscal policy, models of community leadership, the influence of business in the city, urban crime, political cultures, population changes, urban ecology and federal funding for urban research.

389. Coulter, Philip B. "Measuring the Inequity of Urban Public Services: A Methodological Discussion with Applications." *Policy Studies Journal*, 8 (Spring 1980), 683-98.

Attempts to extend the analysis of urban service delivery beyond equality of units of service input to measurement of the equity of both inputs and outputs (impact). Develops an original technique for measuring and indexing service equity. It is applied to police services in Tuscaloosa, Alabama.

390. David, Elizabeth. "Benefit-Cost Analysis in State and Local Investment Decisions." *Public Administration Review*, 39 (January/February 1979), 23-26.

Over the years various methods have been used to guide government investment decision making. These methods have frequently implicitly weighted the costs of implementation of proposed investments against the benefits to be gained. Benefit-cost analysis was developed to make this calculation explicitly.

391. Diggins, William, James D. Wright, and Peter H. Rossi. "Local Elites and City Hall: The Case of Natural Disaster Risk-Mitigation Policy." *Social Science Quarterly*, 60 (September 1979), 203-17.

    Examines the attitudes of 383 elected officials in one hundred local communities toward land-use approaches to the management of natural hazards risk. Emphasizes the role of these officials' perceptions of the views of other community influentials on their own views regarding this issue.

392. Doig, Jameson W. and Michael N. Danielson. "From the Firm Ground of Result and Fact to the Tossing Sea of Cause and Theory: The Role of Government in Urban Development." *Policy Studies Journal*, 8 (Summer 1980), 852-61.

    Summarizes the widely held view that economic forces determine the distribution of jobs and residences in urban areas, and argues that this conclusion involves serious conceptual difficulties.

393. Dornan, Paul B. "Whither Urban Policy Analysis? A Review Essay." *Polity*, 9 (Summer 1977), 503-27.

    Detailed examination of urban public services is a fairly recent focus for political science research. The study of garbage collection, sewage removal, education, police and fire protection produced and/or distributed by local governments was the preserve of urban planners and policy specialists. Today, professional panels and entire issues of professional journals are devoted to the subject of urban service provision.

394. Dowall, David E. "An Examination of Population-Growth-Managing Communities." *Policy Studies Journal*, 9 (Winter 1980), 414-27.

    Examines the fiscal, social, economic and environmental characteristics of 228 cities and counties.

395. Dye, Thomas R. and T.L. Hurley. "The Responsiveness of Federal and State Governments to Urban Problems." *The Journal of Politics*, 40 (February 1978), 196-207.

    This research examines the following: (1) whether total federal outlays in the cities are correlated with any generally accepted measures of social need in cities; (2) whether total federal outlays have a redistributional effect; (3) whether federal outlays by function, specifically outlays for Health, Education and Welfare, Housing and Urban Development, and Office of Economic Opportunity, are related in any way to measures of social need; (4) whether the pattern of federal outlays changes over time; (5) whether federal grants-in-aid to municipal governments are positively associated with economic resources; and finally, (6) whether state grants-in-aid to municipal governments are more responsive to indicators of social need in cities than federal grants-in-aid.

396. ———. "Measuring Responsiveness: A Brief Reply." *The Journal of Politics*, 43 (February 1981), 102-3.

   The authors stand by their position that the federal government is largely unresponsive to generally accepted measures of social need in cities, and fails to redistribute significantly among cities with different resources.

397. Elling, Richard C. "State Party Platforms and State Legislative Performance: A Comparative Analysis." *American Journal of Political Science*, 23 (May 1979), 383-405.

   Assesses the extent to which the parties of Illinois and Wisconsin legislatively fulfill their platform commitments. As hypothesized, the parties of "issue-oriented" and "moralistic" Wisconsin performed more responsibly than those of "job-oriented" and "individualistic" Illinois. Argues that the responsible-parties model be reconceptualized as a multidimensional ideal type, as various findings of the study indicate it is empirically unlikely that a party or party system could be "responsible" with respect to all dimensions simultaneously.

398. Farnham, Paul G. "The Targeting of Federal Aid: Continued Ambivalence." *Public Policy*, 29 (Winter 1981), 75-92.

   The issue of the targeting of federal intergovernmental aid on certain groups in the population has been widely discussed over the past two decades. Although there has been a trend toward the lessening of federal control over grant-in-aid programs, all affected groups have exhibited ambivalent attitudes on this question. This paper illustrates the reasons for this ambivalence.

399. Ferber, Mark and Edmund Beard. "Marketing Urban America: The Selling of the Boston Plan and a New Direction in Federal-Urban Relations." *Polity*, 12 (Summer 1980), 539-59.

   Analyzes the planning, selling, and buying of the Boston Plan for urban revitalization, which was developed and promoted by Mayor Kevin White during 1977-78. In the authors' view the Plan points to ways of coordinating national goals with local realities and needs by meshing federal approval and monitoring with local effectiveness without neglecting community interests.

400. Fitzgerald, Michael R. and Robert F. Durant. "Citizen Evaluations and Urban Management: Service Delivery in an Era of Protest." *Public Administration Review*, 40 (November/December 1980), 585-94.

   Argues that citizen evaluations of municipal services can play a significant role in contemporary municipal administration. A model of the citizen service evaluation and response process is presented and tested with data gathered from a recent survey of urban citizens.

401. Foster, John L. "Regionalism and Innovation in the American States." *The Journal of Politics*, 40 (February 1978), 179-87.

   Perhaps the most significant study of the spread of innovations in American state politics is Jack Walker's "The Diffusion of Innovations in the American States." This paper is a reexamination of one of Walker's more intriguing speculations—the noticeable impact of "regionalism" upon the spread of innovations among the American states.

402. Fowler, E.P. and David White. "Big City Downtowns: The Non-Impact of Zoning." *Policy Studies Journal*, 7 (Summer 1979), 690-700.

   Do land prices determine zoning policy, or vice versa? The case of one big city downtown suggests that it depends on the political climate. Different political climates not only change the determinants of zoning decisions but also the nature of their relationships with those determinants, and the relative importance of zoning itself.

403. Friedman, Judith J. "Central Business District and Residential Urban Renewal: Response to Undesired Change?" *Social Science Quarterly*, 58 (June 1977), 45-59.

   Shows that central business district renewal decreases with retail sales, while residential renewal increases with the percent nonwhite and the decline in the socioeconomic status of the population. Housing conditions are found to be unimportant.

404. Giles, William A., Gerald T. Gabris, and Dale A. Krane. "Dynamics in Rural Policy Development: The Uniqueness of County Government." *Public Administration Review*, 40 (January/February 1980), 24-28.

   Examines the types of counties that are likely to employ contemporary administrative techniques in their struggle to assuage public problems. The analysis touches upon the issue of whether the administrative development is significantly related to the policy of local government.

405. Goering, John M. "Towards a National Policy for Neighborhoods: A Conversation between a Policy Maker and a Social Scientist." *Public Administration Review*, 40 (November/December 1980), 553-60.

   Offers a simulation of a private conversation between a member of the White House domestic policy staff and a prominent urban research specialist on the topic of a national policy for neighborhoods. The conversation was prompted by the release of the National Commission on Neighborhoods report to the President on their fifteen-month, million dollar search for new policies and programs for neighborhoods.

406. Gunlicks, Arthur B., ed. *Local Government Reform and Reorganization: An International Perspective*. Port Washington, N.Y.: Kinnicat Press, 1981.

The most striking reality about metropolitan reform is its lack of impact upon the actual process of local governance. Gunlicks has assembled this series of essays on structural reform of local government in nine other Western democracies in order to provide a comparative context for understanding why this is the case.

407. Hayes, Frederick O. "City and County Productivity Programs." *Public Administration Review*, 38 (January/February 1978), 15-18.

The observations on city and county productivity programs are based primarily upon a study of programs in eight local governments made between July 1975 and March 1976. The eight governments include five large cities, two smaller cities, and one large suburban county. With two governments each in the far west, southwest, midwest, and northeast, only the southeast is unrepresented. The jurisdictions are divided evenly between those with elected chief executives and those with city manager charters.

408. Hudson, William E. "The New Federalism Paradox." *Policy Studies Journal*, 8 (Summer 1980), 900-6.

One of the aims of Nixon's "New Federalism" reforms was to promote political decentralization in the federal system. An examination of the impact of revenue-sharing and block-grant programs in El Paso, Texas reveals that this New Federalism seems to have had the opposite effect in that city.

409. Hutchins, Matthew and Lee Sigelman. "Black Employment in State and Local Governments." *Social Science Quarterly*, 62 (March 1981), 79-87.

The most recent data available in regard to the quantity and quality of black employment in state and local governments across the United States are presented. In most states, black government employment is at least proportional to the black share of the population, but in every state except one, black salaries lag behind those of whites. Variations in the latter are most closely related to region, with blacks doing better outside the South.

410. Ingram, Helen M., Nancy K. Laney, and John R. McCain. *A Policy Approach to Political Representation: Lessons from the Four Corners States*. Baltimore: Johns Hopkins University Press, 1980.

In this empirical application of propositions in Hannah Pitkin's *The Concept of Representation* (1967), the authors investigate the distributions of opinions of voters and state senators on a wide range of policy issues, but particularly those involving development, energy, environment, and water use in Arizona, Colorado, New Mexico, and Utah.

411. Jaros, Dean and Michael A. Baer. "Disaffection for 'State Policy Outputs and Collective Behavior.'" *Social Science Quarterly*, 59 (September 1978), 386-89.

The authors question the control variables selected by Wasserman (1978) and his interpretation of their article (1976).

412. Johnson, William and John J. Harrigan. "Innovation by Increments: The Twin Cities as a Case Study in Metropolitan Reform." *Western Political Quarterly*, 31 (June 1978), 206-18.

Combines a non-incremental with an incremental interpretation to explain the evolution of metropolitan governmental reform in the Minneapolis-St.Paul metropolitan area. This combination of non-incremental with incremental change enabled the achievement of metropolitan reforms that have eluded most metropolitan areas.

413. Johnston, Richard E. and John T. Thompson. "The Burger Court and Federalism: A Revolution in 1976?" *Western Political Quarterly*, 33 (June 1980), 197-216.

Examines the past history of the great powers of the Congress, including taxing, spending, commerce regulation, etc., and then examines the effect which *National League of Cities v. Usury* might have upon the future use of taxing, spending, and commerce regulation in the United States.

414. Johnston, Robert A. "The Politics of Local Growth Control." *Policy Studies Journal*, 9 (Winter 1980), 427-39.

Local growth controls are categorized as controlling class composition, growth location, or growth rate. Literature concerning the motives for adopting these types of growth controls is examined. Four case studies are presented, two involving growth rate controls and two concerned with growth phasing (locational) controls.

415. Jones, E. Terrence. "Block Grants and Urban Policies: Implementation and Impact." *Policy Studies Journal*, 8 (Summer 1980), 906-12.

Using two jurisdictions--St. Louis City and St. Louis County--and two block grant programs--Community Development and Comprehensive Employment and Training--as case studies, this essay describes how differences in local polities affects policy implementation and policy impact.

416. Karnig, Albert K. and Susan Welch. "Sex and Ethnic Differences in Municipal Representation." *Social Science Quarterly*, 60 (December 1979), 465-81.

   Using as a data base several hundred U.S. cities, examines sex and ethnic differences in municipal representation. Several population and political factors, hypothesized to affect female, black and Mexican-American representation, are correlated with the absolute and proportional representation rates of each minority sex-gender group.

417. ―――. *Black Representation and Urban Policy*. Chicago: The University of Chicago Press, 1981.

   This study on black politics and urban governance provides the first comprehensive analysis of changes in black office-holding in American cities between 1970 and 1978.

418. Kasarda, John D. "The Implications of Contemporary Distribution Trends for National Urban Policy." *Social Science Quarterly*, 61 (December 1980), 373-400.

   Kasarda notes that much has been written about how federal policies have shaped the redistribution of U.S. population and commercial activity, and reverses the directionality to discuss how the trends might inform more fruitful policies apropos urban problems and national productivity.

419. Kraemer, Kenneth L. and John L. King. "A Requiem for USAC." *Policy Analysis*, 5 (Summer 1979), 313-49.

   Evaluates the USAC program's philosophy, impacts, successes and failures, and policy implications, with the intent of providing a comprehensive overview of the meaning and lessons of USAC.

420. Lazin, Frederick A. "Administrative Networks and Municipal Service Distributions." *Policy Studies Journal*, 9 (Summer 1981), 1051-58.

   Analyzes the service distribution patterns of Israeli cities during the late 1970's in an effort to gain a better understanding of the potential effects of institutional arrangements on service distribution.

421. Lewis, Carol W. "Service Needs and Municipal Expenditures." *Policy Studies Journal*, 9 (Summer 1981), 1021-30.

   The difficulties involved in assessing the meaning of municipal expenditures are examined in view of the fact that dependency upon municipal services varies among and within jurisdictions.

422. Lewis, Eugene and Frank Anechiarico. *Urban America: Politics and Policy.* New York: Holt, Rinehart and Winston, 1981.

   Provides a general introduction to some significant aspects of the politics, economics, and social life of cities and suburbs. More specifically, the volume examines the history of the American city, the political machine, reform movements, power in urban America, the policy process, public economy, intergovernmental relations, equity, the bureaucracy, and hopes and despairs of metropolitan America.

423. Lineberry, Robert L. "The Impact of Municipal Reformism: A Symposium." *Social Science Quarterly*, 59 (June 1978), 117-77.

   Eight political scientists are concerned with the general question: "Does reformed government make a difference?" The five research efforts are summarized and discussed by Robert L. Lineberry in his introduction and in his commentary.

424. Logan, John R. and Mark Schneider. "Suburban Municipal Expenditures: The Effects of Business Activity, Functional Responsibility and Regional Context." *Policy Studies Journal*, 9 (Summer 1981), 1039-50.

   A wide variety of models exists seeking to explain variation in the level of suburban government activity. Alternative models stress concepts of local stratification and discrimination, the structure of local decision making, ecological position, and public choice, each of which suggests varying hypotheses about which suburbs spend more and which less. The authors summarize and evaluate the relative strength of each of these alternative models, and propose major directions for future research.

425. Lucy, William H., Dennis Gilbert, and Guthrie S. Birkhead. "Equality in Local Service Distribution." *Public Administration Review*, 37 (November/December 1977), 687-97.

   Suggests a framework for administrators to use in analyzing service distribution and offers suggestions for making judgments about the equity of service distribution patterns.

426. McBeath, Gerald A. and Thomas A. Morehouse. *The Dynamics of Alaska Native Self-Government.* Washington, D.C.: University Press of America, 1980.

   A study by two professors of political science at two Alaska universities of Alaska native (Eskimo, Aleut, and Indian) political development from 1959 to 1980, the period of Alaska statehood.

427. Marando, Vincent L. "City-County Consolidation: Reform, Regionalism, Referenda and Requiem." *Western Political Quarterly*, 32 (December 1979), 409-21.

Indicates that city-county consolidation continues to be considered a viable means of metropolitan reorganization although political obstacles often prevent adoption. The argument is made that there is sufficient support for reform, to be considered, but not enough political support for referenda passage. There is a definite regional influence on where consolidations occur, with the West currently replacing the South as the region of most adoptions.

428. ———— and Robert D. Thomas. "County Commissioners' Attitudes toward Growth: A Two-State Comparison." *Social Science Quarterly*, 58 (June 1977), 129-38.

Using the states of Florida and Georgia, the authors' analysis shows that attitudes toward growth are associated more with the state in which county commissioners govern than with the growth characteristics of their counties. Florida commissioners are far more anti-growth than those in Georgia.

429. Marlin, John Tepper. "City Affirmative Action Efforts." *Public Administration Review*, 37 (September/October 1977), 508-11.

The first step in rationalizing national equal employment policy would be to ensure that the federal government speaks to the localities with one voice on the issue. The second step would be to assist localities in dealing with the job-relatedness issue for civil service tests. Finally, the federal government could help local equal employment officials gather the recalcitrants in providing data.

430. Mead, Lawrence M. "Institutional Analysis for State and Local Government." *Public Administration Review*, 39 (January/February 1979), 26-30.

Institutional analysis is a way to study administrative and political factors which affect the implementation of government programs. This kind of research could contribute to the policy analysis public officials need to make decisions about programs. This paper discusses the need for institutional analysis, one possible approach to it, and the contribution it can make to policy analysis for state and local government.

431. Menzel, Donald D. and Irwin Feller. "Leadership and Interaction Patterns in the Diffusion of Innovations among the American States." *Western Political Quarterly*, 30 (December 1977), 528-36.

Two issues relating to the diffusion of innovation in state governments are analyzed: (1) Is "innovativeness" a general timeless phenomenon? Or is it specific to a given time period and function? (2) Is interaction, i.e., adopter-nonadopter contact, a meaningful explanatory variable as presently employed? Data on the date of adoption of two highway technologies (impact attenuators, computer modeling) and two air pollution control technologies (air telemetry systems, computer modeling) were collected for all states.

432. Methe, David T. and James L. Perry. "The Impacts of Collective Bargaining on Local Government Services: A Review of Research." *Public Administration Review*, 40 (July/August 1980), 359-71.

    Empirical research about the effects of collective bargaining on local services is examined. A taxonomy is developed to compare and evaluate the research, the preponderance of which has focused on employee wages.

433. Miller, Gary J. *Cities by Contract: The Politics of Municipal Incorporation*. Cambridge, Mass.: MIT Press, 1981.

    Provides documentation on the Lakewood and similar incorporation movements in California, how state legislation creating incorporation was passed, and how incorporation has worked in recent years; tax differentials between pre- and postwar California cities; and the conflict generally between the tax- and territory-hungry cities and the more affluent unincorporated areas.

434. Mladenka, Kenneth R. "Citizen Demands and Urban Services: The Distribution of Bureaucratic Response in Chicago and Houston." *American Journal of Political Science*, 25 (November 1981), 693-714.

    Do public officials view their control over responsiveness to citizen grievances as a political resource that can be used to reward and punish, or is responsiveness accomplished according to routinized procedures institutionalized in a set of bureaucratic decision rules? Relying upon a variety of data, responsiveness to citizen demands in a machine city and a reformed one is analyzed.

435. ——— and Kim Quaile Hill. "The Distribution of Urban Police Services." *The Journal of Politics*, 40 (February 1978), 112-33.

    Explores the distribution of police services in Houston, evaluates the pattern of municipal service delivery in terms of who get what, establishes standards for equity in resource distribution, and investigates the role of the urban bureaucracy in the distribution of services. These issues are empirically examined.

436. Morgan, David R. and William Lyons. "The Impact of Intergovernmental Revenue on City Expenditures: An Analysis over Time." *The Journal of Politics*, 39 (November 1977), 1088-97.

The increasing dependence of state and local governments on intergovernmental revenue is now widely recognized. The effects of such aid on subnational units of government is far less well understood, however. Of particular interest is the question of whether or not aid may merely be used as a substitute for funds that otherwise might be raised locally. A multivariate analysis over three time periods evaluates the effects of aid on expenditure patterns of city governments when other important socioeconomic and political variables are included.

437. Morgan, David R., John P. Pelissero, and Robert E. England. "Urban Planning: Using a Delphi as a Decision-Making Aid." *Public Administration Review*, 39 (July/August 1979), 380-84.

Reviews the experience of an Oklahoma community with citizen involvement in goal setting for a new comprehensive plan. In addition to a citizen survey in the community, officials successfully used a decision-making method that is rather unique to urban planning--a Delphi exercise, the use of which in policy making is presented.

438. Morgan, David R. and John P. Pelissero. "Urban Policy: Does Political Structure Matter?" *The American Political Science Review*, 74 (December 1980), 999-1006.

An interrupted time-series quasi-experiment is employed to test the basic hypothesis that reformed cities (with city manager, at-large elections, and nonpartisan ballots) tax and spend less than unreformed communities.

439. Mushkin, Selma J. "Policy Analysis in State and Community." *Public Administration Review*, 37 (May/June 1977), 245-53.

Added resources devoted to building management capacity in the state and local governments would facilitate the analysis needed for policy decisions and for insuring that the public services produced meet public demands. Yet, the resources to achieve the needed knowledge are lacking. There continues to be a failure to build the kind of organizational structure that would overcome the barriers, including barriers to creativity, to staff recruiting, and to feeding back evaluations of programs into the decision-making process through policy analysis.

440. Nachmias, David and John P. Blair, eds. *Fiscal Retrenchment and Urban Policy*. Beverly Hills, Calif.: Sage Publications, 1979.

Professor Nachmias is a leading authority in the field of policy analysis. The volume touches on those issues (e.g., erosion of tax base, "white flight") that are of importance to urban America.

441. Neiman, Max. "A Path Analytic Exploration of Income Clustering and Local Inequality." *Policy Studies Journal*, 9 (Summer 1981), 1030-39.

    Explores relationships among income status, economic resources, service needs, and taxing policies for muncipalities and schools in thirty-nine metropolitan suburbs of the Milwaukee SMSA.

442. ——— and Catherine Lovell. "Mandating as a Policy Issue--The Definitional Problem." *Policy Studies Journal*, 9 (Spring 1981), 667-81.

    Mandating of state policies by agencies of the federal government and of local government policies by both state and federal agencies has emerged in recent years as an important policy issue. This conceptualization of mandating behavior offers a typology based upon (1) substantive aspects of the mandate, (2) the method by which a mandate is imposed, and (3) the mode of application. Problems associated with different types of mandates suggest multidimensional effects of intergovernmental relations on state and local policy formulation and implementation.

443. Newman, Monroe and Brinley J. Lewis. "Regional Resource Allocation." *Public Administration Review*, 39 (July/August 1979), 355-62.

    Twelve years of budgetary experience with the Appalachian Regional Development Program are used to inquire whether less detailed congressional constraints on the use of appropriated funds have resulted in a change in state spending priorities. The conclusion is reached that though priorities have clearly changed, other factors have also been in operation.

444. Nivola, Pietro S. "Distributing a Municipal Service: A Case Study of Housing Inspection." *The Journal of Politics*, 40 (February 1978), 59-81.

    Based on 1973 data for one important municipal function (housing inspection) in a major city (Boston), suggests that conventional views of local service distribution need rethinking. In particular, the study implies that the dispensation of city services (sometimes even those most vulnerable to political pressures, such as housing inspection) may best be understood as an autonomous bureaucratic process, over which exogenous actors, including local political leaders, policymakers, and neighborhood interest groups, wield relatively little influence.

445. Pachon, Harry P. and Nicholas P. Lovrich, Jr. "The Consolidation of Urban Public Services: A Focus on the Policy." *Public Administration Review*, 37 (January/February 1977), 38-47.

Reviews the major assertions which the "anti-consolidationists" make in specific reference to the consolidation of urban police departments: (1) that larger police departments are not more efficient or economical; and (2) that citizen satisfaction with urban police services varies inversely with the size of the municipality.

446. Pack, Howard and Janet R. Pack. "The Resurrection of the Urban Development Model." *Policy Analysis*, 3 (Summer 1977), 407-27.

Widespread failure in model development itself or very limited application characterized the earliest use of urban development models. The authors' more recent case studies of eleven model-using regional planning agencies show that land-use models are being successfully developed and incorporated into the analytical work of regional planning agencies.

447. Palley, Marian Lief and Howard A. Palley. *Urban America and Public Policies*. Lexington, Mass.: D.C. Heath, 1981.

Examines a wide variety of policies that are administered at the municipal level of government. Included in the analysis are a general discussion of urban America, social welfare, police services, housing, health care, transportation, environmental protection, and New York City's fiscal crisis.

448. Parkin, Andrew. "Centralization and Urban Services: The Australian Experience." *Policy Studies Journal*, 9 (Summer 1981), 1059-65.

Australian centralism tends to have an equalizing effect, largely due to bureaucratic patterns of service delivery, but has also produced both an insensitivity to specialized local factors and an "organizational fragmentation."

449. Peterson, Paul E. *City Limits*. Chicago: University of Chicago Press, 1981.

The most significant book about urban politics to appear in a long time. Skillfully blends economic and political analysis in a fashion that brings needed integration and fresh perspectives to the discipline's most fragmented field.

450. Roessner, J. David. "Federal Technology Policy: Innovation and Problem Solving in State and Local Governments." *Policy Analysis*, 5 (Spring 1979), 181-200.

   Discusses how public technology policy issues can be conceptualized and analyzed, presents the results of empirical research bearing on the resolution of these issues, and discusses the implications of research findings for federal public technology policy.

451. Rosenbloom, Sandra and Alan Altshuler. "Equity Issues in Urban Transportation." *Policy Studies Journal*, 6 (Autumn 1977), 29-40.

   Examines the problem of equity in urban transportation.

452. Rosenthal, Alan. *Legislative Life: People, Process, and Performance in the States*. New York: Harper & Row, 1981.

   Merges interviews with legislators and staffs, the author's absorption of the political atmosphere in state capitols, and important findings of the political science literature.

453. Sanger, Mary Bryna. "Are Academic Models of Urban Service Distributions Relevant to Public Policy? Lessons from New York." *Policy Studies Journal*, 9 (Summer 1981), 1011-20.

   Presents findings on the determinants of intra-city distribution patterns for sanitation, fire and police services in New York.

454. Savage, Robert L. "Policy Innovativeness as a Trait of American States." *The Journal of Politics*, 40 (February 1978), 212-24.

   There is a suggestion of a certain randomness in the relative speed of adoption of public policies within and among the states, producing a sampling problem. The findings here address these problems with a larger and more representative data base. A total of 181 policy measures, including policies from such areas as agriculture, business regulation, conservation, crime and corrections, education, electoral regulation, governmental structures and operation, local government, health, professional licensing, race relations, taxation, transportation, and welfare are incorporated in the analysis.

455. Sharp, Elaine B. "Citizen Perception of Police Service Delivery: A Look at Some Consequences." *Policy Studies Journal*, 9 (Summer 1981), 971-81.

   What difference does it make if public services are inequitably distributed? Addresses that question by examining the relationships among perceived inequity in service delivery and dissatisfaction with public services on the one hand, and a variety of other attitudes and reports of behavior on the other.

456. Skok, James E. "Federal Funds and State Legislatures: Executive-Legislative Conflict in State Government." *Public Administration Review*, 40 (November/December 1980), 561-67.

    The national movement by state legislatures to appropriate federal funds in line-item detail is analyzed using national sources and information gathered through a case study of one state's efforts to deal with this issue. Arguments supporting and opposing detailed state legislative appropriation of federal funds are presented.

457. Szanton, Peter. *Not Well Advised*. New York: Russell Sage Foundation, 1981.

    Szanton's thesis is that advisers from an academic environment are too abstract and too preoccupied with teaching and long-term research to provide the prompt, practical advice needed by city officials. Raises insightful remarks about scholars as government practitioners.

458. Teitelbaum, Fred. "The Relative Responsiveness of State and Federal Aid to Stressed Cities." *Policy Studies Review*, 1 (1981), 309-22.

    Many federal, urban-oriented programs operate under the assumption that state governments are less responsive to urban needs than is the federal government. Shows that this assumption is most likely fallacious.

459. Thompson, Joel A. "State Compliance with Workmen's Compensation Recommendations." *Policy Studies Journal*, 8 (Winter 1979), 417-30.

    The Occupational Safety and Health Act of 1970 established the National Commission on State Workmen's Compensation Laws. The Commission was directed to "undertake a comprehensive study and evaluation of state workmen's compensation laws in order to determine if such laws provide an adequate, prompt, and equitable system of compensation." In 1972 the Commission issued its report, and criticized many aspects of state workmen's compensation programs. In its report the Commission made eighty-four recommendations for a "modern" workmen's compensation program and designated nineteen of these as "essential." This research traces state progress in complying with each of these nineteen essential recommendations.

460. Turnbull, Augustus B., III. "Staff Impact on Policy Development in the Florida Legislature." *Policy Studies Journal*, 5 (Summer 1977), 450-54.

    Views, from the perspective of a participant observer, the involvement of legislative staff in the development of a key state level policy in a "reformed" legislature.

461. Van Horn, Carl E. "Evaluating the New Federalism: National Goals and Local Implementors." *Public Administration Review*, 39 (January/February 1979), 17-22.

Examines the implementation of three legislative components of the New Federalism in order to determine the broad patterns of benefit distribution and governance resulting from it. The laws are the State and Local Assistance Act or General Revenue Sharing, the Comprehensive Employment and Training Act (CETA), and the Housing and Community Development Act, or CDBG.

462. Walker, David B. *Toward a Functioning Federalism*. Englewood Cliffs, N.J.: Prentice Hall, 1981.

In his excellent appraisal of our federal system, Walker carefully documents the expansion of federal power since the founding of the Republic in four main eras of intergovernmental history: 1790-1860; 1860-1930; 1930-1960; and in the "new federalism," from 1960 to the present, which is the main object of Walker's analysis.

463. Ward, Peter D. "The Measurement of Federal and State Responsiveness to Urban Problems." *The Journal of Politics*, 43 (February 1981), 83-101.

Using a previous study by Dye and Hurley for exemplary purposes, problems in analyzing federal responsiveness to urban need are detailed. Specifically, the use of correlational analyses and data expressed in city-percentage and per capita terms is questioned on grounds of conceptual inadequacy. In addition, problems with the Geographic Distribution of Federal Funds data base are discussed.

464. Ward, Sally K. "National Linkages and City Planning: A Note on the Correlates of Planning Expenditures." *Social Science Quarterly*, 61 (September 1980), 308-16.

Raises issues in regard to the measurement of national linkages and their relationship to a variety of community outputs.

465. Wasserman, Ira M. "State Policy Outputs and Collective Behavior: A Causal Reinterpretation." *Social Science Quarterly*, 59 (September 1978), 379-85.

An earlier article by Jaros and Baer (1976) is the point of departure for this paper by Wasserman, who introduces new control variables, reanalyzes the Jaros and Baer data and questions the original relationships reported between political disaffection and state policy outputs.

466. Weimer, David L. "Federal Intervention in the Process of Innovation in Local Public Agencies: A Focus on Organizational Incentives." *Public Policy*, 28 (Winter 1980), 93-116.

   In the absence of federal intervention, innovation and the diffusion of innovations among local public agencies is likely to proceed at a rate slower than the social optimum. A simple typology describes the various ways that information, funding, and technical assistance can be combined in federal programs to encourage innovation.

467. Welch, Susan and Albert K. Karnig. "The Impact of Black Elected Officials on Urban Social Expenditures." *Policy Studies Journal*, 7 (Summer 1979), 707-14.

   Using a data base of 155 U.S. cities of over fifty thousand population and at least 10 percent black, explores the impact of black mayors and city council members on a variety of social welfare expenditures. An over-time design was used to explore changes in social welfare policies from 1968 to 1975.

468. Welch, Susan and Kay Thompson. "The Impact of Federal Incentives on State Policy Innovation." *American Journal of Political Science*, 24 (November 1980), 715-29.

   Using fifty-seven state public policies as the basis for analysis, assesses the impact of federal incentives on the diffusion rates of these policies throughout the American states. Reveals that policies with federal incentives do diffuse substantially faster than policies that are the preserve of the states, even when the authors controlled for the functional area of the policy.

469. Whisler, Marilyn W. "Growth Management Strategies: Population Policy Implementation by Local Governments." *Policy Studies Journal*, 6 (Winter 1977), 208-16.

   Deals with the efforts of subnational governments to control population growth within their jurisdictions, and with the effectiveness of recently developed growth control mechanisms.

470. White, Michelle J. "Self-Interest in the Suburbs: The Trend toward No-Growth Zoning." *Policy Analysis*, 4 (Spring 1978), 185-203.

   Under the "no-growth" banner, suburban communities have been passing zoning ordinances that severely restrict the construction of any type of new housing. The author contrasts this recent practice with the older practice of exclusionary zoning.

471. Wikstrom, Nelson. "The Mayor as a Policy Leader in the Council-Manager Form of Government: A View from the Field." *Public Administration Review*, 39 (May/June 1979), 270-76.

The argument set forth in this paper, based on field interviews conducted with city mayors and managers in Virginia, is that the mayor, for a variety of reasons, usually functions as a strong policy leader. The implications flowing from the exercise of strong mayoral leadership include the emergence of teamwork governance, the merging of policy making and administration, and the "democratization" of the council-manager plan.

472. Wright, Deil S. and Alfred R. Light. "The Indeterminants of State Revenue Sharing Expenditures: Reactions to the Havick Research Note." *The Journal of Politics*, 39 (May 1977), 457-63.

The difficulty of measuring General Revenue Sharing (GRS) expenditures in the states is especially acute in cases in which GRS may have been used to reduce taxes or to prevent tax increases. Havick tried to calculate a "proportion of the funds explicitly earmarked for tax relief," using the General Accounting Office report. States, however, are not requested nor required to report GRS funds for tax relief on the forms they file with the United States government; but there is no category into which dollar amounts of GRS can be specified for usage as tax relief.

473. Zody, Richard E. "The Quality of Rural Management: Introductory Comment." *Public Administration Review*, 40 (January/February 1980), 13-18.

For a better part of this century, particularly its middle decades, we have focused our attention and resources on large systems. The attention that has been directed to local governments usually has been restricted to large urban settings. As a consequence, our knowledge and understanding of rural administration tends to consist of myths, fugitive studies, or questionable inferences based on our knowledge and understanding of larger entities.

Chapter 9

SEX, DRUGS, AND THE REGULATION OF MORALITY

474. Allen, James E. with Deborah Bender. *Managing Teenage Pregnancy: Access to Abortion, Contraception, and Sex Education.* New York: Praeger, 1980.

   A comparative study of the experience of adults in two communities in coping with increased teenaged pregnancy since the 1950's, this monograph is a welcome addition to the growing literature of empirical studies reporting data in a manner to facilitate the design and evaluation of social policy.

475. Bennett, W. Lance. "Imitation, Ambiguity, and Drama in Political Life: Civil Religion and the Dilemmas of Public Morality." *The Journal of Politics*, 41 (February 1979), 106-33.

   A careful analysis of civil religion shows that the displacement of the high symbols of state would risk the abandonment of a collective and binding moral order in any form. An analysis of the dynamics of the civil religion suggests a set of conditions which would permit the ordinary use of the sacred symbols of state and minimize their abuses. This analysis follows a brief introduction to the concept of civil religion.

476. Bessmer, Sue. "Anti-Obscenity: A Comparison of the Legal and the Feminist Perspectives." *Western Political Quarterly*, 34 (March 1981), 143-55.

   This comparison of traditional legal perspectives on pornography and new feminist perspectives illustrates how inaccessible policy change may be when basic values (in this case, values concerning sexuality), which define and delineate a whole body of legal tradition, are challenged.

477. Brown, Lawrence A. and Susan G. Philliber. "The Diffusion of a Population-Related Innovation: The Planned Parenthood Affiliate." *Social Science Quarterly*, 58 (September 1977), 215-28.

   Focusing upon supply of the innovation, the significant variables are community characteristics pertaining to need for family planning services, knowledge of Planned Parenthood, and presence of persons who would be likely to start an affiliate.

478. Bullough, Vern L. "Challenges to Societal Attitudes toward Homosexuality in the Late Nineteenth and Early Twentieth Centuries." *Social Science Quarterly*, 58 (June 1977), 29-44.

    Using homosexuality as an example, argues that in areas where there are strongly held, emotionally based opinions, traditional beliefs are not easily changed. Instead, even the scientific community is reluctant to incorporate the findings of new scientific data until organized pressure is mounted.

479. Cooper, Terry L. *The Responsible Administrator: An Approach to Ethics for the Administrative Role*. Port Washington, N.Y.: Kennikat Press, 1982.

    Dealing with ethics, is concerned with individual decision making and the freedom of choices within the organization. As a result, both the personal self-interest and administrative necessity for responsible management come through.

480. Craig, Richard B. "Human Rights and Mexico's Antidrug Campaign." *Social Science Quarterly*, 60 (March 1980), 691-701.

    Analyzes four charges leveled against the program and official responses to the accusations. Concludes that narcotics traffic, the campaign to curtail it and the resultant abuse of human rights are symptomatic of outside demand, official concern over regional developments outside government control and neglect of the rural sector.

481. Dean, Gillian. "The Study of Political Feedback Using Nonrecursive Causal Models: The Case of State Divorce Policies." *Policy Studies Journal*, 8 (Summer 1980), 920-27.

    Researchers interested in policy feedback effects can use the nonrecursive modeling strategies proposed here when time series data are not available for assessing feedback dynamics. This strategy is illustrated in a study of the impacts of American state divorce policies on divorce behavior and the responsiveness of policies to divorce rates.

482. Delamater, John and Patricia Maccorquodale. *Premarital Sexuality: Attitudes, Relationships, Behavior*. Madison: University of Wisconsin Press, 1979.

    The survey of sexual behaviors and attitudes was conducted among randomly selected students at the University of Wisconsin-Madison and, unlike previous studies of premarital sexuality, also included a systematic probability sample of nonstudents living in the Madison area. All respondents were eighteen to twenty-three years old and most were white.

483. Doron, Gideon. "Administrative Regulation of an Industry: The Cigarette Case." *Public Administration Review*, 39 (March/April 1979), 163-70.

    Departs from the "public interest" theories of regulation by proposing a third possibility--in some cases while regulation may be initiated in order to advance the interest of the public, the practical consequences may be compatible with the self-interest of the industry. To show this, the effects of the regulation imposed on the cigarette industry are examined.

484. Fairbanks, David. "Religious Forces and 'Morality' Policies in the American States." *Western Political Quarterly*, 30 (September 1977), 411-17.

    An analysis of the determinants of liquor and gambling regulations in the American states. The religious basis of anti-liquor and anti-gambling movements is reviewed and indicators of religious influence are correlated with Guttman scale measures of liquor and gambling laws.

485. ─────. "Politics, Economics, and the Public Morality: Why Some States Are More 'Moral' than Others." *Policy Studies Journal*, 7 (Summer 1979), 714-21.

    The relative restrictiveness of state regulations over liquor, gambling, divorce and birth control is measured by five-item Guttman scales and the resulting state morality scores then correlated with measures of state economic development, political development, and religious culture.

486. Field, Marilyn J. "Determinants of Abortion Policy in the Developed Nations." *Policy Studies Journal*, 7 (Summer 1979), 771-81.

    Although many of the more developed nations of the world have recently liberalized their laws on abortion, considerable variation remains. This variation appears to be linked--at least in the short run--to several political/ideological differences across nations. Economic variables do not dominate political variables in the statistical analysis of policy variation, but they do appear over the longer run to shape policy directions.

487. Hansen, Susan B. "State Implementation of Supreme Court Decisions: Abortion Rates since *Roe v. Wade*." *The Journal of Politics*, 42 (May 1980), 372-95.

    Examines effects of the Supreme Court's 1973 *Roe* decision in the states. Legalizing abortion has had little impact on national abortion or birth rates, but it has reduced interstate differences in access to abortion. A path-analytic model evaluates effects of legislative support, public preferences, Medicaid, and availability of hospital services for abortion in the states.

488. Helms, Robert B., ed. *Drugs and Health: Economic Issues and Policy Objectives.* Washington, D.C.: American Enterprise Institute for Public Policy Research, 1981.

    A collection of studies and conference proceedings on the economic performance of the pharmaceutical industry and the effect of governmental regulation on that performance. An objective of this collection is to provide scientific evidence that will be useful to policymakers attempting to control the use of drugs.

489. Kemp, Kathleen A., Robert A. Carp, and David W. Brady. "The Supreme Court and Social Change: The Case of Abortion." *Western Political Quarterly*, 31 (March 1978), 19-31.

    Examines the impact of the U.S. Supreme Court's abortion decisions upon hospital policies in a major metropolitan area in the United States. In assessing the effect of the *Roe* and *Doe* rulings, the study tries to identify which variables are associated with the hospitals' abortion policies before the Court rulings, the hospitals' post-*Roe* and *Doe* policies, and which factors best explain the change from one time period to another.

490. Kyvig, David E. *Repealing National Prohibition.* Chicago: University of Chicago Press, 1980.

    Represents a serious examination of the Prohibition period but with greater emphasis upon those forces seeking to overturn the Eighteenth Amendment.

491. Louthan, William C. *The Politics of Managerial Morality: A Value-Critical Approach to Political Corruption and Ethics Policy.* Washington, D.C.: University Press of America, 1981.

    For better or for worse, the Watergate scandal has produced a small new literature on political corruption and wrongdoing. This study approaches the question from the point of view of ethics and seeks to demonstrate the continuing ethical tensions by means of a number of well-known case studies.

492. Manning, Peter K. *The Narc's Game: Organizational and Informational Limits on Drug Law Enforcement.* Cambridge, Mass.: MIT Press, 1980.

    Manning spent several months in 1975 interviewing and examining records in two Southeastern city police departments' narcotics units. From these data is drawn a picture of the structural flaws of drug law enforcement generally.

493. Margolis, Michael and Kevin Neary. "Pressure Politics Revisited: The Anti-Abortion Campaign." *Policy Studies Journal*, 8 (Spring 1980), 698-716.

   Focuses on the anti-abortion campaign as an extreme example of pressure group operations. A comparison to the Anti-Saloon League is examined, and the article concludes with speculations about the probable consequences and future of such closely defined single interest groups.

494. Moore, Mark H. "A 'Feasibility Estimate' of a Policy Decision to Expand Methadone Maintenance." *Public Policy*, 26 (Spring 1978), 285-304.

   A major problem with traditional forms of policy analysis is that they ignore political and bureaucratic factors that determine whether a given policy can be adopted and successfully implemented. Four steps are used in evaluating the feasibility of a proposal to expand methadone maintenance.

495. ―――. "Reorganization Plan #2 Reviewed: Problems in Implementing a Strategy to Reduce the Supply of Drugs to Illicit Markets in the United States." *Public Policy*, 26 (Spring 1978), 229-62.

   To restrict supplies of heroin, barbiturates, and amphetamines reaching illicit markets in the United States, a wide diversity of activities of different organizations at different levels of government must be sustained and successfully coordinated. To manage this complex set of activities, the federal government instituted "Reorganization Plan #2," which consolidated federal narcotics enforcement activities within a single agency (the Drug Enforcement Administration). Two years after passage, the hopes for this agency had not yet been fulfilled.

496. Ostheimer, John M. "Abortion and American Population Politics." *Policy Studies Journal*, 6 (Winter 1977), 216-23.

   Investigates some of the unique characteristics of one of the most controversial population issues on the national agenda, abortion.

497. Palley, Howard A. "Abortion Policy: Ideology, Political Cleavage and the Policy Process." *Policy Studies Journal*, 7 (Winter 1978), 224-33.

   Examines the broad political processes surrounding abortion policies in the wake of the Supreme Court's 1973 abortion decisions and the impact of such processes on abortion policies culminating in the withholding of federal Medicaid funds in the case of non-therapeutic abortions in August, 1977.

498. Peek, Charles W. and Sharon Brown. "Pornography as a Political Symbol: Attitudes toward Commercial Nudity and Attitudes toward Political Organizations." *Social Science Quarterly*, 58 (March 1978), 717-23.

   Data from a 1973 national sample of American adults indicate that commercial nudity as a type of pronography is symbolic of orientations toward four important political organizations (the FBI, local police, United States, and Russia), in that attitudes toward commercial nudity are linked to attitudes toward each of these organizations.

499. Shapo, Marshall S. *A Nation of Guinea Pigs*. New York: The Free Press, 1979.

   Makes a powerful case for permanently adding yet another area of activity to the police, defense, and other functions of government. When the public senses the extent of the threat from chemical and drug research and development, it will support the extension of government regulation, for better or worse.

500. Stetson, Dorothy M. "Family Policy and Fertility in the United States." *Policy Studies Journal*, 6 (Winter 1977), 223-30.

   Offers a framework for assessing the impact of indirect government policies (chiefly family policies) on fertility.

501. Strean, Herbert S. *The Extramarital Affair*. New York: The Free Press, 1980.

   Is it possible for a man or woman to have a long-term love affair and maintain a happy marriage? The author, a noted psychoanalyst, comes down strongly on the negative. Most of the evidence presented is based mainly on clinical cases--persons who have come voluntarily to the analytical situation, generally white, middle class or above, prepared for long-term therapeutic relationships. The generalizability of whatever meager objective data there are is severely limited and readers should bear this in mind.

502. Symons, Donald. *The Evolution of Human Sexuality*. New York: Oxford University Press, 1979.

   Argues that distinctions between male and female sexuality have a deeply innate biological base. In a word, the two sexes are programmed differently. Males possess an innate urge for sexual variety. Females, on the other hand, have a greater parental investment in their offspring and seek to attach themselves to a strong, protective male.

503. Tatalovich, Raymond and Byron W. Daynes. *The Politics of Abortion: A Study of Community Conflict in Public Policy Making.* New York: Praeger, 1981.

    Argues, from existing data on policy enactments, that abortion politics is a deviant case. Abortion politics are best analyzed, in the authors' view, when viewed as a sequential process of agenda setting, community conflict, and consensus building.

504. Wardell, William M., ed. *Controlling the Use of Therapeutic Drugs: An International Comparison.* Washington, D.C.: American Enterprise Institute for Public Policy Research, 1978.

    The extent of the controls on drug use being implemented or planned in the United States, together with their rapid increase in number, has important public policy implications that are not widely recognized. This book explores those implications.

505. Warner, Kenneth E. "Clearing the Airwaves: The Cigarette Ad Ban Revisited." *Policy Analysis*, 5 (Fall 1979), 435-50.

    Empirical analysis has led to the conclusion that the ad ban on cigarettes was myopic public policy. Reexamines the wisdom of that policy and considers its relevance, as well as that of closely related alternatives, to the federal government's reinvigorated anti-smoking campaign.

506. Watts, Meredith W. "Anti-Heterodoxy and the Punishment of Deviance: An Explanation of Student Attitudes toward 'Law and Order.'" *Western Political Quarterly*, 30 (March 1977), 93-103.

    Attitudes toward "law and order"--defined as the tendency to prefer punitive treatment of statutory deviance--are conceived as the result of cognitive organization which anchors the individual in the sociopolitical milieu. It is hypothesized that such attitudes can be predicted by anti-heterodoxy, a construct asserted to be similar to Gabennesch's notion of "breadth of perspective." Using a sample of college students, evidence is found that anti-heterodoxy is strongly related to law and order attitudes, thus generally supporting the thesis.

507. Yisai, Yael. "Abortion in Israel: Social Demand and Political Responses." *Policy Studies Journal*, 7 (Winter 1978), 270-90.

    This paper has four purposes: (1) to reveal the factors that made abortion a nondecision issue, preventing its appearance on the public agenda; (2) to explore the factors that have successfully pushed forward abortion to the point that it became a public issue; (3) to study the process that made abortion a subject of legislative public policy; and (4) to examine the implementation (or lack thereof) of this policy.

508. Yondorf, Barbara. "Prostitution as a Legal Activity: The West German Experience." *Policy Analysis*, 5 (Fall 1979), 417-33.

Examines the West German experience with legal prostitution, exploring in detail three questions of particular interest to American policy analysts and public decisionmakers.

Chapter 10

SOCIAL WELFARE POLICY

509. Albritton, Robert B. "Measuring Public Policy: Impacts of the Supplemental Social Security Income Program." *American Journal of Political Science*, 23 (August 1979), 559-78.

   An effort to measure impacts of the Title XX amendments to the Social Security Act in an interrupted time series design. Applications of an Auto-Regressive Integrated Moving Averages (ARIMA) model (Box and Jenkins, 1970) to indicators of welfare policy outputs aid in solving a number of perplexing problems of time series analysis and facilitate estimation of effects of the Supplemental Security Income Program. Results of the analysis show that this welfare policy innovation resulted in dramatic, nonincremental changes in consequential aspects of American welfare policy.

510. Auster, Richard D. and Josephine G. Gordon. "Incentives in a Government-Controlled Health Sector?" *Policy Studies Journal*, 5 (Spring 1977), 295-300.

   Examines the extent to which the high cost of hospital services is due to the absence of a residual claimant who captures the gains from cost decreases and bears the losses from cost increases. Besides explaining much contemporary experience, the analysis sheds insight into the merits of alternative possibilities for public policy.

511. Barmack, Judith A. "The Case against In-Kind Transfers: The Food Stamp Program." *Policy Analysis*, 3 (Fall 1977), 509-30.

   Reviews criteria for the evaluation of public income transfer programs and applies them to an analysis of the Food Stamp Program.

512. Benest, Frank. "One City's Commitment to a Comprehensive Human Services Delivery System: A Case History of Gardena, California." *Public Administration Review*, 37 (March/April 1977), 190-92.

   Ever since California cities were forced in the late 1960's to recognize the physical and human dimensions of urban decay, city councils and municipal administrators have struggled with a whole series of interrelated policy issues. Presents a brief history of the efforts of the Gardena City Council and its municipal administration to develop/coordinate a comprehensive human services delivery system.

513. Berkowitz, Edward D. "The Politics of Mental Retardation during the Kennedy Administration." *Social Science Quarterly*, 61 (June 1980), 128-43.

Notes that President Kennedy used the power of the presidency to make mental retardation a special federal concern. The bureaucratic and ideological constraints that he encountered are analyzed.

514. Bieker, Richard F. "Work and Welfare: AFDC Participation Rates in Delaware." *Social Science Quarterly*, 62 (March 1981), 169-76.

Examines the growth in Aid to Families with Dependent Children (AFDC) participation rates in Delaware over the period 1950-74. The findings of the study provide a basis for exploring several broader welfare policy questions.

515. Blau, Peter. "Implications of Growth in Services for Social Structure." *Social Science Quarterly*, 61 (June 1980), 3-22.

After reviewing his (1977) macrosociological theory of social structure, Blau examines American trends to infer how the growth in services has affected heterogeneity, inequality, and the crosscutting of various forms of differentiation.

516. Bradley, John P. "Shaping Administrative Policy with the Aid of Congressional Oversight: The Senate Finance Committee and Medicare." *Western Political Quarterly*, 33 (December 1980), 492-501.

Focusing on the Senate Finance Committee's oversight of the Medicare program, concludes that the oversight function of Congress may contribute to the accomplishment of policies sought by administrators. Secondly, committee-bureau cooperation was found in opposition to interest groups rather than there being a "cozy triangle" relationship.

517. Burkhauser, Richard V. and Timothy M. Smeeding. "The Net Impact of the Social Security System on the Poor." *Public Policy*, 29 (Spring 1981), 159-78.

Since 1974, Supplemental Security Income (SSI) has provided a universal income floor for the low-income aged. A major feature of this "social welfare" program is that it taxes income from social security (OASI) at virtually 100%. Shows that the current structure of SSI has altered significantly the "social insurance-social welfare" nature of OASI for many low-income workers.

518. Butler, John A. and Richard K. Scotch. "Medicaid and Children: Some Recent Lessons and Reasonable Next Steps." *Public Policy*, 26 (Winter 1978), 3-27.

    Analyzes the recent federal experience in subsidizing health care services for low-income children. The overall equalizing effects of Medicaid are discussed, as are those of Medicaid's component that promotes preventive services for children, the Early and Periodic Screening, Diagnosis, and Treatment program (EPSDT).

519. Chadwin, Mark L., John J. Mitchell, and Demetra S. Nightingale. "Reforming Welfare: Lessons from the WIN Experience." *Public Administration Review*, 41 (May/June 1981), 372-80.

    Examines the employment-related aspects of welfare reform in light of recent research findings on the implementation of the Work Incentive (WIN) program, the current welfare-employment program. Contends that nine lessons can be learned from the WIN research that should be applied to the future design and development of welfare-employment programs, whether or not welfare reform legislation is enacted.

520. Chase, Gordon. "Implementing a Human Services Program: How Hard Will It Be?" *Public Policy*, 27 (Fall 1979), 385-435.

    A framework is presented for examining obstacles to the implementation of human services delivery programs.

521. Derthick, Martha. *Policymaking for Social Security*. Washington, D.C.: The Brookings Institution, 1979.

    A case study on U.S. social security policy, emphasizing the specialness of this policy sphere more or less to the exclusion of broad generalizations of the contextual or comparative sort.

522. Engquist-Seidenberg, Gretchen. "The State Role in Health Care Cost Containment." *Policy Studies Review*, 1 (1981), 275-87.

    Examines the history of health care policy in the U.S., including the Social Security Act of 1935, the Medicaid legislation of 1965, and concludes with an examination of state efforts to link quality of health care with cost containment.

523. Farge, Emile J. "A Review of Findings from 'Three Generations' of Chicano Health Care Behavior." *Social Science Quarterly*, 58 (December 1977), 407-11.

    Tests the hypotheses summarized by Weaver (1973) on a sample of 150 Mexican-American household heads. The findings confirm Weaver's suspicions that most observers wrongly typify this population.

524. Feldstein, Martin. "Social Insurance." *Public Policy*, 25 (Winter 1977), 81-115.

    Begins with a general discussion of the principles of social insurance design, discusses seven ideas that are relevant to all types of social insurance, and then discusses two specific programs, social security and unemployment insurance.

525. Flora, Peter and Arnold J. Heidenheimer, eds. *The Development of Welfare States in Europe and America*. New Brunswick, N.J.: Transaction Books, 1981.

    An important and useful collection of essays produced under the impact of a widely discussed "crisis of the welfare state," the essays are not only international in authorship but also comparative and carefully scientific in execution. The welfare state is seen as a modernizing response to basic, long-term developmental processes.

526. Fox, Peter D. "Options for National Health Insurance: An Overview." *Policy Analysis*, 3 (Winter 1977), 1-24.

    After discussing the rationale for national health insurance, presents the basic options embodied in the major bills in Congress and examines their consequences, then discusses the future of existing federal mechanisms for financing medical services.

527. Friedman, Lee S. "An Interim Evaluation of the Supported Work Experiment." *Policy Analysis*, 3 (Spring 1977), 147-70.

    In this report on interim results from the evaluation of the Supported Work social experiment, the author also reflects on the role and limitations of benefit-cost analysis as it affects program development.

528. Ginzberg, Eli, ed. *Employing the Unemployed*. New York: Basic Books, 1980.

    Provides a collection of perspectives on the Manpower programs of the sixties as they matured in the seventies.

529. Gleeson, Michael E. "Budgeting for Federal Housing Programs: A Problem and What to Do About It." *Public Administration Review*, 40 (July/August 1980), 321-30.

    Argues that budget authority for Section 8, the nation's largest housing construction subsidy program, is not sufficient to meet the full term of commitments. Using even optimistic assumptions, it is estimated that budget authority may need to be increased substantially. Three means of addressing the problem are analyzed.

Social Welfare Policy

530. Green, Barbara B. and Nancy K. Klein. "The Mentally Retarded and the Right to Vote." *Polity*, 13 (Winter 1980), 184-206.

   Sets out to justify the restoration of political rights to the mentally retarded by analyzing the reasons for granting political participation to the common man. Applying the same criteria to the mentally retarded, finds the relevant differences insufficient to justify their political disqualification. Sees the root of the problem in certain widespread feelings and prejudices.

531. Greenberg, George D. "Constraints on Management and Secretarial Behavior at HEW." *Polity*, 13 (Fall 1980), 57-79.

   Considers the impact of administrative discretion and constraint on executive leadership in the departments of the government. Lack of discretion is apt to preclude effective leadership, while unbridled arbitrariness reduces administrative continuity and undermines organizational morale. Analyzes the problem from the perspective of the Department of Health, Education, and Welfare as a case study.

532. Grondbjerg, Kirsten, David Street, and Gerald D. Suttles. *Poverty and Social Change*. Chicago: University of Chicago Press, 1978.

   Provides an incisive, composite history of American social welfare policy. This accomplishment is supplemented by an excellent bibliography and a chronology of major welfare events.

533. Hargrove, Erwin G. and Gillian Dean. "Federal Authority and Grass-Roots Accountability: The Case of CETA." *Policy Analysis*, 6 (Spring 1980), 127-49.

   The Comprehensive Employment and Training Act of 1973 assumed that prime sponsors would join local political accountability and planning for local labor market needs. The new federal role was to be technical assistance in this task.

534. Hausman, Leonard J. "Welfare in Retreat: A Dilemma for the Federal System." *Public Policy*, 25 (Winter 1977), 25-48.

   Considers the record of revisions in the welfare system and the process by which they have been achieved, the financial and other constraints to continuing changes in welfare, and suggestions about the central issues involved in redesigning the welfare system.

535. Haveman, Robert H. "Poverty, Income Distribution, and Social Policy: The Last Decade and the Next." *Public Policy*, 25 (Winter 1977), 3-24.

   It is the purpose of this essay to place the 1965-75 years of the war on poverty into some perspective and, on the basis of both that experiment in policy intervention and recent social trends, to speculate on the nature of social policy over the following decade.

536. Hochschild, Jennifer L. "Why the Dog Doesn't Bark: Income, Attitudes and the Redistribution of Wealth." *Polity*, 11 (Summer 1979), 478-511.

Seeks to explain why poor Americans have failed to demand a redistribution of wealth, contrary to expectations based on classical and liberal political theory, psychological theories, empirical observation, and current politics.

537. Hoffman, Ellen. "Policy and Politics: The Child Abuse Prevention and Treatment Act." *Public Policy*, 26 (Winter 1978), 71-88.

Politics and policy frequently interact to affect substantially the final shape of legislation. In the case of the Child Abuse Prevention and Treatment Act, public hearings and the media focused attention on the problem of abused children, helping to create a climate favorable for action by the Congress. The shapers of the bill deliberately accepted an incremental approach, believing that adequate funding for a more comprehensive attack on child abuse was not forthcoming.

538. Howards, Irving and Henry Brehm. "The Impossible Dream: The Nationalization of Welfare? A Look at Disability Insurance and State Influence over the Federal Government." *Polity*, 11 (Fall 1978), 7-26.

Shows that the administration by states has had at best a nominal impact upon rising costs and uniformity of eligibility decisions. Concludes, first, that the states continue to be a potent force in American federalism and, second, that people in need will apply for and receive benefits regardless of the program's nature or its administering agency.

539. Jennings, Edward T., Jr. "Civil Turmoil and the Growth of Welfare Rolls: A Comparative State Policy Analysis." *Policy Studies Journal*, 7 (Summer 1979), 739-45.

Tests three propositions derived from Francis Fox Piven and Richard Cloward's analysis of the growth of welfare rolls in the 1960's. Regression analysis is used to assess the effects of urban riots, community action agencies, and unemployment levels on relief rolls in the American states.

540. ―――. "Competition, Constituencies, and Welfare Policies in American States." *The American Political Science Review*, 73 (June 1979), 414-29.

Examines the logic underlying formulations of the interparty competition hypothesis in the comparative state policy

Social Welfare Policy   123

        literature, suggests a reformulation which provides some new
        insights into the conditions under which we might expect state
        policies to change as a result of party characteristics, and
        undertakes an initial test of the reformulation.

541.   ———. "Urban Riots and the Growth of State Welfare Expendi-
        tures." *Policy Studies Journal*, 9 (Autumn 1980), 34-40.

        Examines the relationship between urban riots and increases
        in state welfare spending in the 1960's.

542.   Kelly, William J. "Theoretical Foundations for a Reform of Un-
        employment Insurance." *Social Science Quarterly*, 60 (June
        1979), 96-104.

        Discusses adverse work incentives in present state unemploy-
        ment insurance programs and offers a theoretical basis for an
        improved system incorporating a work requirement and taxation
        of benefits.

543.   Kerstein, Robert and Dennis R. Judd. "Achieving Less Influence
        with More Democracy: The Permanent Legacy of the War on
        Poverty." *Social Science Quarterly*, 61 (September 1980),
        208-20.

        Analyzes the long-term impact of the War on Poverty on the
        politics of St. Louis, Missouri, and concludes that the program
        provided a buffering mechanism which focused discontent in the
        ghetto community on the anti-poverty bureaucracy, thus allowing
        established political and economic institutions to escape pro-
        test.

544.   Kirst, Michael W., Walter Garms, and Theo Oppermann. "State
        Services for Children: An Exploration of Who Benefits, Who
        Governs." *Public Policy*, 28 (Spring 1980), 185-206.

        In recent years, equity, choice, and efficiency issues in
        the provision of education have received much attention and
        analysis. Yet, in the area of other state services for chil-
        dren (health, protective services, day care, etc.), there has
        been scant concern for equity, efficiency, or choice, despite
        the fact that out-of-school influences can be crucial in deter-
        mining in-school performance. This paper reports on work in
        progress that reaches certain conclusions.

545.   Knaub, Norman L. "The Impact of Food Stamps and Cash Welfare
        on Food Expenditures, 1971-1975." *Policy Analysis*, 7
        (Spring 1981), 169-82.

        Compares the food expenditure behavior of food stamp recip-
        ients with the behavior of food stamp non-recipients and ana-
        lyzes the impact of bonus food stamps on food stamp recipients.

546. Kushman, John E. "A Public Choice Model of Day Care Center Services." *Social Science Quarterly*, 60 (September 1979), 295-308.

   Notes that this model is relatively simple and yet takes into account the existence of reciprocal externalities. The collective demand for government day care center spaces is estimated using data from North Carolina in 1973, and the implications of the model are tested.

547. Lave, Lester B. *The Strategy of Social Regulation: Decision Frameworks for Policy*. Washington, D.C.: The Brookings Institution, 1981.

   One of the Brookings Institution Studies in the Regulation of Economic Activity. Reflects public concern for health, safety, and environmental problems as worthy of attention by the state.

548. Leman, Christopher. "Patterns of Policy Development: Social Security in the United States and Canada." *Public Policy*, 25 (Spring 1977), 261-91.

   Old age security policies in Canada and the United States have been profoundly influenced by the political contexts in which they have developed. Explores the differences in the political context of the two countries and their implications for the policy-making process.

549. ―――. *The Collapse of Welfare Reform: Political Institutions, Policy, and the Poor in Canada and the United States*. Cambridge, Mass.: MIT Press, 1980.

   In the 1970's both the United States and Canada embarked on political debate and policy design concerned with welfare reform. The thrust of both movements was to extend social assistance to working families via a guaranteed income system, and both movements failed. Argues that despite their common failure, these two movements were really very different and that their difference is explained more by political structure than political culture.

550. Lewis-Beck, Michael S. and John R. Alford. "Can Government Regulate Safety? The Coal Mine Example." *The American Political Science Review*, 74 (September 1980), 745-56.

   The federal government has been directly involved in coal mining safety for over thirty-five years, operating under three major pieces of legislation, enacted in 1941, 1952, and 1969. Opposing opinions regarding the effect of this legislation can be grouped into three categories: radical, reactionary, and reformer. A multiple interrupted time series analysis indicates that, in fact, the 1941 and 1969 regulations significantly reduced the fatality rate in coal mining.

551. Liebhafsky, E.E., John E. Gnuschke, and William L. McKee. "Value Judgments Inherent in Criticisms of CPS Measurement of Unemployment." *Social Science Quarterly*, 61 (September 1980), 237-52.

Shows that changes in concepts, proposed by both the "overstatement" and the "understatement" criticisms, involve value judgments that Bureau of Labor Statistics (BLS) has traditionally avoided and that the BLS insists upon objectivity, continuity of data series, and continuing review of concepts in order to maintain the integrity of the system.

552. Lynn, Laurence J., Jr. and Mark D. Worthington. "Incremental Welfare Reform: A Strategy Whose Time Has Passed." *Public Policy*, 25 (Winter 1977), 49-80.

Reviews the coverage and characteristics of existing income assistance programs and evaluates the major proposals for incremental reform of these programs. The subject is reanalyzed in terms of issues rather than specific proposals in an effort to clarify areas of agreement and disagreement between proponents of different strategies for welfare reform.

553. MacDonald, Marucie and Isabel V. Sawhill. "Welfare Policy and the Family." *Public Policy*, 26 (Winter 1978), 89-119.

Discusses the difficulties of defining and implementing a more neutral family policy and reviews the empirical evidence about the effects of income transfer programs on family behavior.

554. McKinley, Tina M. "One by One: Training the Unemployed." *Public Administration Review*, 39 (November/December 1979), 532-36.

When the author studied to become a planner, she was taught that the world should be approached through a comprehensive plan. Goals should reflect optimal achievement. Activities should be proposed to guide the present to the optimal. In short, what should be, is not. It is, therefore, the responsibility of the planner to assess what should be and to propose alternative ways of getting there. The assessment of "shoulds" (goals) must involve clarifying and quantifying relevant social values.

555. Marmor, Theodore R. "The Politics of National Health Insurance: Analysis and Prescription." *Policy Analysis*, 3 (Winter 1977), 25-48.

Assesses what we can realistically expect NHI to do. After briefly evaluating the "crisis" in American medicine and the major competing NHI bills, proposes a two-pronged plan--national health insurance for preschool children and universal tax-credit catastrophic insurance which is deemed fiscally, administratively, and politically feasible.

556. Meier, Kenneth J. "Executive Reorganization of Government: Impact on Employment and Expenditures." *American Journal of Political Science*, 24 (August 1980), 396-412.

Many public officials have an unshakable belief that the structural reorganization of executive agencies can reduce employment and expenditures. This belief coexists with a fair amount of literature which argues that structural reorganization is unrelated to either economy or efficiency. The research presented here addresses this dispute empirically, with an analysis of sixteen state government reorganizations since 1965.

557. Mendeloff, John. "Welfare Procedures and Error Rates: An Alternative Perspective." *Policy Analysis*, 3 (Summer 1977), 357-74.

Discusses the two main types of welfare errors--errors of stringency and errors of liberality; examines the impact on them of two major procedural changes introduced in California during the past few years; and suggests several remedies for redressing the current inattention to errors that prevent clients from getting benefits to which they are entitled.

558. Moon, Marilyn. "Supplemental Security Income, Asset Tests, and Equity." *Policy Analysis*, 6 (Winter 1980), 1-20.

The treatment of assets and income from assets has important consequences for eligibility in the Supplemental Security Income program for the aged and disabled. Examines the equity effects of several alternative approaches to asset testing, including those advocated in current welfare reform debates.

559. Norgren, Jill. "In Search of a National Child Care Policy: Background and Prospects." *Western Political Quarterly*, 34 (March 1981), 127-42.

The failure to pass a national child care policy illuminates the difficulty of achieving policy change when, despite access, a lobby must simultaneously challenge social myths regarding the family and women's roles in it and reach consensus on the nature of appropriate policy alternatives.

560. O'Loughlin, John. "Black Representation Growth and the Seat-Vote Relationship." *Social Science Quarterly*, 60 (June 1979), 72-86.

Notes that the growth in the number of black elected officials has slowed down now that most black-majority districts have elected black representatives. Once elected, black candidates continue to win with ease. In interracial contests, the proportion of seats won by blacks is higher than the proportion of black votes.

561. Osmond, Marie Withers and Mary Durkin. "Measuring Family Poverty." *Social Science Quarterly*, 60 (June 1979), 87-95.

Maintains that measuring family poverty should involve a minimum of four indicators. Measures based on annual income adjusted for family size, average weeks per year that the household head has been employed, weeks per year that the family has received public assistance and occupation of the household head are shown to be relatively independent and to have specific implications depending upon the race and sex of the head of the family.

562. Perrotta, John A. "Machine Influence on a Community Action Program: The Case of Providence, Rhode Island." *Polity*, 9 (Summer 1977), 481-502.

Examines the theses of the pluralists and their critics through his case study of the Community Action Program in Providence from 1965 to 1969. Finds that members of minority groups, particularly blacks, were able to broaden their power base through the federally sponsored CAP against the centralized political structure of the city. Provides no evidence that deprived groups are excluded from the decision-making process in Providence.

563. Pesso, Tana. "Local Welfare Offices: Managing the Intake Process." *Public Policy*, 26 (Spring 1978), 305-30.

Three areas of concern are found in the performance of two intake units in the Massachusetts Department of Public Welfare: (1) intake clerks deny welfare applications informally; (2) intake workers fail to adequately inform applicants about welfare services and to refer them to such services; and (3) intake workers are not as compassionate as might be wished.

564. Plotnik, Robert D. "Social Welfare Expenditures: How Much Help for the Poor?" *Policy Analysis*, 5 (Summer 1979), 271-89.

Analyzes the growth of government social welfare expenditures and the extent to which they have benefited low-income persons.

565. ——— and Timothy Smeeding. "Poverty and Income Transfers: Past Trends and Future Prospects." *Public Policy*, 27 (Summer 1979), 255-72.

Analyzes the reduction of poverty produced by government transfers during the 1965-76 period and, building upon these past trends, speculates on future anti-poverty effects of transfers.

566. Prager, Edward. "Subsidized Family Care of the Aged: U.S. Senate Bill 1161." *Policy Analysis*, 4 (Fall 1978), 477-90.

Would cash subsidies encourage nuclear families to share their households with elderly kin? This alternative to skilled nursing facility care was proposed by U.S. Senate Bill 1161; yet empirical evidence in the area of family helping behavior and conceptual considerations generated by the body of exchange theory lend little support to such a program.

567. Randall, Ronald. "Presidential Power versus Bureaucratic Intransigence: The Influence of the Nixon Administration on Welfare Policy." *The American Political Science Review*, 73 (September 1979), 795-810.

Many observers routinely assert the relative weakness of presidents before the bureaucracy. The research of this study, guided by a structuralist theory of organizations, provides evidence of the Nixon administration's power to change policy, even over the opposition of the bureaucracy, concerning the Aid to Families with Dependent Children program.

568. Saltzstein, Alan L. "Federal Categorical Aid to Cities: Who Needs It versus Who Wants It." *Western Political Quarterly*, 30 (September 1977), 377-83.

The amount of federal categorical aid to cities is analyzed to assess the importance of the need for aid and the interest in and efforts expended in acquiring aid by members of the city government. A survey of attitudes and practices of city managers and city council members in twenty cities is used to measure attitudes and practice.

569. Sapolsky, Harvey M. "America's Socialized Medicine: The Allocation of Resources within the Veterans' Health Care System." *Public Policy*, 25 (Summer 1977), 359-82.

Following World War II, budgetary strategies pursued by the Veterans Administration have intensified the veterans' health care system's involvement with acute medicine. Examines the bureaucratic origins of these strategies and their implications for the care of veterans and for the nation's overall health policy.

570. Schantz, Harvey L. and Richard H. Schmidt. "The Evolution of Humphrey-Hawkins." *Policy Studies Journal*, 8 (Winter 1979), 368-77.

Outlines the major changes made in Humphrey-Hawkins from its introduction in June 1974 to its enactment in October 1978, the contents of the Full Employment and Balanced Growth Act of 1978, and the politics surrounding its passage.

571. Schroeder, Larry D., David L. Sjoquist, and Paula E. Stephan. "The Allocation of Employment and Training Funds across States." *Policy Analysis*, 6 (Fall 1980), 395-407.

Substantial variations exist in the state-by-state allocation of federal employment and training program grants per capita and per poor. The research discussed here indicates that the variables in the funding formula are not significant in explaining the variations in grants per capita, while important explanations can be found in the funding process.

572. Sigelman, Lee and Carol K. Sigelman. "Social Service Innovation in the American States: Deinstitutionalization of the Mentally Retarded." *Social Science Quarterly*, 62 (September 1981), 503-15.

Analyzes the extent to which American states have deinstitutionalized their mentally retarded populations. An index of deinstitutionalization displays substantial variation among the states. Comparison of the index to a similar index for juvenile offenders indicates that they are substantially unrelated, suggesting the non-existence of any statewide deinstitutionalization dimension. Examination of effects coefficients in a three-variable regression model indicates that two political/institutional factors--political culture and legislative capability--are the most and affluence the least decisive determinants of the extent to which states rely on community-based facilities for the retarded.

573. Sinclair, Barbara D. "The Policy Consequences of Party Realignment--Social Welfare Legislation in the House of Representatives, 1933-1954." *American Journal of Political Science*, 22 (February 1978), 83-105.

Burnham's theory of the policy consequences of realignments is applied to social welfare legislation during the New Deal realignment and its aftermath. As predicted, social welfare legislation does emerge as a direct response to the depression. The most clearly nonincremental programs were passed during the height of the realigning era (1935-38) and little nonincremental legislation passed during the remaining years under study.

574. Stonecash, Jeff and Susan W. Hayes. "The Sources of Public Policy: Welfare Policy in the American States." *Policy Studies Journal*, 9 (Spring 1981), 681-98.

The conceptualization of political and economic determinants of public policy as interactive rather than sufficient causes is subjected here to a comparative state analysis. An examination of interactive effects of culture, wealth, and gubernatorial power on AFDC grants and Medicaid benefits offers empirical illustration of Stonecash's reconceptualization of the classic politics-process-policy model.

575. Struyk, Raymond J. *A New System for Public Housing: Salvaging a National Resource.* Washington, D.C.: Urban Institute Press, 1980.

   Uses twenty-nine large public housing authorities, rated as "badly distressed" by HUD, to demonstrate two central themes. Argues that public housing in the largest cities is definitely in trouble and that what is needed is a comprehensive strategy aimed at alleviating problems and improving PHA management capacity.

576. ———— and Marc Bendick, Jr., eds. *Housing Vouchers for the Poor: Lessons from a National Experiment.* Washington, D.C.: Urban Institute Press, 1981.

   Authorized by Congress in 1970, the Experimental Housing Allowance Program shows that housing vouchers are administratively workable, that they will be used by needy families, and that the per-unit cost of such housing is less than the per-unit cost of subsidized housing built specifically for the poor. The experiment also indicated that vouchers do not have an inflationary effect on the housing market.

577. Thompson, Joel A. "Outputs and Outcomes of State Workmen's Compensation Laws." *The Journal of Politics*, 43 (November 1981), 1129-52.

   In attempting to overcome shortcomings of previous research, this study identifies potentially important forces within states. It utilizes both party competition and interest group involvement as indicators of political characteristics, and investigates the linkage between policy outputs and policy impacts. The study concludes that, at least for workmen's compensation, measures of policy outputs are not important determinants of policy impacts.

578. Thompson, Lawrence H. "Toward the Rational Adjustment of Social Security Benefit Levels." *Policy Analysis*, 3 (Fall 1977), 485-508.

   Under the law in effect, social security benefits for workers retiring in the future tend to be overadjusted every time prices rise and underadjusted every time wage levels rise. Explains the features in the current law that give rise to this result, examines the effect on the long-run costs of the program, and explores ways in which future benefit levels can be brought under greater control.

579. Van Horn, Carl E. "Implementing CETA: The Federal Role." *Policy Analysis*, 4 (Spring 1978), 159-83.

   Assesses the federal government's role in implementing the first two years of the Comprehensive Employment and Training

Act, following a discussion of CETA and the New Federalism with an analysis of the impact of the U.S. Department of Labor on major CETA policy issues.

580. Van Loon, Rick. "Reforming Welfare in Canada: The Case of the Social Security Review." *Public Policy*, 27 (Fall 1979), 469-504.

   From 1973 to 1978 a major review of welfare policy in Canada aimed to improve social-insurance programs, inaugurate a "Community Employment Strategy," provide better funding for personal social services, expand existing demogrant programs and, most important to its planners, introduce a program of income supplementation for the working poor. The review was begun partly because of problems within the welfare system but in large measure because of broader political considerations.

581. Vickery, Clair. "The Changing Household: Implications for Devising an Income Support Program." *Public Policy*, 26 (Winter 1978), 121-51.

   Focuses on the policy implications of the changing household structure for the formulation of an income support program. A standard for comparing the need of various types of households is described and used to develop a broad outline of an income support program that satisfies both equity and efficiency criteria.

582. Waite, Linda J., Larry E. Suter, and Richard L. Shortlidge, Jr. "Changes in Child Care Arrangements of Working Women from 1965 to 1971." *Social Science Quarterly*, 58 (September 1977), 302-11.

   Indicates that the location of care by nonrelatives shifted from inside to outside the child's home, but that women prefer to use personal friends or family rather than formal day care centers. Concludes that trends in women's employment and living patterns may be adding pressure for formal day care arrangements, but any future increases in the use of such arrangements may be determined as much by their supply as by demand for them.

583. Weissert, William G. "Toward a Continuum of Care for the Elderly: A Note of Caution." *Public Policy*, 29 (Summer 1981), 331-40.

   The search for better ways to care for the chronically ill elderly has led to "alternatives to institutional care." A study of geriatric day care and homemaker services finds that they were used as an add-on to existing care, few patients benefited, and costs were 60 to 71 percent higher than costs of a control group.

584. Williams, Walter with Betty Jane Narver. *Government by Agency: Lessons from the Social Program Grants-in-Aid Experience.* New York: Academic Press, Inc., 1980.

   The authors are concerned with the management of the welfare state. Their point of departure is the perception of many that the structural essence of the welfare state, federal grants to local authorities, has failed.

585. Wynne, Edward A. *Social Security: A Reciprocity System under Pressure.* Boulder, Colo.: Westview Press, 1980.

   The cross-cultural and historical data Wynne presents supports his thesis that the current reciprocity systems have become depersonalized and bureaucratic. Posits recommendations to insure that old age in America is accompanied by true social security. Offers creative insight into theoretical and practical dimensions of social exchange processes.

Chapter 11

TAXING AND COLLECTING PUBLIC REVENUES

586. Anton, Thomas J., Jerry P. Cawley, and Kevin L. Kramer. *Moving Money: An Empirical Analysis of Federal Expenditure Patterns.* Cambridge, Mass.: Oelgeschlager, Gunn & Hain, 1980.

"At the present time, no one really knows where federal money is spent." The investigators proceed to demonstrate in detail the extensive range and exotic variety of "authoritative" spending reports that are inconsistent, incomplete, and often not relevant, one to another.

587. Auten, Gerald E. "Capital Gains Taxes and Realizations: Can a Tax Cut Pay for Itself?" *Policy Studies Journal,* 9 (Autumn 1980), 53-60.

Concerns itself with the effects of capital gains taxes on realizations of accrued capital gains. Previous empirical studies are summarized and exploratory new research using pooled cross-section and time-series tax data is presented.

588. Bond, Jon R. "Oiling the Tax Committees in Congress, 1900-1974; Subgovernment Theory, the Overrepresentation Hypothesis, and the Oil Depletion Allowance." *American Journal of Political Science,* 23 (November 1979), 651-64.

Tests an overrepresentation hypothesis derived from a subgovernment theory of policy making in an effort to explain the adoption and maintenance of the oil depletion allowance over time. Oil states do not tend to be overrepresented on tax committees of Congress during expected periods. The condition of oil state representation on tax committees and/or in key leadership positions is not associated with variation in the oil depletion allowance over time.

589. Break, George F. *Financing Government in a Federal System.* Washington, D.C.: The Brookings Institution, 1980.

Purports to cover the financing of government in a federal system. There are excellent chapters on tax coordination, the economics of intergovernmental grants, the federal aid system, and urban fiscal systems.

590. Brennan, Geoffrey. "Inflation, Taxation, and Indexation." *Policy Studies Journal*, 5 (Spring 1977), 326-32.

Examines proposals to index the income tax system so that inflation will no longer automatically produce increases in real rates of tax. Some analysts have argued that without indexation public spending will increase too rapidly, at least within existing democratic political institutions. Considers indexing as a possible constraint on democratic processes of budgetary choice.

591. Dye, Thomas R. "Taxing, Spending, and Economic Growth in the American States." *The Journal of Politics*, 42 (November 1980), 1085-1107.

This research on differential rates of growth in the states in income, employment, and productivity, suggests that age itself--the length of time a state has been settled, developed, and politically organized--is an influential determinant of economic growth. State taxing policies have little discernible effect on state economic growth. However, state spending for capital infrastructure, especially outlays for highways, has an independent, stimulative effect on state economies.

592. Eilbott, Peter and William Kempey. "New York City's Tax Abatement and Exemption Program for Encouraging Housing Rehabilitation." *Public Policy*, 26 (Fall 1978), 571-97.

Reports on a study of a New York City tax abatement and exemption program whose purpose is to encourage both major and minor rehabilitation of multiple dwellings.

593. Formuzis, Peter and Anil Puri. "Inflation, Progressivity, and State Income Tax Revenues." *Policy Studies Journal*, 9 (Autumn 1980), 19-25.

Shows that the ratio of income tax revenues to personal income has grown significantly more in states with progressive income tax structures than those with proportional tax structures.

594. Gilbert, D.A. "Property Tax Base Sharing: An Answer to Central City Fiscal Problems?" *Social Science Quarterly*, 59 (March 1979), 681-89.

When a property tax base sharing plan similar to the one used in Minneapolis-St.Paul is applied to other metropolitan areas, relatively small fiscal benefits are produced for most cities. Concludes that tax base sharing is neither a solution to central city fiscal problems nor a fiscal alternative to metropolitan governmental reorganization.

Taxing and Collecting Public Revenues 135

595. Goetz, Michael L. "The Normative Bases of Tax Reform: A Constitutional Perspective." *Policy Studies Journal*, 9 (Autumn 1980), 48-53.

    Examines the explicit and implicit ideological content of tax reform embodied in three views of taxation.

596. Hellawell, Robert, ed. *United States Taxation and Developing Countries*. New York: Columbia University Press, 1980.

    The two principal tax issues discussed in this book are: (1) should U.S. taxpayers be allowed to credit foreign income taxes paid during the taxable year against their U.S. tax liability; and (2) should foreign subsidiaries of U.S. corporations be allowed to defer the payment of U.S. taxes on foreign-earned income until their earnings are remitted to the United States. The book is concerned primarily with their application to developing countries.

597. Hickam, Dale, Robert Berne, and Leanna Stiefel. "Taxing over Tax Limits: Evidence from the Past and Policy Lessons for the Future." *Public Administration Review*, 41 (July/August 1981), 445-53.

    It is generally thought that across-the-board tax limits, while encouraging fiscal restraint, create hardships for jurisdictions with above average and uncontrollable needs. The conclusion is difficult to confirm empirically. This article provides a test of the conclusion based on a study of New York State city school districts where limits long in effect were suspended between 1970 and 1978 because of unusual local behavior and legislative action.

598. Hill, Kim Quaile. "Taxpayer Support for the Presidential Election Campaign Fund." *Social Science Quarterly*, 62 (December 1981), 767-78.

    Presents the first accurate estimates of taxpayer participation in the presidential election campaign fund. Those estimates show public participation to be considerably higher than previously believed. A modest positive relationship between level and participation is also demonstrated. These findings are related to participation rates for other forms of mass political activity and to reformers' intentions regarding public financing of election campaigns.

599. LeLoup, Lance T. *The Fiscal Congress: Legislative Control of the Budget*. Westport, Conn.: Greenwood Press, 1980.

    A carefully organized book to explain the substantive and procedural changes, the differences between the House and the

Senate, and the impact on the tax and appropriations committees. Statistics and tables are used intelligently to highlight the historical record on macroeconomic policy, budget resolutions, floor amendments, committee action, and other indices.

600. Levine, Charles H. and Irene Rubin, eds. *Fiscal Stress and Public Policy.* Beverly Hills, Calif.: Sage Publications, 1980.

    Twelve original articles address the single most important public policy problem of the 1980's: the financing of government in a period of increasing resistance.

601. Lineberry, Robert L. "On Tax Revolts: Two Views." *Social Science Quarterly*, 59 (March 1979), 690-703.

    The victory of Proposition 13 in California in 1978 was the stimulus for position papers on "The Taxpayer Revolt" by James M. Buchanan, university distinguished professor at Virginia Polytechnic Institute and Richard Musgrave, H.H. Burbank Professor of political economy at Harvard University. Editorial Board members Robert L. Lineberry and William R. Allen were instrumental in arranging this discussion of an important issue.

602. Lowery, David and Lee Sigelman. "Understanding the Tax Revolt: Eight Explanations." *The American Political Science Review*, 75 (December 1981), 963-74.

    Extracts eight explanations of the tax revolt from the literature, each of which assumes that the tax revolt is a systematic national phenomenon that is a function of individual-level social, economic, and political factors. Having tested these explanations by means of a discriminant analysis of data from the 1978 American National Election Study, finds little empirical corroboration for any of them.

603. McLure, Charles E. "Integrating the Income Taxes: An Introduction to the Issues." *Public Policy*, 25 (Fall 1977), 459-77.

    Integration, whether applied only to distributed corporate-source income or to all such income, would improve resource allocation, but at the expense of substantial revenue loss and reduced progressivity of the tax system. Hence, it would be acceptable only if accompanied by tax reform that would substantially reduce the preferential treatment available to high-income taxpayers and recoup some of the revenue lost in integration.

604. ―――. "Tax Restructuring Act of 1979: Time for an American Value-Added Tax?" *Public Policy*, 28 (Summer 1980), 301-22.

    Chairman Al Ullman of the House Ways and Means Committee proposed substitution of a tax on value added for part of the personal and corporate income taxes and the payroll taxes used to finance Social Security, but at some cost.

605. MacManus, Susan A. "Tax Structures in American Cities: Levels, Reliance, and Rates." *Western Political Quarterly*, 30 (June 1977), 263-87.

   Describes and contrasts variations in tax structures of the central cities of 243 Standard Metropolitan Statistical Areas (1970). The results indicate that tax levels, reliance, and effective property tax rates are all greatest among central cities located in the Northeast, with populations over one million, having either manufacturing or industrial economic bases, unreformed governmental charters, and financial responsibility for education, welfare, and hospitals.

606. ―――. "Special District Governments: A Note on Their Use as Property Tax Relief Mechanisms in the 1970s." *The Journal of Politics*, 43 (November 1981), 1207-14.

   Examines the fiscal effects of special district governments in the South in the 1970's. Results show that creation of special districts tended to stabilize the rate of increase in city and county property tax levels, keep down the level of local government spending, and compensate for state restrictions on municipal taxing and borrowing powers.

607. Miner, Ralph E. with Donald R. Chalice. "Tax Reform Policy and Legislative Voting Behavior." *Policy Studies Journal*, 5 (Spring 1977), 308-14.

   Examines why tax reform customarily takes the form of a complex set of tax changes, which might be called loophole-opening, rather than general or broad-based changes, which might be called loophole-closing. While these latter types of changes dominate normative proposals for reform, suggests that an awareness of the political framework within which tax policy emerges can give insight into why the former types of changes generally prevail in legislative assemblies.

608. Pechman, Joseph A., ed. *What Should Be Taxed: Income or Expenditure?* Washington, D.C.: The Brookings Institution, 1980.

   In a 1974 *Harvard Law Review* article, William Andrews proposed a practical method of administration of a progressive consumption tax. This seminal article has provoked a lively debate on the relative merits of the consumption tax. *What Should Be Taxed: Income or Expenditure?* is part of that debate.

609. Penniman, Clara. *State Income Taxation*. Baltimore: Johns Hopkins University Press, 1980.

   Directs our attention to the subtle effects of organizational structure on the operation of state income tax and sets out to examine the organizational structure and operation of state income tax offices.

610. Peters, B. Guy. "Determinants of Tax Policy." *Policy Studies Journal*, 7 (Summer 1979), 787-93.

   Posits three principal functions of tax policies adopted by governments, and seeks to find the determinants of these policy choices. The three principal functions are raising revenue, retaining office for incumbent politicians, and redistributing income.

611. Phares, Donald. *Who Pays State and Local Taxes?* Cambridge, Mass.: Oelgeschlager, Gunn & Hain, 1980.

   A massive empirical study that comprehensively answers the question posed by the title. In providing it, develops effective tax rates, each a ratio of tax payments to income for ninety-three categories of state and local taxes, in the fifty states and for fourteen income classes.

612. Portney, Kent E. "State Tax Preference Orderings and Partisan Control of Government." *Policy Studies Journal*, 9 (Autumn 1980), 87-95.

   Using scattered analyses linking partisan control of political institutions to taxation decisions as the point of departure, examines patterns of tax preferences in American states.

613. Quester, Aline O. "Women's Behavior and the Tax Code." *Social Science Quarterly*, 59 (March 1979), 665-80.

   Argues that the present code provides incentives for wives' work behavior that widen gender inequalities in earnings and proposes a return to an individual basis of taxation as well as an earned-income allowance.

614. Radian, Alex and Ira Sharkansky. "Tax Reform in Israel: Partial Implementation of Ambitious Goals." *Policy Analysis*, 5 (Summer 1979), 351-66.

   A study of disparities between a tax reform and its implementation in Israel, and of how organizations adapt to policies they can neither implement fully nor ignore.

615. Rasche, Robert H. "Financing the Government Deficit." *Policy Studies Journal*, 9 (Autumn 1980), 60-67.

   Examines the relationship between the U.S. government deficit on a unified budget basis and the various available sources of financing. Identifies those sources of financing other than private domestic capital markets that are available, and develops measures of the financing responses of both domestic and foreign monetary authorities to the continuing U.S. budget deficits of the past fifteen years.

Taxing and Collecting Public Revenues   139

616. Schick, Allen. *Congress and Money: Budgeting, Spending, and Taxing.* Washington, D.C.: Urban Institute, 1980.

Reviews the background of the Congressional Budget and Impoundment Control Act (1974), the struggles involved in implementing it, and problems created by it.

617. Straussman, Jeffrey D. and Robert Rodgers. "Public Sector Unionism and Tax Burdens: Are They Related?" *Policy Studies Journal*, 8 (Winter 1979), 438-48.

One factor that has affected state and local politics since the 1960's is the growth of public sector unionism. Conventional wisdom assumes that the "fist generation" of public unionism has been a major cause of the fiscal problems faced by many state and local governments in the 1970's. State level cross-sectional analysis (1960-71) questions this widely held assumption with respect to the impact of strike activity and collective bargaining legislation on the tax burden across the states.

618. Thomas, John C. "The Growth of American Public Expenditure: Recent Trends and Their Implications." *Public Administration Review*, 40 (March/April 1980), 160-65.

Despite growing concern over the growth of American public expenditures, there is no consensus on the nature of that growth. Attempts to define the nature of that growth through an analysis of recent trends in American public spending.

619. Wagner, Richard E. "Tax Policy toward Private Foundations: Confused Principles and Unfortunate Legislation." *Policy Studies Journal*, 5 (Spring 1977), 314-19.

Explores the impact of tax policy upon private foundations. An important distinction in the tax treatment of charitable organizations is that between public charities and private foundations. While the intent of present tax practices is to strengthen competitive pressures in the foundation sector, actual policies will not have this effect, and, moreover, will even bring about a relative shrinkage in the foundation sector. Concludes by exploring some alternative approaches to tax policy toward foundations.

620. Walzer, Norman and Samuel K. Gove. "State Financing and Taxing Policies." *Policy Studies Review*, 1 (1981), 335-46.

Identifies three periods of state finance and taxing policies--the 30's were the states dominated Congress; the 60's when federally funded programs exploded onto the scene; and the current period which is characterized by referendum-mandated spending limits and tax reductions.

621. Wildavsky, Aaron. *How to Limit Government Spending.* Berkeley, Calif.: University of California Press, 1980.

Wildavsky's argument is straightforward: growth of government, particularly at the expense of the private sector, is not desirable. He argues that controlling the expansion of federal spending will reduce inflation, lower taxes, and enhance efficiency.

Chapter 12

POLICY ANALYSIS

622. Anderson, Charles W. "The Place of Principles in Policy Analysis." *The American Political Science Review*, 73 (September 1979), 711-23.

Any theory of policy evaluation has to address the problem of the choice of criteria for decision making. In most theories of policy rationality, derived from economic theories of the utility-maximizing individual and a positivist conception of valuation, such values are to be regarded as the "preferences" of the policymaker. The stipulation and ordering of standards of judgment is not considered to be part of policy rationality itself.

623. Anderson, James E., David Brady, and Charles Bullock. *Public Policy and Politics in America*. North Scituate, Mass.: Duxbury Press, 1978.

A general introduction to the field of public policy. It is of such a nature that it would make an excellent introductory text for students interested in the relationship of politics and public policy. Covers energy, environmental, welfare, economic, business, consumer protection, education, government and labor, and agricultural policies.

624. Anderson, James E., ed. *Cases in Public Policy Making*. New York: Holt, Rinehart and Winston, 1982.

A collection of some excellent essays which examine problems facing policy analysts, policy agenda setting, policy formulation, adoption, implementation, and evaluation.

625. Angrist, Shirley S. and Shelby Stewman. "Problem Solving for Public Policy: Learning by Doing." *Policy Analysis*, 5 (Winter 1979), 97-117.

Describes project courses taught future public managers and analysts at the School of Urban and Public Affairs at Carnegie-Mellon University.

626. Axelrod, Robert, Davis B. Bobrow, Heinz Eulau, Charles O. Jones, and Martin Landau. "The Place of Policy Analysis in Political Science: Five Perspectives." *American Journal of Political Science*, 21 (May 1977), 415-33.

In view of the increasing professional interest in policy analysis, five authors were asked to address the question: "What is policy analysis, and how does the analysis of policy contribute to theories of politics?" Their responses to this question comprise a short symposium on the subject.

627. Ballard, Steven C., Allyn R. Brosz, and Larry B. Parker. "Social Science and Social Policy: Roles of the Applied Researcher." *Policy Studies Journal*, 8 (Summer 1980), 951-57.

Outlines four roles--substantive expert, information processor, change agent, and scholar--which have helped to increase the potential usefulness of our research while maintaining linkages to the academic community.

628. Bingham, Richard D. and Robert W. Biersack. "Field Experience for Policy Studies." *Policy Studies Journal*, 6 (Spring 1978), 359-67.

Deals with the need to provide empirical data on which students can exercise themselves as they attempt to master the necessary concepts and methods.

629. Bingham, Richard D. and Marcus E. Ethridge. *Reaching Decisions in Public Policy and Administration*. New York: Longman, 1982.

Introduces the reader to several methodological approaches to the analysis of public policy. Includes discussions on survey research, the Delphi Technique, nominal group techniques, scenario writing, simulation, technology assessment, cost-benefit analysis, decision analysis, organization development, MBO, path analysis, and program evaluation and review technique.

630. Blair, John P. and Steven M. Maser. "Axiomatic versus Empirical Models in Policy Studies." *Policy Studies Journal*, 5 (Spring 1977), 282-89.

Compares deductive and empirical approaches to policy analysis, and suggests that deductive modeling is presently underutilized. Besides articulating a rationale for placing greater emphasis upon the use of deductive models in the articulation of policy advice, provides several particular illustrations of the fruitfulness of deductive modeling.

631. Blissett, Marlan, Jurgen Schmandt, and David Warner. "The Policy Research Project at the LBJ School of Public Affairs." *Policy Analysis*, 7 (Winter 1981), 103-24.

Students in the Master of Public Affairs program at the Lyndon B. Johnson School of Public Affairs, University of Texas at Austin, are required to participate in two year-long policy research projects. These studies of evolving policy issues are undertaken by faculty-student teams, generally for a client agency, and often lead to a published report. The authors review the LBJ School's experience with this alternative to case-study teaching.

632. Cary, Charles D. "An Introductory Course in Evaluation Research." *Policy Analysis*, 3 (Summer 1977), 429-44.

Describes the course in evaluation research that the author has taught to students in the Master of Arts in Public Affairs program at the University of Iowa. The course provides an overview of what is involved in evaluating the performance of, and support for, public programs: it treats the conception, execution, and use of evaluation and is intended to train students to competently manage rather than actually conduct evaluation research.

633. Clark, Terry N. "Policy Research and Urban Public Policy." *Policy Analysis*, 4 (Winter 1978), 67-90.

Distinguishes centralized and decentralized policy contexts, illustrating the latter with three brief case studies, and outlines strategies to enhance the utilization and to constrain the bias of policy analyses.

634. Cohen, Larry J. and Robert M. Rakoff. "Teaching the Contexts of Public Policy: The Need for a Comparative Perspective." *Policy Studies Journal*, 6 (Spring 1978), 319-25.

Suggests that an imbalance exists in the teaching of policy studies because the social, economic and political context in which policies evolve is not adequately explored. Attributing this lack to the "instrumentalism" in the policy literature, calls for treatment of the economic, institutional, and cultural-ideological contexts in the policy studies curriculum. Argues that comparative studies is a most effective way to introduce the context of policy. Not rejecting the instrumentalist approach of policy studies, the authors call for even more openness of the curriculum.

635. Dubnick, Mel. "Comparing Policy Alternatives." *Policy Studies Journal*, 6 (Spring 1978), 368-75.

Describes how the work of Elinor Ostrom and her colleagues at Indiana University has been adapted to the classroom. Students are provided with a framework through which they can dissect alternative policy proposals by expressing propositional linkages in a flow-chart format.

636. Dye, Thomas R. *Understanding Public Policy.* Englewood Cliffs, N.J.: Prentice-Hall, 1978.

   Probably the best general introductory work on public policy analysis. Special emphasis is given to topical policy areas, the policy-making process, the impact of policy, and systems analysis.

637. ———. *Power and Society.* North Scituate, Mass.: Duxbury Press, 1979.

   Presents the reader with an excellent analysis of the relationship of power to such policy concerns as race, sex, poverty, powerlessness, crime, violence, the international system, and the quality of life. The volume includes a series of "social indicators" which could be of enormous help to many policy analysts.

638. ———. *Policy Analysis: What Governments Do, Why They Do It, and What Difference It Makes.* Tuscaloosa: University of Alabama Press, 1980.

   A collection of engaging essays by one of the leading authorities in the field of policy analysis. The essays grew out of a series of lectures at the University of Alabama, where the participants felt these lectures deserved a wider audience; hence, the publication of this stimulating volume.

639. ——— and Virginia Gray, eds. *The Determinants of Public Policy.* Lexington, Mass.: D.C. Heath, 1980.

   Nineteen essays which examine a wide variety of concerns to policy analysts. Specifically, addresses itself to presenting an overview of the literature, examining the theoretical concerns in discovering the determinants of public policy at both the state and local, as well as the national levels of government. Concludes with an excellent appraisal of the literature by Virginia Gray.

640. Edwards, George C., III. "Disaggregation in Policy Research." *Policy Studies Journal,* 7 (Summer 1979), 675-83.

   Disaggregation has gained considerable prominence in policy research, but it is sometimes flawed by invalid and unreliable measures of policy and improper inferences derived from policy data. Examines examples of policy studies which disaggregate within a level of analysis; between levels of analysis; or within a level of analysis, making inferences between levels of analysis.

641. Fairchild, Erika S. "Modular Learning for Policy Studies."
    Policy Studies Journal, 6 (Spring 1978), 341-48.

    Describes the characteristics of a modular approach and why it is particularly suited for policy studies.

642. Fisher, Gene H. "Methods and Practices." *Policy Analysis*, 3 (Winter 1977), 107-14.

    If cost analysis is to continue to be an effective, integral part of policy analysis, several problem areas will have to receive increasing attention. Discusses the issues and briefly considers their implications for synthesizing and presenting study results.

643. Foster, John L. "An Advocate Role Model for Policy Analysis."
    Policy Studies Journal, 8 (Summer 1980), 958-64.

    Outlines an alternate advocacy analysis model which assumes that many policy problems are matters of competing self-interests and that analysts will often be sought to provide the strongest possible case for a client's preference. Also reviews questions of feasibility, credibility, appropriate training, and ethics for an advocacy analysis profession.

644. Fry, Brian R. "Some Notes on the Domain of Public Policy Studies." *Policy Studies Journal*, 6 (Spring 1978), 305-13.

    References, among others, the historical work of the George's, the conceptual work on bureaucracies of Merton, the psychological perspective of Janis and the computer simulations work of Davis, Dempster and Wildavsky, as well as Crecine. The content of policy studies is expressed as a matrix in which the rows are the levels of analysis and the columns, policy processes. Whether or not the authors succeed in their particular formulation, they do introduce many of the concepts now active in the field.

645. Greenberg, George D., Jeffrey A. Miller, Lawrence B. Mohr, and Bruce C. Vladeck. "Developing Public Policy Theory: Perspectives from Empirical Research." *The American Political Science Review*, 71 (December 1977), 1532-43.

    There has been considerable interest in the development of theories of public policy formation, but theoretical efforts to date have not demonstrated adequate recognition of the distinctive qualities of the dependent variable as a focus of research. Attempts to test hypotheses with some rigor, which demonstrated that public policy becomes troublesome as a research focus because of inherent complexity--specifically because of the temporal nature of the process, the multiplicity of participants and of policy provisions, and the contingent nature of theoretical effects.

646. Hambrick, Ralph S., Jr. and William P. Snyder. "Communications Skills and Policy Analysis: Exercises for Teaching." *Policy Studies Journal*, 6 (Spring 1978), 313-19.

Deals with what everyone agrees is a major educational goal--communications with decisionmakers. Presents a clear statement of what the specific communications skills are and what can be done about presenting them.

647. Jones, Charles. *An Introduction to the Study of Public Policy.* North Scituate, Mass.: Duxbury Press, 1977.

A general introduction to the study of public policy. Professor Jones is considered to be one of the most knowledgeable scholars in the field, and this volume lives up to his reputation.

648. Jones, Thomas E. *Options for the Future: A Comparative Analysis of Policy-Oriented Forecasts.* New York: Praeger, 1980.

The title gives only an inadequate indication of the contents: the book is simultaneously a pioneering analysis of the role implicit assumptions can play in distorting policy-oriented forecasts and a superb one-volume history of, and guide to, the debate among American futurists about the shape of "post-industrial society."

649. Klass, Gary M. "The Determination of Policy and Politics in the American States, 1948-1974." *Policy Studies Journal*, 7 (Summer 1979), 745-52.

A path model of the causes and effects of changes in taxation and education spending demonstrates the advantages to policy determination research of analytic and methodological refinements of customary research strategies.

650. Lehman, Edward W. and Anita M. Waters. "Control in Policy Research Institutes: Some Correlates." *Policy Analysis*, 5 (Spring 1979), 201-21.

What type of control of key decisions is most likely to enhance the impact of policy research institutes on government programs? The authors studied a sample of thirty-three research centers, classified the centers according to bureaucratic, semi-bureaucratic, semicollegial, and collegial control structures, and identified the correlation of control type to other structural traits and to links with the political and economic systems.

651. Leinhardt, Samuel and Stanley S. Wasserman. "Quantitative Methods for Public Management: An Introductory Course in Statistics and Data Analysis." *Policy Analysis*, 4 (Fall 1978), 549-75.

   Describes the development, content, and evaluation of an introductory course in quantitative methods that the authors have taught to students in the Master of Public Policy and Management program at the School of Urban and Public Affairs, Carnegie-Mellon University.

652. Leman, Christopher. "How to Get There from Here: The Grandfather Effect and Public Policy." *Policy Analysis*, 6 (Winter 1980), 99-116.

   A little-studied technique in policy design, the "grandfather effect," exempts a particular group from a law.

653. Lewis-Beck, Michael S. "The Relative Importance of Socioeconomic and Political Variables for Public Policy." *The American Political Science Review*, 71 (June 1977), 559-66.

   Since Dawson and Robinson, a dominant issue in the quantitative study of public policy has been the relative importance of socioeconomic and political variables for determining policy outcomes. It is argued here that past efforts to resolve this issue have been unsatisfactory, largely because they relied on inadequate statistical techniques, i.e., simple correlation, partial correlation, or multiple regression.

654. Lindbloom, Charles and David K. Cohen. *Usable Knowledge: Social Science and Social Problem Solving.* New Haven, Conn.: Yale University Press, 1979.

   One of the groundbreaking efforts in the field of policy analysis was Lindbloom's earlier work, *The Policy Making Process.* This volume shows the reader which current methodological skills may be applied to many of the problems facing policy analysts which were noted in Lindbloom's earlier work.

655. Lineberry, Robert L. *American Public Policy.* New York: Harper and Row, 1977.

   Develops two themes in this work: (1) "the notion that policy studies fix our attention on what government is doing and how well it does it," and (2) "the use of the policy approach to say something important about political issues." Examines how policy is shaped, implemented, and distributed. Presents both concepts and techniques used in the analysis of public policy.

656. MacRae, Duncan, Jr. "Introducing Undergraduates to Public Policy Analysis by the Case Method." *Policy Studies Journal*, 6 (Spring 1978), 353-59.

   Discusses the author's use of the case method as a teaching technique.

657. ———— and James Wilde. *Policy Analysis for Public Decisions*. Monterey, Calif.: Brooks/Cole, 1979.

   An interdisciplinary pioneering work which looks at the cycle of policy analysis, defining policy problems, models, enactment of public policy and implementation of policy. Also examines the criteria used for making policy choices as well as defining just exactly what policy analysis does.

658. Maynard-Moody, Steven and Charles C. McClintock. "Square Pegs in Round Holes: Program Evaluation and Organizational Uncertainty." *Policy Studies Journal*, 9 (Spring 1981), 644-66.

   Argues that variation in uncertainty about social program goals and causal processes should influence the selection of evaluation designs and methods. Eighteen prominent evaluation reports are examined to contrast predicted evaluation strategies derived from theory about organizational uncertainty with the actual evaluation methods used.

659. Mazmanian, Daniel A. and Paul A. Sabatier. "A Multivariate Model of Public Policy-Making." *American Journal of Political Science*, 24 (August 1980), 439-68.

   Applies Hofferbert's six-stage model to a specific policy area: environmental-protection and land-use regulation by the powerful California Coastal Commissions. The results suggest the general usefulness of the model in guiding both conceptual thinking and data analysis. Also suggests several important areas where refinement and greater specificity of the model is needed.

660. Menzel, Donald C. "Guided Design." *Policy Studies Journal*, 6 (Spring 1978), 375-81.

   Discusses the application of a procedure first developed for the engineering curriculum, which involves a set of steps described as a "decision structure," a scenario and some group interactions.

661. Morehouse, Sarah McCally. *State Politics, Parties and Policy*. New York: Holt, Rinehart and Winston, 1981.

   Addresses both the question of policy variations across the states and the question of equity. The author's thesis is that states with competitive, vigorous political parties tend to be more likely to produce redistributive policies than states that lack healthy party systems.

662. Nachmias, David. *Research Methods in the Social Sciences.* New York: St. Martin's Press, 1981.

 Many of the research techniques covered in this volume are applicable methodologies for the field of public policy analysis.

663. Nagel, Stuart. *Policy Analysis in Social Science Research.* Beverly Hills, Calif.: Sage Publications, 1979.

 An excellent overview of the place of policy analysis in the social science constellation.

664. ———. "The Policy Studies Perspective." *Public Administration Review,* 40 (July/August 1980), 391-96.

 The core curriculum of policy studies training programs often includes four courses or subjects. They are: (1) policy studies in general, (2) policy studies substance of issues, (3) policy studies process, and (4) policy studies methods. One purpose of this review essay is to review a key book often used to cover each of those four courses or subjects. A second purpose is to indicate the important relations between policy studies and public administration.

665. ——— and Marian Neef. What Is and What Should Be in University Policy Studies?" *Public Administration Review,* 37 (July/August 1977), 383-90.

 Is designed to fit two purposes: (1) to describe what is happening in university policy studies activities within political science departments and within interdisciplinary programs and (2) to analyze a set of prescriptions for improving policy studies activities which have been recommended by academics and by government practitioners.

666. ———. "Finding an Optimum Choice, Level, or Mix in Public Policy Analysis." *Public Administration Review,* 38 (September/October 1978), 404-12.

 Analyzes some general matters concerning how to arrive at an optimum choice, level, or mix when confronted with alternative policy decisions, especially decisions relating to the legal process.

667. ———, eds. *Policy Grants Directory.* Urbana, Ill.: Policy Studies Organization, 1977.

 An indispensable reference volume for policy analysts who wish to know who and where to turn to for financial assistance when considering research projects.

668. ———, eds. *Policy Studies Directory.* Lexington, Mass.: D.C. Heath, 1980.

A standard reference source covering information pertaining to the various policy programs at colleges and universities in the U.S. Every political science and public administration department should have a copy available for the use of their students, if for no other reason.

669. Nagel, Stuart and Nancy Munshaw, eds. *Policy Studies Personnel Directory.* Urbana, Ill.: Policy Studies Organization, 1979.

A most useful reference source, including biographical data on most of the personnel engaged in some aspect of public policy analysis.

670. Nedwek, Brian T. and Steven Puro. "Problems in Developing a Ph.D. Program in Policy Studies for Practitioners." *Policy Studies Journal,* 6 (Spring 1978), 387-92.

Describes the conceptual and the administrative-political problems the authors faced in developing a multi-disciplinary Ph.D. program at Saint Louis University.

671. Newcomer, Kathryn E. and Richard J. Hardy. "Analyzing Policy Impact: Selection of a Linear Trend Model." *Policy Studies Journal,* 8 (Summer 1980), 928-41.

Examines three linear trend models which have been used to depict policy impact through time-series analyses, and identifies the relative advantages and disadvantages associated with the use of each model.

672. Newell, Charldean and James J. Glass. "A Modular Approach to Applied Policy Research." *Policy Studies Journal,* 6 (Spring 1978), 348-53.

Provides a concrete example of how the authors have adapted a modular approach to the difficult task of teaching applied policy research.

673. Nichols, David A. "Pluralism and Post-Pluralism in the Study of Public Policy." *Polity,* 10 (Winter 1977), 274-80.

Policy studies will surpass the limits of pluralism and give us a full understanding of the forces that shape all policy only to the extent that they treat as political the institutions and policies of corporate capitalism. It will not do to point to the exceptions that prove the rule: continued neglect of the issue.

674. Obler, Jeffrey. "The Odd Compartmentalization: Public Opinion, Aggregate Data, and Policy Analysis." *Policy Studies Journal*, 7 (Spring 1979), 524-40.

   Examines some of the assumptions that underlie the use of aggregate data for policy analysis. In particular, explores the consequences of the assumption of antagonistic attitudes between "haves" and "have nots" on social welfare policies.

675. O'Donnell, Tom. "Information-Gathering Skills for Policy Studies Students." *Policy Studies Journal*, 6 (Spring 1978), 333-41.

   Outlines the entire range of information collection skills that students ought to acquire in any policy studies curriculum. The essay states the obvious, but far too few students who complete undergraduate or graduate problems have been introduced to the information collection skills which are specified.

676. Ostrom, Elinor. "Is It B or Not-B? That Is the Question." *Social Science Quarterly*, 61 (September 1980), 198-202.

   The author expresses reservations in regard to Steinberger's (*SSQ*, 1980) perspective.

677. Palumbo, Dennis J. "The State of Policy Studies Research and the Policy of the New *Policy Studies Review*." *Policy Studies Review*, 1 (1981), 5-10.

   A general introduction in the inaugural issue of the *Policy Studies Review* journal. Informs the reader of the purposes of this new journal and provides a general state-of-the-art essay.

678. Parker, Steven. "Public Policy and Administration: New Perspectives on a Perennial Issue." *Polity*, 13 (Spring 1981), 484-94.

   The relationship of public administration and public policy has long been a major concern of students of the political process. Taken together the five titles reviewed here provide a comprehensive overview of the relationship between policy and administration.

679. Quade, E.J. *Analysis for Public Decisions*. New York: Elsevier, 1982.

   A well-known scholar offers the student of policy analysis an excellent view of the juxtaposition of the decision-making sciences and policy analysis.

680. Radin, Beryl A. "On Teaching Policy Implementation." *Policy Analysis*, 4 (Spring 1978), 261-73.

   It is possible to devise a course in policy implementation organized around some generally agreed upon questions. Such a course, offered at the Lyndon B. Johnson School of Public Affairs, University of Texas at Austin, includes readings, class exercises, guest lecturers, and assignment of a series of five well-defined papers.

681. Rein, Martin and Sheldon H. White. "Policy Research: Belief and Doubt." *Policy Analysis*, 3 (Spring 1977), 239-71.

   Examines the twin themes of belief and doubt in the usefulness of social research in the shaping of governmental decisions and the efforts at reform that have been designed to reduce the gap between them.

682. Schick, Allen. "Beyond Analysis." *Public Administration Review*, 37 (May/June 1977), 258-63.

   The contemporary boom in policy analysis has its primary source in the huge growth of American governments, not in the intellectual development of the social sciences.

683. Schneider, Mark and David Swinton. "Policy Analysis in State and Local Government: Introductory Comments." *Public Administration Review*, 39 (January/February 1979), 12-16.

   Despite limitations, the authors believe there exist encouraging signs concerning the future use of policy analysis in state and local governments. Technical problems concerning the use of policy analyses are much better understood than in the past and the exaggerated claims for policy analysis seem to have abated. New and less dogmatic modes of investigating the policy process are being developed.

684. Scioli, Frank P., Jr. "Problems and Prospects for Policy Evaluation." *Public Administration Review*, 39 (January/February 1979), 41-45.

   At all levels of government, arguments are being made for improvements in the efficiency and effectiveness of service delivery. These arguments invariably translate into a plea for increased attention to policy evaluation. This paper discusses several of the problems inhibiting policy evaluation at the state and local levels, as well as the prospects for overcoming them and recommendations for facilitating the tasks.

685. Sharkansky, Ira. "Where You Sit Shapes What You See and What You Do--Maybe." *Social Science Quarterly*, 61 (September 1980), 203-5.

   A more favorable reaction to Steinberger (*SSQ*, 1980).

686. Smith, Bruce L.R. "The Non-Governmental Policy Analysis Organization." *Public Administration Review*, 37 (May/June 1977), 253-58.

The "non-governmental policy analysis organization" is a category of broad scope and fuzzy boundaries. Many exist in one policy arena--e.g., health, education, environment--with little in common with sister organizations in another arena; some few aspire to a more comprehensive reach across the spectrum of governmental activity. The range in quality is striking; some of the most experienced analysts are to be found in the non-governmental organizations as well as some of the most incompetent.

687. Smith, David G. "Policy Analysis and Liberal Arts." *Policy Studies Journal*, 6 (Spring 1978), 381-87.

Attempts to find a place for policy studies in the liberal arts curriculum by arguing that it serves as a third culture between the humanities and the natural sciences.

688. Steinberger, Peter J. "Typologies of Public Policy: Meaning Construction and the Policy Process." *Social Science Quarterly*, 61 (September 1980), 185-97.

Suggests an alternative to traditional approaches and argues that the selection of policy meanings by relevant participants may well be a key to understanding the relationship between substance and process, a relationship with which typological theorists have been especially concerned.

689. ―――――. "A Reply to Ostrom and Sharkansky." *Social Science Quarterly*, 61 (September 1980), 206-7.

The author of "Typologies of Public Policy: Meaning Construction and the Policy Process" responds to criticism.

690. Stonecash, Jeff. "Politics, Wealth and Public Policy: The Significance of Political Systems." *Policy Studies Journal*, 7 (Summer 1979), 670-75.

The argument presented here is that the role of politics and wealth as "determinants" of public policy has been misconceived theoretically and misspecified in empirical analyses.

691. Tufte, Edward R. *Political Control of the Economy*. Princeton, N.J.: Princeton University Press, 1978.

Scholars have been noting the strong relationship between economic variables and policy outcomes for the past two decades. Tufte, a leading figure in policy analysis, has produced a work which continues in the aforementioned school of thought.

692. Ukeles, Jacob B. "Policy Analysis: Myth or Reality?" *Public Administration Review*, 37 (May/June 1977), 223-28.

    The purpose is to present an overview of policy analysis that may shed some light on its growth. The article is divided into two parts: (1) current views of policy analysis--what it is and what its intellectual and pragmatic roots are; and (2) an assessment of the state of policy analysis--how these problems might enhance American governance.

693. Wildavsky, Aaron. *Speaking Truth to Power: The Art and Craft of Policy Analysis*. Boston: Little, Brown, 1979.

    A gold mine of insightful and provocative writing about the role of policy analysts, the kind of subjects they deal with, and the way they should practice their craft.

694. Zeckhauser, Richard and Edith Stokey, eds. *A Primer for Policy Analysis*. New York: W.W. Norton, 1978.

    A good introduction to the study of policy analysis. Zeckhauser (a well-known scholar) and Stokey have compiled a collection of some of the best essays in the field.

Chapter 13

POLICY MAKING

695. Anderson, James E. *Public Policy Making*. New York: Holt, Rinehart and Winston, 1979.

Professor Anderson is a leading authority in the field of public policy analysis. This work represents an excellent general introduction to the field.

696. Baum, Lawrence. "Policy Goals in Judicial Gatekeeping: A Proximity Model of Discretionary Jurisdiction." *American Journal of Political Science*, 21 (February 1977), 13-35.

Research on the federal and state supreme courts has indicated that their decisions whether to grant hearings to appellants are based largely on judges' efforts to achieve their policy preferences. In this paper, a model of these gatekeeping decisions is developed, based upon the premise that judges' responses to petitions for hearing are based solely upon their policy goals.

697. Beckman, Norman. "Policy Analysis for the Congress." *Public Administration Review*, 37 (June 1977), 237-44.

The purposes of this presentation are to: (1) examine the main policy analysis institutions available to the Congress; (2) identify factors that affect the use of policy analysis by the Congress; and (3) describe some current reform proposals aimed at strengthening the policy analysis capability of the Congress.

698. Behn, Robert D. "How to Terminate a Public Policy: A Dozen Hints for the Would-Be Terminator." *Policy Analysis*, 4 (Summer 1978), 383-413.

Public policies are difficult to terminate. Suggests some political strategies that may help policy terminators achieve their objectives, but cautions that they should not be misinterpreted as "Behn's Ironclad Rules That Guarantee Termination," and examines the need for additional research.

699. ———. "Policy Analysis and Policy Politics." *Policy Analysis*, 7 (Spring 1981), 199-226.

   The policy analyst is concerned with efficiency and outputs, and ignores sunk costs; the policy politician is concerned with distribution and inputs, and seeks to justify sunk costs. These differences can be derived from the analyst's indifference to constituencies and the politician's devotion to them.

700. Brigham, John and Don W. Brown, eds. *Policy Implementation: Penalties or Incentives?* Beverly Hills, Calif.: Sage Publications, 1980.

   Twelve papers drawn from a symposium dealing with the capacity of the law to alter behavior, for those interested in the argument of incentive versus coercion strategies these essays are a welcome addition. The research is current and anticipates much of the supply side economics debate.

701. Bunker, Douglas R. "Organizing to Link Social Science with Public Policy Making." *Public Administration Review*, 38 (May/June 1978), 223-32.

   Scientists and public policymakers jointly recognize that close collaboration between the realms of science and government is difficult. Though many trained as social scientists now participate in the federal bureaucracy, and other public officials have grown used to various forms of systematic analysis, which borrow from the language and methods of science, the goals, decision processes and operating norms of scientific and democratic institutions diverge.

702. Burstein, Paul. "Some 'Necessary Conditions' for Popular Control of Public Policy: A Critique." *Polity*, 12 (Fall 1979), 23-37.

   According to most voting studies, the control of public policy by the electorate presupposes a number of conditions: (1) voters must know where candidates stand with respect to public issues; (2) voters must let the candidates' stand determine their choice; (3) voters must have a choice between opposing views; and (4) voters must be able to count on candidates' keeping their promises if elected. Shows that such conditions are neither necessary nor sufficient to insure popular control of public policy.

703. Caldwell, Lynton K. "Biology and Bureaucracy: The Coming Confrontation." *Public Administration Review*, 40 (January/February 1980), 1-12.

   Biology and the new science of sociobiology now compel lawmakers, administrators, and judges to consider issues that were once beyond the pale of political response. Biological findings continue to undermine assumptions long accepted in public law and policy. In effect, biology and bureaucracy are approaching a confrontation comparable to the philosophical conflict between physical science and the medieval church.

704. Califano, Joseph A. *Governing America: An Insider's Report from the White House and the Cabinet.* New York: Simon and Schuster, 1981.

Former Secretary of Health, Education and Welfare Califano provides the first detailed insider's report on the Carter presidency. Although primarily anecdotal in format, this lively and readable book presents a comprehensive but none too flattering view of Carter and his White House. This book is more than just a look inside the administration: it must also be considered as an examination of the policy process and the factors making for success and failure.

705. Campbell, Vincent N. and Daryl G. Nichols. "Setting Priorities among Objectives." *Policy Analysis*, 3 (Fall 1977), 561-78.

Wise allocation of resources implies knowledge of which actions will yield the highest net benefit. Predicting benefit requires comparing objectives for their importance and setting priorities among them. Discusses ways in which policymakers can set priorities rationally.

706. Conway, M. Margaret. "Participatory Democracy and the Democratic Party in the House of Representatives: Implications for Policy Making." *Policy Studies Journal*, 5 (Summer 1977), 459-64.

The possibility of maximizing responsibility (the formulation and enactment of policies which will solve or substantially alleviate policy problems) and accountability (the ability of citizens to be informed about policy and to vote in congressional elections on the basis of whether their representatives acted in accord with their policy preferences), the author argues, potentially has been reduced by two changes in the Democratic party's rules and procedures in the House of Representatives. These two changes are: (1) the revised method of selecting standing committee chairpersons; and (2) the use of caucus instructions to shape the content of legislation being considered by a standing committee or the Rules Committee.

707. Coombs, Fred S. "The Bases of Noncompliance with a Policy." *Policy Studies Journal*, 8 (Summer 1980), 885-92.

Policies have impact only if they are successful in changing the behavior of target individuals. If one focuses upon the prescription imbedded in any policy, it is possible to gauge the success of implementation by assessing the degree of compliance with the prescription. The target individual may not comply, however. Appropriate remedies will depend upon the type of noncompliance encountered.

708. Costain, W. Douglas and Anne N. Costain. "Interest Groups as Policy Aggregators in the Legislative Process." *Polity*, 14 (Winter 1981), 249-72.

    The emphasis of most interest-group research on the role of groups as articulators of discrete interests has understated the impact of interest groups on the legislative system. By considering an aggregative dimension to interest-group behavior, this paper suggests that groups play a more important role in the formulation of congressional policy than has generally been supposed.

709. deLeon, Peter. "Public Policy Termination: An End and a Beginning." *Policy Analysis*, 4 (Summer 1978), 369-92.

    Defines what is meant by policy termination and discusses both why it has received so little analytical attention and why it warrants more.

710. Dye, Thomas R. *Politics in State and Communities*. Englewood Cliffs, N.J.: Prentice-Hall, 1977.

    Examines the principal policies that the states are responsible for administering. Among the policies included are education, highways, social welfare, control of crime, civil rights and taxing.

711. ———. "Oligarchic Tendencies in National Policy-Making: The Role of the Private Policy-Planning Organizations." *The Journal of Politics*, 40 (May 1978), 309-31.

    The purpose of this essay is to contribute to the development of a more specific and useful version of the "elitist" model of the policy-making process. Endeavors to: (1) set forth a more detailed, working model of oligarchy in national policy making; (2) identify the organizations which contribute to cohesion and consensus among top corporate, financial, and governmental leaders; (3) identify the individuals by name who direct these organizations and to note their linkages with the corporate and financial worlds; (4) observe their role in recruiting individuals for high government positions; and (5) specify some of the key decisions in which these private policy-planning organizations have been influential.

712. ———. *Who's Running America: The Carter Years*. Englewood Cliffs, N.J.: Prentice-Hall, 1979.

    Represents a groundbreaking effort in identifying the elite power structure in America. It is recommended for those interested in the relationship of power to policy making and analysis.

713. Edwards, George C., III. "Congressional Responsiveness to Public Opinion: A Policy Perspective." *Policy Studies Journal*, 5 (Summer 1977), 485-91.

Examines evidence of congressional responsiveness to public opinion and its consequences for policy making and public policy.

714. ―――――. *Implementing Public Policy*. Washington, D.C.: Congressional Quarterly, 1980.

Lists the obstacles to effective implementation of public policy as difficulty of communications, the limitation of resources, the dispositions of the administrative staff, and the fragmented nature of the bureaucratic structure. Each of these factors is examined in detail with examples from actual programs.

715. Erbring, Lutz, Edie N. Goldenberg, and Arthur H. Miller. "Front-Page News and Real-World Cues: A New Look at Agenda-Setting by the Media." *American Journal of Political Science*, 24 (February 1980), 16-49.

Introduces an "audience-effects" model which treats issue-specific audience sensitivities as modulators, and news coverage as a trigger stimulus, of media impact on issue salience, issue by issue. An analysis of "most important national problem" mentions in the 1974 National Election Study, augmented by data on front-page content in the newspapers read by respondents and on "real-world' conditions in the respondents' communities, provides considerable empirical support for the proposed audience-contingent effects model.

716. Gordon, Lawrence A. and Allen Schick. "Executive Policy-Making Authority and Using Zero-Base Budgeting for Allocating Resources." *Policy Studies Journal*, 7 (Spring 1979), 554-68.

Examines how executive policy-making authority is affected by allocating public resources via zero-base budgeting (ZBB). After reviewing the concept and rationale of ZBB, compares incremental policy making with scientific policy making. This review and comparison are then used to draw implications of using ZBB.

717. Ingram, Helen M. and Scott J. Ullery. "Policy Innovation and Institutional Fragmentation." *Policy Studies Journal*, 8 (Spring 1980), 664-82.

Argues that fragmented and decentralized policy-making structures can generate major policy innovation as well as can centralized structures.

718. Ingram, Helen M. and Dean E. Mann, eds. *Why Policies Succeed or Fail: Sage Yearbooks in Politics and Public Policy.* Vol. 8. Beverly Hills, Calif.: Sage Publications, 1980.

 The Policy Studies Organization's 1980 Yearbook raises a crucial question--why policies succeed or fail. A lot of ground is covered: what is policy; how policy is formulated, implemented and evaluated; urban dimensions of policy; and how policy is made.

719. Johnson, Arthur T. "Potential Groups and Agenda Responsiveness." *Polity*, 12 (Winter 1979), 349-58.

 Gaining formal agenda status is not a guarantee that a preferred policy will be adopted, but without it there is no hope of success. Although a public problem may achieve agenda status in a variety of ways, the primary and most frequent sponsor is the formal interest group. Organization is the basis of political power, as well as the mobilization of bias.

720. Kozak, David D. and John D. Macartney, eds. *Congress and Public Policy.* Homewood, Ill.: The Dorsey Press, 1982.

 A source book of both scholarly and governmental documents and readings. Covers a wide variety of sources of Congress's impact on the policy-making process. Principal efforts are directed toward the legislative process as well as organizational dynamics.

721. Kritzer, Herbert M. "Federal Judges and Their Political Environments: The Influence of Public Opinion." *American Journal of Political Science*, 23 (February 1979), 194-207.

 Beverly Cook (1977) presented evidence that federal district judges "responded" to public opinion in their sentencing of draft offenders during the Vietnam War. This article raises questions about Cook's conclusions. It reexamines both her national level analysis and her district (state) level analysis, and concludes that there is no evidence to support her contention that judges responded to public opinion.

722. Light, Paul Charles. *The President's Agenda: Domestic Policy Choice from Kennedy to Carter (with Notes on Ronald Reagan).* Baltimore: Johns Hopkins University Press, 1982.

 Provides the first attempt at systematic study of the domestic policy-making process in the post-Eisenhower era, when a series of presidencies have begun to organize internally around the task of framing and advancing more or less extensively elaborated domestic programs. This work stresses limits on presidential achievement rather than the intrinsic strengths of the presidency.

723. Mezey, Michael L. "Legislative Policy-Making through the Imposition of Constraints." *Policy Studies Journal*, 5 (Summer 1977), 402-7.

Two things are implicit in any discussion of political reform: a model of the way the institution or activity in need of reform should operate, and a perception of the way it does operate at variance with that model. To close the gap between the ideal model and the less than ideal reality must be the goal of any reform that is not simply aimless tinkering. Analyses of legislatures around the world are examined to identify three legislative models, each characterized by a particular kind of policy-making relationship between the legislature and the executive.

724. Montgomery, John D. "The Populist Front in Rural Development: Or Shall We Eliminate the Bureaucrats and Get on with the Job?" *Public Administration Review*, 39 (January/February 1979), 58-65.

Distrust of the bureaucracy as an instrument of progress is nothing new. But it is flourishing with extraordinary vigor in this era when little else is taken for granted. There is a fashionable turn in the old populism that rejects, in the United States and abroad, technicians and administrators, along with politicians and judges.

725. Montjoy, Robert S. and Laurence J. O'Toole, Jr. "Toward a Theory of Policy Implementation: An Organizational Perspective." *Public Administration Review*, 39 (September/October 1979), 465-76.

Numerous studies have documented the difficulty of converting public policy into appropriate action. While problems usually appear during implementation, some of them may be predictable from the nature of the policies themselves. If so, prospective policies could be analyzed in terms of their implementability. In this paper, the authors explore one approach to such a theory by applying propositions derived from the organization literature to a major category of implementation problems. They illustrate the generality of their ideas with a variety of reported cases.

726. Moore, Nancy A. "The Public Administrator as Policy Advocate." *Public Administration Review*, 38 (September/October 1978), 463-68.

If the available resources are to be tapped and if public administrators are to participate as policy advocates, the concept which public organizations must turn to is organizational democracy, and the techniques they must seek to master are those of organizational development.

727. Nagel, Stuart. *Policy Evaluations: Making Optimum Decisions.* New York: Praeger, 1982.

   Presents an engaging analysis of the interrelationship of the policy and decision-making sciences.

728. Peters, John G. and Susan Welch. "Legislative Reform and Public Policy: An Overview." *Policy Studies Journal*, 5 (Summer 1977), 408-14.

   Maintains that neither the case studies nor the macro approach, which examines all states, provide reason to be optimistic about possible dramatic positive effects of legislative reform at the state level. These studies should caution those who still believe that better paid, more professional state legislatures will differ dramatically in policy output from the amateur ill-equipped legislatures of twenty years ago.

729. Rathjen, Gregory J. and Harold J. Spaeth. "Access to the Federal Courts: An Analysis of Burger Court Policy Making." *American Journal of Political Science*, 23 (May 1979), 360-82.

   Attempts to ascertain what factors have motivated the Burger Court Justices in their policy choices. Through the use of cumulative scaling, finds that none of the authors' hypothesized influences explain the access choices of the Court as a whole. The Justices, rather, march to the beat of individualized drums.

730. Ripley, Randall B. "Policy Leadership in the U.S. Senate: The Potential for Expanded Policy Committee Activity." *Policy Studies Journal*, 5 (Summer 1977), 464-69.

   The nature of Congress, particularly the Senate, in many ways militates against a strong policy leadership role for party leaders. There are, however, important opportunities for party leaders to increase their substantive policy role (including their role in both providing and using policy analysis) despite the constraints created by congressional practices, norms, and incentives.

731. ———— and Grace Franklin. *Congress, the Bureaucracy, and Public Policy.* Homewood, Ill.: The Dorsey Press, 1980.

   Examines policy making at the national level with particular emphasis placed on the interaction of Congress and the bureaucracy. Focuses on policy formulation and legitimation. Examined are distributive policy, protective policy, redistributive policy, and foreign and defense policy.

Policy Making

732. ———, eds. *National Government and Policy in the United States.* Itasca, Ill.: F.E. Peacock, 1977.

Presents an excellent introductory essay on government and policy, then a series of essays on the role of the public, mass media, political parties, and interest groups in making policy demands. There are also essays on the impact of the presidency, bureaucracy, Congress, and the courts on the making of public policy. The final section of the book examines both domestic and foreign and defense policy.

733. Schuck, Peter H. "Public Interest Groups and the Policy Process." *Public Administration Review*, 37 (March/April 1977), 132-40.

Public policy emerges best from a process in which the generation of relevant data is maximized, basic assumptions are questioned, expert witnesses are cross-examined, and a broad spectrum of values is advanced. Public interest groups are a necessary, if not always sufficient, condition of this process. If adequately funded, their activities should continue to improve, at least marginally, the quality of agency decision making, and should affect the direction of substantive agency policy.

734. Schulman, Paul R. *Large-Scale Policy Making.* New York: Elsevier, 1980.

Despite other progress, policy analysts have yet to produce convincing and generally useful taxonomies for the policies they analyze. Schulman offers no comprehensive solution to the general problem, but he makes a strong case for accommodating at least one visible feature of policy, namely, "largeness-of-scale."

735. Sharkansky, Ira. "Policy Making and Service Delivery on the Margins of Government: The Case of Contractors." *Public Administration Review*, 40 (March/April 1980), 116-23.

Focuses on contractors who work for government agencies in the United States. Identifies both manifest and latent functions of contractors, deals with issues of government control over contractors, and examines several possibilities for reform.

736. ———. *Public Administration: Agencies, Policies, and Politics.* San Francisco: W.H. Freeman and Co., 1982.

One of the leading figures in the field of policy analysis presents a volume which should be of particular interest to readers who are interested in the rational model of policy making, the decision-making sciences and the growth of policy making by non-governmental consultants (i.e., "government on the margins").

737. Shumavon, Douglas H. "Policy Impact of the 1974 Congressional Budget Act." *Public Administration Review*, 41 (May/June 1981), 339-48.

The 1974 Budget and Impoundment Control Act was a significant piece of legislation passed during one of the most stressful times in American politics. The act specifically delineates two processes affecting federal congressional-executive relations--both dealing with the economic and fiscal matters of the budgetary process. In the budget estimates from the Congressional Budget Office and the Office of Management and Budget there are differences in information presented from each organization. To explain these differences, interviews were conducted with employees in both CBO and the executive branch.

738. Sinclair, Barbara Deckard. "Who Wins in the House of Representatives: The Effect of Declining Party Cohesion on Policy Outputs, 1959-1970." *Social Science Quarterly*, 58 (June 1977), 121-28.

Examines the voting vehavior of northern Democrats, southern Democrats, eastern Republicans and non-eastern Republicans. The results show that the majority segments of the two parties are internally cohesive and that the two segments seldom vote together. The two minority segments are, however, increasingly defecting from the positions taken by their party colleagues. This has resulted in the majority segment of the majority party being increasingly unable to control policy outcomes.

739. Sindler, Allan P. *American Politics and Public Policy*. Washington, D.C.: Congressional Quarterly, 1982.

Consists of seven case studies that were selected because they are topics that are usually covered in American government and public policy courses. Included are analyses of the electoral college system, the role of political party leaders in formulating policy, the FDA, energy, abortion, and defense.

740. Sloan, John W. and Jonathan P. West. "The Role of Informal Policy Making in U.S.-Mexico Border Cities." *Social Science Quarterly*, 58 (September 1977), 270-82.

Describes the interactions, attitudes, and policy behavior of border officials and analyzes the factors that facilitate bicommunity cooperation to deal with common problems.

741. Starling, Grover. *Managing the Public Sector*. Homewood, Ill.: The Dorsey Press, 1977.

A well-known scholar exposes the reader to just how strongly bureaucratic discretion in implementing legislation is intertwined with the making of public policy. In two parts, Part I looks at the techniques used in policy analysis and Part II presents several intriguing case studies.

Policy Making   165

742. Steiner, Barry H. "Policy Organization in American Security
     Affairs: An Assessment." *Public Administration Review*, 37
     (July/August 1977), 357-67.

     Outlines five major ways in which national security policy
     making affects American security interests and evaluates their
     effectiveness. The article then proceeds with a survey of pol-
     icy making since World War II, focusing on the National Secu-
     rity Council and its development.

743. Stevens, John M. and Robert D. Lee, Jr. "Patterns of Policy
     Analysis Use for State Governments: A Contingency and De-
     mand Perspective." *Public Administration Review*, 41 (Novem-
     ber/December 1981), 636-44.

     Indicates that policymakers and policy analysts will have
     to work together to: orient analyses to real governmental and
     state needs as determined through a dialogue between analysts
     and decisionmakers; identify the priority of competing internal
     and external influences on governmental functions; determine
     and make explicit what is feasible given political and economic
     demands; set mutually agreeable performance objectives for the
     analysis using applicability to the demand/contingency as a cri-
     terion; and acquire top level support by demonstrating that the
     benefits of the analysis exceed the costs.

744. Thayer, Ralph E. "The Local Government Annual Report as a Pol-
     icy Planning Opportunity." *Public Administration Review*,
     38 (July/August 1978), 373-76.

     A local government annual report appears both feasible and
     practical even if its precise shape and use are still open to
     discussion. Performance statistics and their association with
     financial data by function and agency could be a most encourag-
     ing vehicle by which to judge local government responsiveness
     and accountability.

745. Tutchings, Terrence R. *Rhetoric and Reality: Presidential Com-
     missions and the Making of Public Policy*. Boulder, Colo.:
     Westview Press, 1979.

     Classifies commissions by: issue area; temporal variations
     in demand; size of commission staff; use of consultants, hear-
     ings, and new research; representation of types of elites; type
     of policy recommendations and their political manipulation re-
     quirements. The cross-classification of these variables gener-
     ates a number of suggestive findings.

746. Van Horn, Carl E. *Policy Implementation in the Federal System:
     National Goals and Local Implementors*. Lexington, Mass.:
     D.C. Heath, 1979.

     Taking the General Revenue Sharing program, the Comprehen-
     sive Employment and Training Act, and the Community Development

Block Grant, Van Horn develops and applies a model of intergovernmental policy implementation to analyze what transpires in the implementation process of these three important cornerstones of the New Federalism.

747. Versel, Mark J. "Zero-Base Budgeting: Setting Priorities through the Ranking Process." *Public Administration Review*, 38 (November/December 1978), 524-27.

The budget process for most public sector organizations traditionally has served as a mechanism for the "true" expression of policy priorities. Into this arena of "choices for making choices" comes zero-base budgeting and its requirement that managers set their budgetary priorities through ranking. Ranking has been the most controversial aspect of zero-base budgeting.

748. Weiss, Carol H. "Research for Policy's Sake: The Enlightenment Function of Social Science Research." *Policy Analysis*, 3 (Fall 1977), 531-45.

Data from three recent studies suggest that the major use of social research is not the application of specific data to specific decisions. Rather, government decisionmakers tend to use research indirectly, as a source of ideas, information, and orientations to the world.

749. Williams, Bruce A. "Beyond 'Incrementalism,' Organizational Theory and Public Policy." *Policy Studies Journal*, 7 (Summer 1979), 683-89.

Suggests that a closer analysis of bureaucratic organizations' role in the public policy process may aid in resolving the long-standing debate between advocates of incremental policy models and advocates of rational/synoptic policy models.

part iii:
indices

AUTHOR INDEX

Adams, Bruce, 372
Adams, William, 36
Agnew, Ann C., 354
Albin, Suzanne, 36
Albritton, Robert B., 509
Alford, John R., 550
Allen, Irving, 373
Allen, James E., 474
Allen, Michael P., 122
Altshuler, Alan, 161, 451
Ambler, John S., 168
Amidjaya, Imat R., 379
Anderson, Charles W., 622
Anderson, James E., 623, 624, 695
Anderson, Patricia S., 379
Anderson, Paul A., 310
Andrews, Richard N.L., 207
Anechiarico, Frank, 422
Angel, William D., Jr., 374
Angrist, Shirley S., 625
Anton, Thomas J., 586
Anwyll, James B., 136
Aron, Joan B., 208
Auster, Richard D., 510
Auten, Gerald E., 587
Aviel, Joanne F., 1
Axelrod, Regina S., 209
Axelrod, Robert, 626

Baer, Judith A., 37
Baer, Michael A., 411
Bahl, Roy, 375
Baker, Paula C., 148
Ballard, Steven C., 306, 627
Bardes, Barbara Ann, 311, 344, 345
Barmack, Judith A., 511
Baugh, William H., 312
Baum, Lawrence, 696
Beard, Edmund, 399
Beck, Paul A., 210
Becker, Susan D., 38
Beckman, Norman, 697
Beecher, Janice A., 376

Beer, Samuel H., 377
Behn, Robert D., 698, 699
Bender, Deborah, 474
Bendick, Mark, Jr., 576
Benedict, Robert, 211
Benest, Frank, 512
Bennett, W. Lance, 475
Berk, Richard A., 41
Berkowitz, Edward D., 513
Berne, Robert, 169, 597
Berry, Linda, 212
Berry, Marvin P., 213
Berry, R. Albert, 2
Bessmer, Sue, 476
Bieker, Richard F., 514
Biersack, Robert W., 628
Bingham, Richard D., 378, 628, 629
Birkhead, Guthrie S., 425
Black, Merle, 39
Blair, John P., 123, 440, 630
Blau, Peter, 515
Blissett, Marlan, 631
Bloomfield, Lincoln P., 313
Bobrow, Davis B., 314, 626
Boles, Donald E., 3
Bond, Jon R., 588
Bone, Hugh, 211
Boneparth, Ellen, 40
Bonnicksen, Thomas M., 214
Boone, Robert, 18
Boruch, Robert F., 379
Boschken, Herman L., 215
Boss, Michael O., 170
Boulay, Harvey, 380
Bowman, Ann, 216
Bozeman, Barry, 273
Bradley, John P., 516
Brady, David, 489, 623
Break, George F., 589
Brecher, Charles, 381
Brehm, Henry, 538
Brennan, Geoffrey, 590
Brenner, Michael J., 315

Bresnick, David, 171
Bridges, William P., 41
Brigham, John, 700
Brisbane, Richard A., Jr., 44
Broadnax, Walter D., 382
Bronfman, Lois Martin, 212
Brosz, Allyn R., 627
Brouthers, Lance Eliot, 383
Brown, Anthony, 384
Brown, Don W., 700
Brown, Lawrence A., 477
Brown, Lawrence D., 42
Brown, Michael K., 43
Brown, Sharon, 498
Browne, William P., 4, 11
Brunner, Ronald D., 217
Bryan, Frank M., 385
Bucknell, Howard, 218
Buell, Emmett H., Jr., 44
Bullock, Charles S., III, 45, 46, 100, 172, 623
Bullough, Vern L., 478
Bunce, Valeri, 124
Bunker, Douglas R., 701
Burkhauser, Richard V., 517
Burstein, Paul, 125, 702
Butler, John A., 518
Butler, John S., 47
Buttel, Frederick H., 140, 219
Butterworth, Robert Lyle, 316
Button, James, 48, 49

Caldwell, Lynton K., 703
Califano, Joseph A., 704
Calvert, Jerry W., 220
Camp, Roderic A., 50
Campbell, Bruce A., 51
Campbell, Vincent N., 705
Canby, Steven L., 317
Carp, Robert A., 489
Carver, Joan S., 52
Cary, Charles D., 632
Castells, Manuel, 126
Cataldo, Everett S., 64
Catau, John C., 188
Cawley, Jerry P., 586
Cayer, N. Joseph, 53, 386
Chadwin, Mark L., 519
Chalice, Donald R., 607
Chambers, M.M., 173
Charney, Jonathan I., 221
Chase, Gordon, 520
Chia, Tiang Ping, 103
Childs, Robin, 331
Chomsky, Noam, 318

Cigler, Beverly A., 222
Cingranelli, David L., 387
Citrin, Jack, 294
Claggett, William, 54
Clark, Cal, 63
Clark, Janet, 63
Clark, Terry, 388, 633
Clarke, Susan E., 127
Cleary, Robert E., 174
Cline, William R., 2
Coffey, Joseph I., 319
Cohen, David K., 654
Cohen, Larry J., 634
Cohen, Ronald D., 175
Colasanto, Diane, 60
Comer, James P., 176
Comfort, Louise K., 177
Conrad, Jon M., 223
Convisser, Martin, 224
Conway, M. Margaret, 706
Conway, Nicholas T., 225
Cook, Constance E., 226
Cook, Earl, 227
Coombs, Fred S., 707
Cooper, Patrick, 137
Cooper, Terry L., 479
Cortner, Hanna J., 228
Costain, Anne N., 55, 56, 57, 708
Costain, W. Douglas, 708
Coulter, Philip B., 389
Craig, Richard B., 480
Crandall, Robert W., 128
Critchley, W. Harriet, 320
Cuzan, Alfred G., 229

Dahlbert, Kenneth A., 5
Daneke, Gregory A., 230
Danielson, Michael N., 392
David, Elizabeth, 390
Davidson, Dorothy K., 236
Davis, James A., 363
Daynes, Byron W., 503
Dean, Gillian, 481, 533
Deese, David A., 231
de la Garza, Rudolfo O., 321
Delamater, John, 482
deLeon, Peter, 709
Del Sesto, Steven L., 232, 233
Dentler, Robert A., 178
Derthick, Martha, 521
Diggins, William, 391
Doerksen, Harvey, 234
Doig, Jameson W., 392
Doran, Charles F., 235
Dornan, Paul B., 393

Author Index

Doron, Gideon, 483
Dowall, David E., 394
Drew, Joseph, 253
Dubnick, Mel, 635
Durant, Robert F., 400
Durkin, Mary, 561
Duval, Robert D., 322
Dye, Thomas R., 58, 236, 395, 396, 591, 636, 637, 638, 639, 710, 711, 712

Edgmon, Terry D., 237
Edmunds, Stahrl W., 129, 238
Edwards, George C., III, 640, 713, 714
Ehrlich, Paul R., 130, 239
Eilbott, Peter, 592
Elam, Rick, 273
Elling, Richard C., 397
Engelbert, Ernest A., 179
England, Robert E., 102, 437
Engquist - Seidenberg, Gretchen, 522
Erbring, Lutz, 715
Erickson, Kenneth P., 240
Erie, Steven P., 43, 59
Ertur, Omer S., 180
Ervin, Osbin L., 131
Esseks, J.D., 6
Etheredge, Lloyd S., 323
Ethridge, Marcus E., 629
Eulau, Heinz, 626

Fairbanks, David, 484, 485
Fairchild, Erika S., 641
Farge, Emile J., 523
Farley, Reynolds, 60
Farnham, Paul G., 398
Feldstein, Martin, 524
Feller, Irwin, 431
Ferber, Mark, 399
Field, Marilyn J., 486
Fisher, Gene H., 642
Fitzgerald, Michael R., 400
Flora, Peter, 525
Flowers, George A., Jr., 132
Formuzis, Peter, 593
Foster, John L., 401, 643
Fowler, E.P., 402
Fowler, Kenneth S., 241
Fox, Peter, D., 526
Fox, William F., 152
Franklin, Grace, 731, 732
Friedman, Judith J., 403
Friedman, Lee S., 527

Fry, Brian F., 644
Frye, Hardy T., 61
Fuhrman, Susan, 198

Gabris, Gerald R., 404
Game, Kingsley W., 242
Garcia, John A., 62
Garcia, Jose A., 63
Gardner, David P., 181
Garms, Walter, 544
Gatlin, Douglas S., 64, 182
Gelb, Joyce, 65
Gilbert, D.A., 594
Gilbert, Dennis, 425
Gilchrist, C. Jack, 300
Giles, Micheal W., 64, 182
Giles, William A., 404
Gillespie, J. David, 66
Ginsburg, Helen, 133
Ginzberg, Eli, 528
Gist, John R., 134
Githens, Marianne, 67
Glass, James L., 672
Gleeson, Michael E., 529
Gnuschke, John E., 551
Goering, John M., 405
Goetz, Michael L., 595
Goldenberg, Edie N., 715
Goldman, Alan H., 68
Goldstein, Leslie F., 69
Goodwin, Craufurd D., 243
Gordon, Josephine G., 510
Gordon, Lawrence A., 716
Gordon, Robert M., 7
Gottheil, Dianne Levitt, 114
Gove, Samuel K., 620
Graves, Philip E., 244
Gray, Virginia, 639
Green, Barbara B., 530
Green, Phyllis Strong, 135
Greenberg, George D., 531, 645
Greenberg, Saadia R., 253
Greenberg, Stanley B., 70
Greer, Darryl G., 183
Gremillion, Lee L., 245
Griffin, Kenyon N., 246
Grondbjerg, Kirsten, 532
Groth, Alexander, 331
Gruhl, John, 71
Guither, Harold D., 8
Gunlicks, Arthur B., 406
Gustafson, Thane, 9, 247
Guth, James L., 10

Hadwiger, Don R., 11

Hall, Grace, 72
Hall, Timothy A., 306
Hambrick, Ralph S., Jr., 646
Hamilton, Mary A., 248
Handley, David H., 77
Hanke, Steve H., 7, 136
Hanks, Michael, 73
Hansen, Susan B., 137, 487
Hardin, Charles M., 12
Hardy, Richard J., 74, 90, 671
Hargrove, Erwin G., 533
Harkavy, Robert, 324
Harrigan, John J., 412
Harrison, David, 249
Hausman, Leonard J., 534
Haveman, Robert H., 535
Hayes, Frederick O., 407
Hayes, Susan W., 574
Heidenheimer, Arnold J., 525
Hellawell, Robert, 596
Helms, Robert B., 488
Henderson, Lenneal J., 75
Hensler, Carl P., 105
Hershey, Marjorie R., 76
Hevener, Natalie, 325
Hickam, Dale, 597
Hill, Kim Quaile, 435, 598
Hill, Stuart, 280
Hochschild, Jennifer L., 536
Hoffman, Ellen, 537
Hollander, Edward, 189
Hollick, Ann L., 326
Holsti, Ole R., 327
Hoole, Francis W., 77
Horton, Raymond D., 381
Howards, Irving, 538
Huckle, Patricia, 78
Huddleston, Mark W., 138
Hudson, William E., 408
Hula, Richard C., 139
Humphrey, Craig R., 140
Hunt, Janet G., 79
Hunt, Larry L., 79
Hurley, T.L., 395, 396
Hutchins, Matthew, 409

Ingram, Helèn M., 250, 251, 252, 293, 410, 717, 718

Jackman, Mary R., 80, 184
Jacobs, David, 81
Jansson, Douglas, 379
Jaros, Dean, 411
Jennings, Edward T., Jr., 539, 540, 541

Johnson, Arthur T., 719
Johnson, D. Gale, 13
Johnson, Loch, 328
Johnson, Roberta Ann, 110
Johnson, William, 412
Johnston, Richard E., 413
Johnston, Robert A., 414
Jones, August J., 82
Jones, Bryan D., 253
Jones, Charles O., 626, 647
Jones, E. Terrence, 415
Jones, Lamar B., 14
Jones, Thomas E., 648
Jorgensen, Joseph G., 254
Joseph, Lawrence B., 83
Jud, G. Donald, 185
Judd, Dennis R., 270, 543

Kaiser, Fred M., 329
Karnig, Albert K., 416, 417, 467
Kasarda, John D., 418
Kassiola, Joel, 84
Kaufman, Clifford, 253
Keehn, Norman H., 141
Kegley, Charles W., Jr., 354
Kelly, William J., 542
Kemp, Kathleen, 142, 489
Kempey, William, 592
Kenski, Henry C., 143, 255
Kenski, Margaret C., 255
Kerrigan, Mark L., 256
Kerstein, Robert, 543
Keyserling, Leon H., 144
Kiewiet, D. Roderick, 145
Kihl, Young W., 334
Kinder, Donald R., 294
King, Joel, 361
King, John L., 419
Kirst, Michael W., 186, 544
Kiser, Larry, 148
Klass, Gary M., 649
Klein, Nancy K., 530
Knaub, Norman L., 545
Korb, Lawrence J., 330
Kozak, David C., 720
Kraemer, Kenneth L., 419
Kramer, Kevin L., 586
Krane, Dale A., 404
Kritzer, Herbert M., 721
Krumm, Ronald J., 244
Kushman, John E., 331, 546
Kyvig, David E., 490

Laird, Roy D., 15
Lambright, W. Henry, 257

Landau, Martin, 626
Laney, Nancy K., 252, 410
Lave, Charles A., 258
Lave, Lester B., 547
Lazin, Frederick A., 420
Leavel, Willard, 211
Lee, Robert D., Jr., 743
Legge, Jerome S., Jr., 132
Lehman, Edward W., 650
Leinhardt, Samuel, 651
LeLoup, Lance T., 599
Leman, Christopher, 548, 549, 652
Levine, Charles H., 600
Levine, Erwin L., 187
Lewis, Brinley J., 443
Lewis, Carol W., 421
Lewis, Eugene, 422
Lewis-Beck, Michael S., 146, 550, 653
Liebhafsky, E.E., 551
Light, Alfred R., 259, 472
Light, Paul Charles, 722
Lindbloom, Charles, 654
Lineberry, Robert L., 376, 423, 601, 655
Livingston, John C., 85
Logan, John R., 424
Long, James E., 86
Lopez, Manual Mariano, 87
Lord, J. Dennis, 101, 188
Louthan, William C., 491
Lovell, Catherine, 442
Lovrich, Nicholas P., Jr., 445
Lowery, David, 602
Lucy, William H., 425
Lunch, William M., 332
Lurie, Jonathan, 16
Lynn, Laurence J., Jr., 552
Lyon, Larry, 88
Lyons, William, 436

Macartney, John D., 720
McBeath, Gerald A., 426
McCain, John R., 250, 251, 252, 410
McCalla, Alex F., 17
McCarrick, Earlean M., 89
McClintock, Charles C., 658
McCormick, James M., 328, 333, 334
Maccorquodale, Patricia, 482
McCrone, Donald J., 74, 90
MacDonald, Marucie, 553
MacEwen, Ann, 260

MacEwen, Malcolm, 260
McGee, Leo, 18
McKean, Margaret A., 261
McKean, Roland N., 262
McKee, William L., 551
McKenney, James L., 245
McKinley, Tina M., 554
McLure, Charles E., 603, 604
MacManus, Susan A., 605, 606
McNeil, Dixie M., 360
McNeil, Mary, 263
MacRae, Duncan, Jr., 656, 657
McTighe, John J., 147
Madar, Daniel, 335
Maggiotto, Michael A., 216
Mann, Dean E., 718
Manning, Peter K., 492
Manus, Lawrence, 189
Mansbach, Richard W., 336
Marando, Vincent L., 427, 428
Margolis, Michael, 493
Marlin, John Tepper, 429
Marmor, Theodore R., 555
Martin, Dolores T., 264
Martin, John Frederick, 91
Maser, Steven M., 630
Maynard-Moody, Steven, 658
Mazmanian, Daniel A., 659
Mead, Lawrence M., 430
Medler, Jerry, 265
Meier, Kenneth J., 19, 92, 556
Mendeloff, John, 557
Menzel, Donald C., 266, 431, 660
Merelman, Richard M., 190
Methe, David T., 432
Mezey, Michael L., 723
Michie, Aruna Nayyar, 20
Migdal, Joel A., 337
Milbrath, Lester W., 267
Miller, Arthur H., 715
Miller, Gary J., 433
Miller, Jeffrey A., 645
Miller, Trudi C., 191
Milward, H. Brinton, 93
Miner, Ralph E., 607
Mitchell, John J., 519
Mitchell, Michael L., 66
Mitnick, Barry M., 268
Mladenka, Kenneth R., 434, 435
Modelski, George, 338
Mohl, Raymond A., 175
Mohr, Lawrence P., 645
Molineu, Harold, 339
Montgomery, John D., 724
Montjoy, Robert S., 725

Moon, Marilyn, 558
Moore, Mark H., 494, 495
Moore, Nancy A., 726
Morehouse, Sally McCally, 661
Morehouse, Thomas A., 426
Morgan, David R., 436, 437, 438
Morgan, Patrick M., 192, 340
Morris, David, 269
Most, Benjamin A., 341
Munshaw, Nancy, 669
Murray, Richard, 94
Musgrove, Frank, 193
Mushkatel, Alvin, 265, 270
Mushkin, Selma J., 439

Nachmias, David, 123, 440, 662
Nagel, Stuart, 663, 664, 665, 666, 667, 668, 669, 727
Narver, Betty Jane, 584
Nau, Henry R., 342
Navarro, Peter, 271
Neary, Kevin, 493
Nedwek, Brian T., 670
Neef, Marian, 665, 666, 667, 668
Neiman, Mark, 441, 442
Nelkin, Dorothy, 272, 343
Newacheck, Paul W., 194
Newcomer, Kathryn E., 671
Newell, Charldean, 672
Newman, Monroe, 443
Nichols, Darryl G., 705
Nichols, David A., 673
Nightingale, Demetra S., 519
Nikolai, Loren A., 273
Nivola, Pietro S., 274, 444
Nogee, Joseph, 364
Norgren, Jill, 559
Nye, Joseph E., 231

Oakerson, Ronald, 148
Obler, Jeffrey, 674
Odell, Morgan, 195
O'Donnell, Tom, 675
Okrent, David, 275
Oldendick, Robert, 311, 344, 345
O'Loughlin, John, 560
Olson, Janice, 99
Olson, Laura K., 276
O'Neill, Timothy J., 95
Oppermann, Theo, 544
Orbell, John M., 277
Orfield, Gary, 196
Orr, David W., 278, 279, 280
Orr, Lloyd D., 281
Ortiz, Isidro D., 21

Osmond, Marie Withers, 561
Ostheimer, John M., 496
Ostrom, Charles W., Jr., 77, 346
Ostrom, Elinor, 148, 676
Ostrom, Vincent, 148
O'Toole, Laurence J., Jr., 725

Paarlberg, Don, 22, 23, 24
Paarlberg, Robert L., 25
Pachon, Harry P., 445
Pack, Howard, 446
Pack, Janet R., 446
Palley, Howard A., 447, 497
Palley, Marian Lief, 65, 447
Palumbo, Dennis J., 677
Parker, Larry B., 627
Parker, Steven, 678
Parkin, Andrew, 448
Parks, Roger B., 148
Pastor, Robert A., 149
Payne, William C., Jr., 26
Pechman, Joseph A., 608
Peek, Charles W., 498
Pelissero, John P., 437, 438
Penniman, Clara, 609
Percy, Stephen L., 148
Perrotta, John A., 562
Perry, Charles S., 282
Perry, James L., 432
Pesso, Tana, 563
Peters, B. Guy, 610
Peters, John G., 728
Peterson, Paul E., 449
Pettman, Ralph, 347
Phares, Donald, 611
Pharr, Susan J., 96
Philliber, Susan G., 477
Picard, Louis A., 348
Pierce, John C., 283
Pipes, Richard, 349
Plotnick, Robert D., 564, 565
Pollack, Michael, 343
Porter, Laurellen, 27
Porter, Roger B., 28, 150
Portney, Kent E., 612
Prager, Edward, 566
Prestage, Jewel L., 67, 197
Preston, Michael B., 97
Price, Robert M., 98
Prysby, Charles L., 151
Puri, Anil, 593
Puro, Steven, 670
Pyburn, Philip J., 245

Quade, E.J., 679

Author Index

Quandt, William B., 350
Quester, Aline O., 99, 613
Quester, George H., 351

Radian, Alex, 614
Radford, Paul E., 132
Radin, Beryl A., 680
Rakoff, Robert M., 634
Randall, Ronald, 567
Ransom, Harry Howe, 352
Rasche, Robert H., 615
Rathjen, Gregory J., 729
Rector-Owen, Holley, 88
Regens, James L., 100, 284, 285
Reid, J. Norman, 152
Rein, Martin, 681
Renick, James, 58
Rent, George S., 101
Reppy, Judith, 353
Rhoads, Steven E., 153
Rice, G. Randolph, 14
Rice, Ross, 211
Rich, Michael J., 376
Richard, John B., 29
Richardson, Neil R., 354
Rider, Robert, 286
Rindskopf, David, 379
Ripley, Randall, 730, 731, 732
Robinson, Ted, 102
Robinson, Thomas S., 214
Rochester, J. Martin, 355
Rockman, Bert A., 356
Rodgers, Robert, 617
Roessner, J. David, 450
Roof, Wade Clark, 115
Rosberg, Carl G., 98
Rose, Winfield, H., 103
Rosenau, James N., 327
Rosenbaum, Walter A., 287
Rosenbloom, Sandra, 451
Rosenthal, Alan, 198, 452
Rossi, Peter H., 391
Rothstein, Robert L., 357
Rourke, John T., 358
Rubin, Irene, 600
Rupnow, Gary L., 3
Rushefsky, Mark E., 30
Russell, Clifford S., 288
Rycroft, Robert W., 285, 289, 290

Sabatier, Paul, 291, 659
Saltzstein, Alan L., 72, 568
Sampson, R. Neil, 31
Sanger, Mary Byrna, 453
Sapolsky, Harvey M., 569

Savage, Robert L., 454
Sawhill, Isabel V., 553
Schaefer, Roger L., 386
Schaller, David A., 292
Schantz, Harvey L., 570
Scher, Richard, 49
Schick, Allen, 616, 682, 716
Schlozman, Kay Lehman, 154
Schmandt, Jurgen, 631
Schmidt, Richard H., 570
Schneider, Mark, 424, 683
Schoen, Robert, 104
Schooler, Dean, 293
Schoultz, Lars, 359
Schramm, Sarah Slavin, 199
Schroeder, Larry D., 571
Schuck, Peter H., 733
Schulman, Paul R., 734
Schuman, David, 200
Scioli, Frank P., Jr., 684
Scotch, Richard K., 518
Scott, Marvin B., 178
Sears, David O., 105, 294
Sederberg, Peter C., 155
Segers, Mary C., 106
Semyonov, Moshe, 107
Shapo, Marshall S., 499
Sharkansky, Ira, 614, 685, 735, 736
Sharp, Elaine B., 455
Shefrin, Bruce M., 156
Shelton, Robert B., 246
Shepsle, Kenneth A., 157
Sherman, Betsy, 372
Sherman, Joel D., 201
Shortlidge, Richard L., Jr., 582
Shumavon, Douglas H., 737
Sigelman, Carol K., 572
Sigelman, Lee, 53, 360, 409, 572, 602
Simay, Gregory L., 225
Simon, Julian L., 295
Sinclair, Barbara D., 573, 738
Sindler, Allan P., 739
Siverson, Randolph M., 361
Sjoquist, David L., 571
Skok, James E., 456
Slater, Jerome, 362
Slawson, John, 108
Sloan, John W., 740
Smeeding, Timothy, 517, 565
Smith, Bruce L.R., 686
Smith, David G., 687
Snyder, William P., 363, 646
Solomon, Arthur P., 158

Spaeth, Harold J., 729
Spanier, John, 364
Speer, Leslie K., 105
Sperlich, Peter W., 332
Spohn, Cassia, 71
Starling, Grover, 741
Starr, Harvey, 341
Starr, John Bryan, 365
Stein, Robert M., 159
Steinberger, Peter J., 688, 689
Steiner, Barry H., 742
Stephan, Paul E., 571
Stetson, Dorothy M., 500
Stevens, John M., 743
Stewart, Debra W., 109
Stewart, Joseph, Jr., 46, 172
Stewman, Shelby, 625
Stiefel, Leanna, 169, 597
Stoff, Michael B., 296
Stokey, Edith, 694
Stonecash, Jeff, 574, 690
Stoper, Emily, 110
Straussman, Jeffrey D., 617
Strean, Herbert S., 501
Street, David, 532
Struyk, Raymond J., 575, 576
Stucker, James P., 297
Suter, Larry E., 582
Suttles, Gerald D., 532
Swanson, Cheryl, 93
Swanson, Gerald C., 298
Swinton, David, 683
Symons, Donald, 502
Szanton, Peter, 457

Tassey, Gregory, 160
Tatalovich, Raymond, 503
Taylor, Marcia Whicker, 155
Teal, Roger, 161
Teich, Albert H., 257
Teigen, Ronald L., 162
Teitelbaum, Fred, 458
Thayer, Ralph W., 744
Thelin, John, 195
Thomas, John C., 618
Thomas, Robert D., 428
Thompson, Frank J., 111
Thompson, Joel A., 459, 577
Thompson, John T., 413
Thompson, Kay, 468
Thompson, Kenneth W., 366, 367
Thompson, Lawrence H., 578
Thompson, William R., 322
Thurow, Lester C., 163
Trice, Robert H., 368

Tropman, John E., 202
Tufte, Edward R., 691
Turnbull, Augustus B., III, 460
Tutchings, Terrence R., 745
Tyler, Tom R., 294

Uhlman, Thomas M., 112
Ukeles, Jacob B., 692
Ullery, Scott J., 717

Vandivort, Martha B., 148
Van Horn, Carl E., 461, 579, 746
Van Loon, Rick, 580
Vasquez, John A., 336
Vedlitz, Arnold, 94
Verba, Sidney, 154
Versel, Mark J., 747
Vickery, Clair, 581
Vietor, Richard H.K., 299
Vladeck, Bruce C., 645
von Beyme, Klaus, 369

Wade, L.L., 164
Wagner, Richard E., 619
Waite, Linda J., 582
Waldman, Loren K., 113
Walker, David B., 462
Walker, James L., 185
Wallerstein, Mitchel B., 32
Wallich, Henry C., 165
Walzer, Norman, 620
Wandesforde-Smith, Geoffrey, 291, 301
Ward, Peter D., 463
Ward, Sally K., 464
Wardell, William M., 504
Wardwell, John M., 300
Warner, David, 631
Warner, Kenneth E., 505
Wasserman, Ira M., 465
Wasserman, Stanley S., 651
Waters, Anita M., 650
Watts, Meredith W., 506
Watts, Nicholas, 301
Weatherford, M. Stephen, 166, 203
Weimer, David L., 466
Weinbaum, Marvin G., 33
Weingast, Barry R., 302
Weintraub, Sidney, 370
Weiss, Carol H., 748
Weissert, William G., 583
Welch, Susan, 71, 114, 416, 417, 467, 468, 728
Wengert, Norman I., 303
Wenner, Lettie M., 304

Author Index

West, Jonathan P., 740
Wexler, Elizabeth M., 187
Weyant, John P., 305
Whisler, Marilyn W., 469
Whitaker, Gordon P., 148
White, David, 402
White, Irvin L., 306
White, Michelle J., 470
White, Sheldon H., 681
Wiggins, Charles W., 4
Wikstrom, Nelson, 471
Wilcox, Fred, 307
Wilcox, Jerry, 115
Wildavsky, Aaron, 621, 693
Wilde, James, 657
Williams, Bruce A., 749
Williams, Walter, 584
Wilson, Graham K., 34
Wilson, James Q., 167
Wilson, Kenneth L., 47
Wilson, L.A., II, 277
Wilson, Rick, 148
Wilson, Robert B., 308
Wilson, William Julius, 116

Wiltsee, David H., 132
Wise, Arthur E., 204
Wittkopf, Eugene R., 371
Wohlenberg, Ernest H., 117
Wolf, Eleanor P., 205
Worcester, Dean A., Jr., 118
Worthington, Mark D., 552
Wright, Deil S., 472
Wright, Erik Olin, 206
Wright, Gerald C., 119
Wright, James D., 391
Wynne, Edward A., 585

Yandle, Bruce, 309
Yisai, Yael, 507
Yondorf, Barbara, 508
Youngberg, Garth, 35

Zashin, Elliott M., 120
Zeckhauser, Richard, 694
Zeigler, Harmon, 170
Zetterbaum, Marvin, 121
Zody, Richard E., 473

SUBJECT INDEX

Abortion policy, 497
  anti-abortion, 493
  in developed nations, 486
  implementation of, 487
  in Israel, 507
  politics of, 503
  and population politics, 496
  and social change, 489
Affirmative action, 85
  city efforts for, 429
  constraints on, 92
  and federal personnel systems, 120
  and higher education, 197
  impact of, on organizational behavior, 93
  and municipal employees, 386
Aged
  care of, 583
  by the family, 566
Agenda setting
  agricultural, 22, 23
  executive, for domestic policy, 722
  gaining agenda status in, 719
  by the media, 715
Agricultural policy, 13, 34
  and alternative agriculture, 30
  and Congress, 27
  and economic inequality, 20
  food policy in, 23, 24, 33
  pricing in, 12
Agriculture
  and agenda setting, 22, 23
  collective bargaining in, 21
  corporate, land ownership of, 3
  and economic equality, 20
  and the environment, 5
  in U.S.S.R., 9
  and foreign policy, 15, 28
  and interest groups, 4, 34
  politics of, 11
  in Britain, 34
  and productivity, 2

Agriculture (*continued*)
  research in, 17
  and water resources, 29
Agriculture, U.S. Department of
  and federal nondiscrimination policies, 26
  and interest groups, 19
Aid to Families with Dependent Children
  the Nixon administration's influence on, 567
  participation rates growth in, 514
Alliances, national, and war, 361
Allocation
  of employment and training funds, 571
  of resources
    regional, 443
    in veterans' health care system, 569
    zero-base budgeting for, 716
Alternative agriculture, 30, 35
Analysis
  equity, 169
  institutional, 430
  values, and environmental policy, 207
Antitrust policy, 146
Apartheid, 98
Appropriations
  and Congressional budget reform, 138
  politics of, 134
  state, legislative, 456
Arms control, 340
  and the cruise missile, 319
  impact statements, 316
  policy, 313, 314, 324
Athletics
  and educational achievement, 73
  and women, 107
Attitudes
  toward county growth, 428

Subject Index

Attitudes (continued)
toward the environment, 220
foreign policy, structure of, 311, 344, 345, 371
toward homosexuality, 478
toward law and order, 506
toward minority hiring, 111
toward nuclear power, 211, 232
political, 51
and pornography, 498
toward premarital sexuality, 482
racial, 100
toward the welfare state, 219

Biopolitics, 347
Blacks
and Congressional voting, 45
and economic equality, 48
economic polarization of, 59
as elected officials, and public policy, 97
and federal social policy, 43
impacts on
of the civil rights movement, 49
of the Equal Employment Opportunity Act of 1972, 103
and the NDPA, 61
occupational mobility of, 88
and racial inequality, 115
representation of, on school boards, 102
and residential segregation, 60
and rural landownership, 18
as trial judges, 112
urban, religious affiliation and militancy among, 79
Block grants, and urban policy, 415
Boston Plan, the, and federal-urban relations, 399
Britain
and agricultural policy, 34
higher education in, 168
governance of, 181
Budgeting
federal, 162
for housing programs, 529
legislative control of, 599
impacts
of Congressional reform on appropriations, 138
of elite succession on priorities, 124

Budgeting (continued)
models, 77
national defense, 330
and voting behavior of school districts, 180
zero-base
for resource allocation, 716
and setting priorities, 747
Bureaucracy
and agricultural price policy, 12
and Congress, in policy making, 731
and education, 204
and rural development, 724
and sociobiology, 703
in U.S. Department of Agriculture, 19
Burger Court, the
and federalism, 413
politics of, toward women, 69
and sexual equality, 37
Busing
and national policy, 196
politics of, 203
whites' opposition to, 105

Capitalism
development of, race and state in, 70
economic crisis in, 126
Chicanos
and health care behavior, 523
impacts on, of employment policy, 63
self-identity of, 62
and U.S. foreign policy, 321
Child Abuse Prevention and Treatment Act, politics of, 537
Child care policy, national, 559
Civil Rights Act of 1964
impact of, on women, 74
implementation of Title VI, 82
Civil rights movement
impacts of, on black municipal services, 49
and liberalism, 91
Civil rights policy, and racial economic equality, 90
Class
and economic deprivation, 154
and education, 185, 193, 206
and income determination, 206
and political response to recession, 166

Clean Air Act, 242, 271
Coal
  and environmental policies, 299
  resource development, 131
  severance tax policy, 246
Collective bargaining
  and agriculture, 21
  impacts of, on local services, 432
  in the public sector, and tax burdens, 617
Commodities exchanges, federal regulation of, 16
Communities, characteristics of, 394
Community Action Program, machine influence on, 562
Compliance, policy, and bases of noncompliance, 707
Comprehensive Employment and Training Act of 1973
  and accountability, 533
  implementation of, 579
Congress
  and agricultural policy, 27
  and energy policy, 274
  and foreign policy, 328, 358, 364
  economic, 149
  and money, 616
  and nuclear power, 302
  partisanship in, 143
  policy analysis for, 697
  political parties in, 125
  and the Presidency, 364
  and public policy, 720
  and the bureaucracy, 731
  voting of, 45
Congressional Budget and Impoundment Control Act of 1974, 616
  policy impact of, 737
Conservation
  of energy, 210, 282
  in national parks, 214, 260
  and national seashores and lakeshores development, 214
Corporations
  agricultural, 3
  elite structure of, 122
Crime policy, urban, 376
Crisis, international definition of, 333

Dairy policy
  and consumer organizations, 10

Dairy policy (continued)
  and milk marketing, 7
Day care
  arrangements for, of working women, 582
  centers, model of, 546
Decentralization
  of energy policies, 217
  institutional, and policy innovation, 717
  and land use, 286
Decision making
  federal, and women, 65
  foreign policy, 310
  government, use of social research in, 748
  presidential, 360
  and the economy, 150
  in energy regulation, 256
Defense policy, national, 313
  and the defense budget, 330
Deficit, the government, financing of, 615
Democracy
  and anti-inflation policy, 141
  and electoral succession, 124
  participatory, and policy making, 706
Democratic Party, the
  and liberalism, 91
  and policy making in the House, 706
Desegregation, school, 178, 205
  and busing, 196
  impact of, on local school financing, 201
  and intra-school district migration, 188
  and the Department of Justice, 46
  and policy support, 64
  politics of, 44
  and public policy compliance, 182
Detente, 349, 369
Developing countries
  agrarian structure in, 2
  and developing agriculture, 5
  and economic policies, 164
  policy successes in, 337
  and U.S. foreign policy, 357, 370
  and U.S. taxation, 596
Diffusion
  of innovations, 431, 477

Subject Index

Diffusion (continued)
  and spread of war, 341
Disarmament, 313
Discount rate, 136
  and public investment, 157
Discrimination
  and employment, 118
    of Spanish-origin males, 86
    of women, 36
  reverse, 66, 68, 84
  and schooling, 172, 185
  sexual, in education, 55
  in USDA, 26
Distribution
  of services, 455
    local, 425
    municipal, 387, 420, 444, 453
    urban police, 435
  trends in national urban policy, 418
Divorce policy, state, 481
Drugs
  and health, 488
  law enforcement, 492
  methadone maintenance, expansion of, 494
  Mexico's antidrug campaign, 480
  Reorganization Plan #2, 495
  therapeutic, controlling the use of, 504

Ecology
  and agricultural development, 5
  the crisis of, and society, 280
  educational, 227
  and environmental policy, 238, 239
  and man, 278
Economic crisis
  in American society, 126
  in U.S. steel industry, 128
Economic policy
  analysis of, 153
  in developing countries, 164
  foreign, 149
  no-growth in, 155
  orientations, 151
  and pluralism, 163
  presidential, 150
  targeting funds in, 132
  and unemployment, 144
  and venture capital markets, 160
Economists
  and economic issues, 130

Economists (continued)
  and policy analysis, 153
Education
  and athletics, 73
  and black representation, 102
  discrimination in,
    class, 185
    racial, 172, 184, 185
    sexual, 55
  government regulation of, 204
  and the handicapped, 187
  higher
    politicization of, 168
    social environment of, 227
  reform in, 175, 176
  school grades in, 202
  and the sexes, 99
  and socialization, 190, 193
  and tolerance, 80
Education for All Handicapped Children Act of 1975, 187
Educational policy
  evaluation of, 177
  in higher education, 174, 183, 198
  making of, and influence power, 170
  states' role in, 186
  and Title I, 171
Effluent charges, 281, 288, 304
Elementary and Secondary Education Act, 171
Elites, succession of, and impact on budgetary priorities, 124
Emissions, automotive, controlling of, 249, 304
Employment
  and equality
    of minorities, 53, 58, 63, 72, 75, 86
    of race, 48, 66, 103
    of women, 36, 53, 63, 75
  full, as a policy, 133
  and labor market mobility, 88
  and the sexes, 99
Energy, 218
  as a concept, in policy and administration, 237
  conservation of, 210
  consumption, 240
  crisis, the, and political system support, 294
  management of, local, 222
    and boom town growth, 303
    and the national defense, 218

Energy (*continued*)
  and population distribution, 300
  and public policy, 287
  regulation, management of, 256
  research and development, 225, 257
  security, 231, 296
  technology, 212
  and transportation, 258
  and urban America, 269
  usage, and the environment, 209
Energy policy, 237, 243
  attitudes toward, and legislative action, 220
  and the Carter administration, 259
  and Congress, 274
  decentralization of, 217
  and energy conservation, 210, 282
  and the Federal Energy Administration, 285, 289, 290
  formulating and/or implementing of, 284, 285
    in the Four Corners states, 228
    quantitative models in, 305
  impacts of, and the 55 MPH speed limit, 264
  for Indian lands, 274
  politics of, 279, 287
  intergovernmental, 208
  in the public-private sector, 248
  of states, 236, 284
  technology assessment in, 306
  U.S. foreign, 342
Entrepeneurship, urban, 374
Environment, the
  attitudes toward
    and economic growth and the welfare state, 219
    and legislative action, 220
    and citizen protest, in Japan, 261
  disruption or repair of, 295
  and health, 244, 263
  and nuclear power, 226
  and public policy, 276
  social, and American education, 227
  and the social sciences, 239
  and transportation, 224

Environmental policy
  and coal, 299
  and ecology, 238
  and enforcement, 262
  local, 253
  formulating and/or implementing of, 291
    and the impacted public, 267
  and growth/no-growth, 140
  impacts of, 209
    the Clean Air Act of 1970, 271
    social, 254
  orientations, to air pollution, 216
  and quality control, 281, 288
  and the U.S. House of Representatives, 255
  in the U.S.S.R., 247
  and values, 207, 301
Environmental Protection Agency, 250
Equal Employment Opportunity Act, impacts of, 118
  on federal black employment, 103
  and organizational practices, 109
  on women and minorities, 63, 75
Equal Rights Amendment, 38
  ratification of, 117
Equality
  economic
    and agricultural policies, 20
    and public policy, 81
  and race, 48, 90
  in federal health care policy, 42
  and human need, 121
  and individual rights, 89
  language of, 95
  in local service distribution, 425
  of opportunity, 83
    educational, 191, 199
    for the sexes, 106, 199
  and public policy
    economic, 81
    sexual, 106
  sexual, 106
    and the Burger Court, 37
    and income, 41
Equity analysis, 169
Ethics policy
  for the administrative role, 479

Ethics policy (*continued*)
  and political corruption, 491
Ethnics
  in capitalist development, 70
  in municipal representation, 416
  in residential segregation, 87
  stratification of, 104
  urban groups, suburban preference of, 373
Evaluation
  citizen, and municipal services delivery, 400
  policy
    and decision making, 727
    problems and prospects for, 684
  program, and organizational uncertainty, 658
  research, introductory course in, 632
Expenditures
  defense, 346
  federal
    control of, 134
    and interregional benefits, 152
    limiting of spending, 621
    and party balance, 125
    patterns, analysis of, 586
  government, 377
  social welfare, 564
  municipal
    impact of intergovernmental revenue on, 436
    and service needs, 421
    suburban, 424
  planning, correlates of, 464
  policy, 165
  public, American, growth of, 618
  social, urgan, 467
  state, 137
    revenue sharing, 472
  welfare, state, growth of, 541

Family policy
  and fertility, 500
  and welfare policy, 553
Farmland preservation, 6, 31
Federal aid
  allocations, 159
  categorical, to cities, 568
  targeting of, 398
Federal Energy Administration, 285, 289, 290

Federalism, 462
  and the Burger Court, 413
  and government expenditures, 377
  and nationalization of welfare, 538
Feedback, policy, 481
Feminism, 38, 110
Finance policy
  governmental, 589
  higher education, 173
  school
    and desegregation impacts, 201
    equity of, 169
    reform of, 194
Financing
  of government, 600
    federal, 589, 615
    urban, 375
  higher education, 173
  school
    and desegregation impacts, 201
    reform, 194
  state, and tax policies, 620
Fiscal policy, 165
  impacts of, local, 131
  urban, 123, 440
Food
  aid, 32
  crisis, world, 1
  interest groups, 8
  policy, 13, 23, 24
  and food lobbyists, 8
  in the Middle East, 33
  politics of, 11
  in foreign policy, 15, 25, 28, 32
Food Stamp Program, 511
  impacts of, on recipients' expenditures, 545
Foreign policy
  and morality, 367
  Saudi Arabian, 350
  Soviet, 349
Foreign policy, U.S.
  attitudes, dimensions of, 311, 344, 345, 371
  behavior, 354
  and IGO's, 334
  beliefs of women in, 327
  and Chicanos, 321
  and China, 365
  commentary on, 318
  Congressional participation in, 328, 358, 364
  and the Presidency, 364

Foreign policy, U.S. (continued)
  decision making, justification in, 310
  economic, 149, 369, 370
  energy, 342
  and food, 25, 32
  grain and the U.S.S.R., 15, 28
  and the House Committee on International Relations, 329
  and human rights, 325, 359, 366
  and interest groups, 368
  and international relations, 355
  and Latin America, 359
  making of, 356
  and oil, 296, 350
  personality effects on, 323
  and size of nation-state, 322
  and the Third World, 357, 370
  and UNCLOS III, 326
France, higher education in, 168
Fuel
  crisis, world, 1
  efficiency standard, 309
Future, the
  policy-oriented forecasts for, analysis of, 648

Gas, natural, offshore exploration for, 308
Gasoline tax, 297
Government
  council-manager, mayor in, 471
  county, and rural policy development, 404
  expenditures, 377
  federal
    financing of, 589
    spending, limiting of, 621
  financing of, 600
    federal, 589
    urban, 375
  international, and policy making, 77
  investment decisions, 390
  local,
    annual report, for policy planning, 744
    and citizen-initiated contacts, 253
    and corporate agriculture, 3
    employment in
      of blacks, 409
      of minorities, 53
      of women, 53

Government (continued)
  local (continued)
    and energy research and development, 225
    fiscal effects on,
      of coal resource development, 131
      of FmHA business loans, 132
    institutional analysis for, 430
    reform of, 406
  municipal
    employment in,
      of minorities, 72, 75
      of women, 75
    and public policy in the U.S., 732
    reorganization impacts of, executive, 556
    responsiveness, to urban problems, 395, 396, 458, 463
    role of, in urban development, 392
    scholars as practitioners in, 457
    self-, Alaska native, 426
    special district, 606
  state
    employment in
      of blacks, 409
      of minorities, 53, 63
      of women, 53, 63
    innovations diffusion among, 431
    institutional analysis for, 430
  urban, finance, 375
Grants-in-aid, federal, 584
Growth
  of American public expenditure, 618
  attitudes toward, county, 428
  economic, 156
    in developing countries, 164
    and state taxing, 591
    and venture capital markets, 160
    and the welfare state, 219
  growth/no-growth, sociology of, 140
  impacts of, energy boom town, 303
  management
    characteristics of, 394
    local, 414, 469
    policies, 135
    state, 127
  no-growth,
    and the American economy, 156
    political economy of, 155
    zoning, 470

Subject Index   187

Growth (continued)
  in social services, 515
Harvest policies of trees, 241
Health
  and drugs, 488
  and the environment, 244, 263
Health care policy
  and cost containment, state, 522
  government-controlled, incentives in, 510
  national health insurance, 526
  politics of, 555
  and the veterans' health care system, 569
Higher education
  and affirmative action, 197
  in Britain and France, politicization of, 168
  federal involvement in, 174, 181, 189, 192
    and state coordinating boards, 183
  financing of, 173
  leadership in, state, 198
  planning, statewide, 195
  policy
    analysis of, 200
    federal, 174
    the policy analysis field in, 179
Hispanics
  impacts on, of employment policy, 63
  and self-identity, 62
Home credit, 139
Homosexuality, attitudes toward, 478
House Committee on International Relations, 329
Housing programs
  budgeting for, federal, 529
  experimental, vouchers in, 576
  public, 575
Human rights
  and Mexico's antidrug campaign, 480
  policy, 339
  in U.S. foreign policy, 325, 359, 366
Humphrey-Hawkins, evolution of, 570

Impacts, policy
  of affirmative action, 93

Impacts, policy (continued)
  analysis of, 671
  on Congressional appropriations, of budget reform, 138
  of the 1974 Congressional Budget Act, 737
  of desegregation on school financing, 201
  on employment
    of blacks, 103
    of minorities, 63
    of women, 63
  of equal employment opportunity, 103
  of growth management, 135
  of municipal reformism, 423
  social, of environmental legislation, 254
  of Supplemental Security Income Program, 509, 517
Implementation, policy, 700, 714, 725
  of abortion policy, 487
  of CETA, 579
  of energy policy, 228, 285
  of higher education policy, 183
  of human services delivery programs, 520
  of nondiscrimination policies, 26
  and policy, teaching of, 680
  of pollution control, 304
  Sunset, 372
  of Surface Mining Control and Reclamation Act of 1977, 266
  of Title VI, 82
  of Title IX, 55
Income
  and class structure, 206
  clustering, and local inequality, 441
  differences in
    male-female, 41
    and public policy, 81
    male, black and white, 90
  support program, 581
Incorporation, municipal, 433
Incrementalism, and the policy process, 749
India, agricultural modernization in, and economic equality, 20
Individual rights, 89
Industry
  policies of, U.S. steel, 128
  regulation of, 142, 483

Inequality
  and affirmative action, 85
  educational, and income, 206
  local, and income clustering, 441
  and minority relations, 108
  and public policy, 81
  racial, 115
  types and measures of, 113
Inflation
  and anti-inflation policy, 141
  costs of, 129
  and taxation, 590
Innovation, policy
  adoption of
    by local government, 378
    by states, 454
  diffusion of
    population-related, 477
    among states, 431
    and institutional fragmentation, 717
  in metropolitan reform, 412
  process of, federal intervention in, 466
  and regionalism, in state politics, 401
  state, 468
Integration
  and policy commitment, 184
  and tolerance, 80
Intelligence agencies, U.S., 352
Interest groups
  and agenda responsiveness, 719
  agricultural, 4, 8, 19, 29, 34
  anti-abortion, 493
  dairy, 10
  economic, 122
  environmental, 226
  and foreign policy, 368
  and public policy, 733
    Congressional formulation of, 708
  and water resources, 29
  women's, 55, 56, 57, 65
International relations, and U.S. foreign policy, 355
Israel, food and fuel policy making in, 1

Japan, political women in, 96
Justice, U.S. Department of, and school desegregation, 46

Labor
  agricultural, 14, 21

Labor (continued)
  market, mobility of, 88
Land
  agricultural, 31
  improvement of, Soviet, 9
  ownership of, corporate, 3
  rural, black ownership of, 18
Land use
  control of, public, 215
  policy, 291
    state, 270
  planning, 286
    urban-rural conflict in, 265
  urban, 215
Legislatures, state
  and federal funds, 456
  legislators' lives, 452
Liberalism
  and anti-inflation policy, 141
  and the Democratic Party, 91
Long cycles, 338

Management
  behavior, constraints on, 531
  energy, local, 222
  of energy regulation, 256
  growth
    characteristics of, 394
    policy impacts of, 135
    strategies, 469
  natural disaster, 391
  public
    cutback strategies in, 147
    of growth, state, 127
    quantitative methods for, 651
  rural, 473
  urban, and municipal services delivery, 400
  water resources, 213, 229, 234, 250, 251, 252, 293
Mandating, federal, 442
Manpower programs, 528
Marriage, and the extramarital affair, 501
Medicaid, and children, 518
Medicare, and the Senate Finance Committee, 516
Mental retardation
  deinstitutionalization of the mentally retarded, 572
  politics of, 513
  and the right to vote, 530
Mexican-Americans
  impacts on, of employment policy, 63
  and self-identity, 62

Subject Index

Mexico
—U.S. border cities, informal policy making in, 740
women and political leadership in, 50
Middle East, agricultural and food policies in, 33
Military, the
and race relations, 47
research and development of, 353
Military policy
the all-volunteer force, 363
strategic value concept in, 320
Minorities
and agricultural policy, 26
employment of
attitudes toward, 111
and economic status of, 86
in state and/or local government, 53, 63, 72, 75
urban, 58
Missiles
cruise, and arms control, 319
strategic, basing modes for, 312
Models
budgeting, 77
in energy policy formulation, 305
U.S. defense expenditure, 346
Monetary policy, and fiscal policy, interface, 165
Morality
and foreign policy, 367
policy, and religious forces, 484
public
and civil religion, 475
and politics and economics, 485

National defense
and energy, 218
policy, and the defense budget, 330
National Forest System, program planning in, 245
National parks
and conservation, 214
in England and Wales, 260
and shores development, 214
National security policy, 742
NATO, defense strategy of, 317
Natural disaster policy, local, 319

Natural Gas Policy Act of 1978, 274
Natural resources
development of, 220
protection of, 291
Neighborhood policy, national, 405
New Federalism, 382, 408, 461, 462
and policy implementation, 746
Noncompliance, policy, bases of, 707
Non-proliferation, nuclear, 315
Nuclear power
attitudes toward, 232
and voting, 211
development and political economy of, 230
and the environment, 226
and non-proliferation, 315
opposition to, 307, 343
and reactor safety, 232, 233, 272, 275
and Three Mile Island, 272
regulation of, 302

Obscenity, anti-, 476
Oil
depletion allowance, 588
and energy security, 231, 296
exploration, offshore, 308
policy, 296
cartel, of OPEC, 235
foreign, 296
spills, 223
Outputs, policy
effect of declining party cohesion in the House on, 738
state, 465
of workmen's compensation laws, 577

Parties, political
balance of, in Congress, 125
black, 61
platforms, state, 397
realignments, policy consequences of, 573
Partisanship
and ideology, in the Revenue Act of 1978, 143
and state tax preference orderings, 612
and women's enfranchisement, 54
Planned Parenthood, 477
Planning
local, 744
program, 407

Planning (*continued*)
  urban, 437, 464
Pluralism
  and economic policy, 163
  in policy studies, 673
Policy analysis, 638, 682, 692, 693, 694
  an advocate role model for, 643
  aggregate data use for, 674
  applied, technology assessment, 306
  and the Congress, 697
  and the decision-making sciences, 679
  of economic variables and policy outcomes, 691
  and the environment, 276
  equity analysis, 169
  in higher education, 200
  as an educational field, 179
  and liberal arts, 687
  methods and practices, 642
  organization, non-governmental, 686
  place of
    in political science, 626
    principles in, 622
  and policy politics, 699
  for public decisions, 657
  of public policy, 629, 636
  research, grants for, 667
  in state and community, 439, 683
  teaching of, use of case method in, 656
  urban, 388, 393
  use patterns of, for states, 743
Policy making, 695, 734
  cases in, 624
  Congressional, 713
  educational, influence power in, 170
  executive, 704, 722
    authority of, and zero-base budgeting, 716
  and government on the margins, 735, 736
  informal, in U.S.-Mexico border cities, 740
  Israeli, during 1972-74 food/fuel crisis, 1
  judicial, 696
    the Burger Court, 729
  legislative, 723

Policy making (*continued*)
  national, 732
    Congress and the bureaucracy in, 731
    and the elite power structure, 712
    oligarchic tendencies in, 711
    and presidential commissions, 745
  for national security, 742
  and participatory democracy, 706
  public
    cases in, 624
    models, 659
    and organizational theory, 749
    and social science, 701
    and public administration, 736, 741
  setting priorities in, 705
  women in, as trial judges, 71
Policy research, 681
  the all-volunteer force, 363
  disaggregation in, 640
  institutes, control in, 650
  projects, in the LBJ School of Public Affairs, 631
Policy studies
  activities, in universities, 665
  directory, 668
  personnel, 669
  the domain of, 644
  field experience in, 628
  guided design in, 660
  models in, 630
  modular learning for, 641
  perspective, 664
  pluralism in, 673
  program, Ph.D., developing of, 670
  of public policy, introduction to, 647
  research, 677
  students of, information-gathering skills for, 675
Political systems, and international travel, 331
Politics
  in America, and public policy, 623, 739
  international, analysis of, 336
  policy, and policy analysis, 699
  rural, 385
  state, and parties and policy, 661
  urban, 449
    social control theories of, 380

Subject Index   191

Pollution
  air, 291
    control of, 304
    state, 242
    and health, 244
    policy orientations to, 216
    -control tax incentive, 273
  marine, and Antarctica, 221
  water, 291
    marine, 221
    river, 277
Population
  distribution of, and energy, 300
  growth, management of, 394
  politics, and abortion, 496
Pornography, as a political symbol, 498
Poverty
  family, measuring of, 561
  and government transfers, 565
Power, political
  analysis of relationship to society, 637
  and black parties, 61
  and minority employment, 58
  and women, 40
Pregnancy policy, 78
  managing teenage pregnancy, 474
Presidency, the, and Congress, 364
Presidential election campaign fund, taxpayer support for, 598
Price policy
  agricultural, 12, 24
  dairy, 10
Problem solving
  for public policy, 625
  social, and social science, 654
Production policy
  agricultural, 24, 31
  in developing countries, 2
Productivity
  programs, city and county, 407
  and relative economic status, 86
Program
  planning and/or evaluating, 658
  local, 379
  productivity, city and county, 407
Prohibition, repealing of, 490
Prostitution, legal, 508
Public administration, 736
  the administrator as policy advocate in, 726

Public administration (continued)
  politics and/or policy, 298
  and public policy, 678, 741
  reaching decisions in, 629
Public Law 94-142, 187
Public management
  cutback strategies in, 147
  of growth, state, 127
Public policy, 732
  American, 655
  analysis of, 629, 636, 666
  and black economic polarization, 59
  and black elected officials, 97
  and Congress, 720
  determinants of, 639, 690
  development, state, staff impact on, 460
  economic, analysis of, 153
  and economic inequality, 81
  and energy, 209, 287
  consumption of, and industrialized society, 240
  and the environment, 209, 276
  and equal employment opportunity, 106
  and fiscal stress, 600
  and the grandfather effect, 652
  innovativeness, states', 454
  and interest groups, 733
  and legislative reform, 728
  in New York City, 381
  outputs, state, 411
  and political representation, 410
  and politics in America, 623, 739
    determination of, 649
  popular control of, 702
  problem solving for, 625
  and public administration, 298, 678
  socioeconomic and political variables for, 653
  state, 710
    and politics and parties, 661
    success or failure of, 718
  teaching of, contexts, 634
  termination of a, 698, 709
  theory, developing of, 645
  typologies of, 676, 685, 688, 689
  and urban America, 447
  urban, and policy research, 633
  and women, 40, 114

Race
  attitudes toward, 100
  and welfare policy, 119

Race (continued)
  discrimination by, and impact
    of school quality, 185
  and domination, 98
  and education, achievement in,
    and athletics, 73
  in employment, 66
  and integration
    residential, 60, 101
    tolerance of, 80
  relations, and the military, 47
  and sex roles, 76
  significance of, 116
  and socioeconomic status, 51
  and voting participation, 94
  and state, in capitalist de-
    velopment, 70
  and support for federal voting
    rights legislation, 39
Recession, political responses
  to, 166
Reform
  budget, Congressional, 138
  city-county consolidation in,
    427
  educational, 175, 176
  legislative, and public policy,
    728
  local government, 406
  metropolitan, 412
  municipal, impact of, 423
  regulatory, in air trans-
    portation, 161
  school finance, 194
  tax, 595, 607
    in Israel, 614
  of unemployment insurance, 542
  welfare
    incremental, 552
    in U.S. and/or Canada, 549,
      580
    the Work Incentive Program,
      519
Regionalism, and innovation, in
  state politics, 401
Regulation
  and chemical and drug research
    and development, 499
  of cigarette industry, 483
  of education, governmental,
    204
  environmental, 268
  federal
    of commodities exchanges, 16
    of energy, 256

Regulation (continued)
  of nuclear power, 302
  politics of, 167
  reform of, in air transportation,
    161
  safety, in coal mines, 550
  social, strategy of, 547
  state, industrial, 142
Religion
  civil, and public morality, 475
  forces of, and morality policies,
    484
Religious affiliation, and urban
  black militancy, 79
Representation
  black, 560
  and urban policy, 417
  municipal, sex and ethnic differ-
    ences in, 416
  political, 410
Resource management, coal, 131
Responsiveness
  agenda, to potential interest
    groups, 719
  to citizen demands, 434
  Congressional, to public opinion,
    713
  government, to urban problems,
    395, 396, 458, 463
  of judges, to public opinion,
    721
Revenue Act of 1978, 143
Revenue
  intergovernmental, impact of, on
    city expenditures, 436
  state
    and expenditure growth, 137
    sharing, expenditures, measur-
      ing of, 472

SALT I, 348
Segregation, residential
  interethnic, in the Southwest, 87
  racial, 60, 101
Senate, U.S., policy leadership in,
  730
Services, human
  delivery of, 520
  municipal, 512
Services, public
  coproduction in, 148
  distribution of,
    inequity in, 455
    local, 425
    municipal, 387, 420, 444
    urban, 435, 453

Services, public (*continued*)
  local, impacts of collective
    bargaining on, 432
  municipal
    black, 49
    needs and expenditures, 421
  urban
    analysis of, 393
    and centralization, 448
    and citizen demands, 434
    consolidation of, 445
    delivery of, 383, 389, 400
    police, 435
Services, social
  growth of, 515
  state, for children, 544
Sex
  and educational achievement,
    73
  human sexuality, evolution of,
    502
  and income, 41
  and municipal representation,
    416
  premarital, attitudes toward,
    482
  roles, racial differences in,
    76
  and work, 99
Social policy
  federal, and blacks, 43
  and social science, 627
Social science
  and public policy making, 701
  research
    government use of, 748
    methods in, 662
    policy analysis in, 663
  and social policy, 627
  and social problem solving, 654
Social security, 585
  benefits, adjustment of, 578
  policy, 524
    development of, 548
    making of, 521
Sociobiology, 347
  and bureaucracy, 703
Socioeconomics
  and race, 51, 116
  and voting participation, 94
  urban, 158
South, the
  black electorate in, 39, 45, 94
  black employment in, 48
  racial inequality in, 115

Southwest, the
  agricultural labor in, 14
  ethnics in
    and Mexican-origin self-
      identity, 62
    and residential segregation,
      87
Speed limit, 55 MPH, 264
Spills policy, oil, 223
State, U.S. Department of, and
  policy planning, 335
Strategic policy, U.S., 351, 362
  and long cycles, 338
  and strategic value, 320
Sunbelt, the, and urban entrepeneurship, 374
Supplemental Security Income
  Program
  equity in, 558
  impacts of, 509, 517
Supported Work experiment, evaluation of, 527
Surface Mining Control and Reclamation Act of 1977, implementation
  of, 266

Targeting
  of federal aid, 398
  of funds, 132
Tax policy, 165
  the coal severance tax, 246
  determinants of, 610
  gasoline, 297
  toward private foundations, 619
  reform, and legislative voting
    behavior, 607
  and the Revenue Act of 1978, 143
  and state financing, 620
  the tax abatement and exemption
    program, 592
Taxing
  an American value-added tax, 604
  burdens, and public sector
    unionism, 617
  capital gains, 587
  code, and women's behavior, 613
  and economic growth, state, 591
  income
    integration of, 603
    state, 609
    revenues of, 593
  and inflation, 590, 593
  and limiting government spending,
    621
  oil depletion allowance, 588

Taxing (continued)
 preference ordering, and
  partisan control, 612
 progressive consumption, 608
 property, relief mechanisms,
  606
 reform, 595, 607, 614
 state and local, 611
 structures, of 1970 SMSA's,
  605
 tax base sharing, 594
 over tax limits, 597
 in U.S. and developing
  countries, 596
Taxpayer
 revolt, 601, 602
 support, for presidential
  election campaign fund, 598
Teaching
 communication skills in, and
  policy analysis, 646
 policy implementation, 680
 public policy contexts, 634
Technical assistance, delivery
 of, rural, 384
Technology assessment, 306
Technology policy
 federal, 450
 and the U.S. venture capital
  market, 160
Termination, public policy, 698,
 709
Three Mile Island, 272
Title I, 171
Title VI, 82
Title IX, 55
Tobacco industry
 regulation of, cigarettes, 483
 and ad ban policy, 505
Tolerance, racial, 80
Transfers
 income, government, 565
 in-kind, Food Stamp Program,
  511
Transportation
 air, regulation of, 161
 and energy, 258
 and the environment, 224
 urban, equity issues in, 451
Travel, international, and
 political systems, 331

UNCLOS III, and U.S. foreign
 policy, 326
Unemployment
 and economic policy, 144

Unemployment (continued)
 insurance, reform of, 542
 and Manpower programs, 528
 measurement of, 551
 political consequences of, 154
 training of unemployed, 554
Urban development
 model, 446
 and role of government, 392
Urban policy, 422, 447
 and black representation, 417
 and block grants, 415
 and energy sources, 269
 and fiscal retrenchment, 123,
  440
 national, distribution trends
  for, 418
 in reformed cities, 438
 zoning, downtown, 402
Urban politics, 449
Urban problems, government responsiveness to, 395, 396, 458, 463
Urban renewal
 the Boston Plan, 399
 central business district, 403
 residential, 403
 and urban-federal relations, 399
USAC, evaluation of, 419

Veterans' health care, allocation
 of resources in, 569
Vietnam War, and American public
 opinion, 332
Voting
 and attitudes toward nuclear
  power, 211
 behavior
  racial, 94
  school district, budgetary,
   180
 Congressional, and the Southern
  black electorate, 45
 and economic conditions, 145,
  166
 and partisanship, 54
 rights, 39, 530
 and women, 54

War
 and national alliances, 361
 spread of, 341
War on Poverty, 535, 543
Water resources
 and agriculture, 29
 management of, 213, 229, 234,
  250, 251, 252, 293

Water resources (*continued*)
 planning, 229
 politics of, 283
Wealth, redistribution of, and
 poor Americans, 536
Welfare policy
 and economic growth and
  environmentalism, 219
 and the family, 553
 and interparty competition,
  state, 540
 and the Nixon administration,
  567
 and racism, 119
 reform of, in Canada, 580
 sources of, 574
 and the War on Poverty, 535
Welfare state
 attitudes toward, 219
 development of, 525
Welfare system
 growth of welfare rolls in,
  539
 procedures
  errors in, 557
  intake, managing of, local,
   563
 revisions in, 534
Women
 and athletics, 107

Women (*continued*)
 behavior of, and the tax code,
  613
 and the Burger Court, 69
 educational equity of, 199
 enfranchisement of, and
  partisanship, 54
 impacts on, policy
  civil rights, 74
  employment, 63, 75, 78
  pregnancy, 78
 interest groups for, 56, 57,
  65
 and labor market mobility, 88
 in politics, 67, 110
  in Florida, 52
  in Japan, 96
  in Mexico, 50
 and public policy, 40, 114
 as trial judges, 71
 in the workforce, 36, 53, 63
Work Incentive Program, and
 welfare reform, 519
Workmen's compensation, state
 compliance in, 459
 outputs and outcomes, 577
Zoning policy
 and big city downtowns, 402
 no-growth, 470

Ref Z 7161 R59 1984
Robey, John S.
 Public policy analysis: an
annotated bibliography